Competitiveness and Growth in Europe

INFER ADVANCES IN ECONOMIC RESEARCH

The International Network for Economic Research (INFER) was established in 1998 as an independent, non-profit research network. It supports high-profile research in all fields of economics and related areas through congresses, seminars, workshops and publications. The main objective of INFER is to foster interactions among academics, business practitioners and policy makers with a view to finding solutions to economic problems. Further details are available from the INFER web site at: www.infer-research.net

The INFER Advances in Economic Research series publishes cutting-edge research findings in all aspects of economics. A multi-stage referee process and a Scientific Advisory Board of distinguished academics, business practitioners and policy makers ensure the quality of the publications.

The INFER Advances in Economic Research series is edited on behalf of the Board of INFER by Michael Pickhardt.

Members of the Scientific Advisory Board:

Jurgen G. Backhaus, *University of Erfurt, Erfurt, Germany*

John Bradley, *The Economic and Social Research Institute, Dublin, Ireland*

Inge Kaul, *United Nations Development Programme, Office of Development Studies, New York*

Gordon Tullock, *George Mason University, Fairfax, Virginia, USA*

Competitiveness and Growth in Europe

Lessons and Policy Implications for the Lisbon Strategy

Edited by

Susanne Mundschenk
ZEI, University of Bonn, Germany and London School of Economics, UK

Michael H. Stierle
European Commission and INFER

Ulrike Stierle-von Schütz
RWTH Aachen University, Germany and INFER

Iulia Traistaru
ZEI, University of Bonn, Germany and INFER

INFER ADVANCES IN ECONOMIC RESEARCH

Edward Elgar
Cheltenham, UK•Northampton, MA, USA

Published by
Edward Elgar Publishing Limited
Glensanda House
Montpellier Parade
Cheltenham
Glos GL50 1UA
UK

Edward Elgar Publishing, Inc.
136 West Street
Suite 202
Northampton
Massachusetts 01060
USA

A catalogue record for this book
is available from the British Library

ISBN-13: 978 1 84542 662 X
ISBN-10: 1 84542 662 2

Printed and bound in Great Britain by MPG Books Ltd, Bodmin, Cornwall

Contents

v

Editors

Susanne Mundschenk is Research Fellow at the Center for European Integration Studies (ZEI) of the University of Bonn. Previously she has worked for the Association for the Monetary Union of Europe based in Paris. She is currently research scholar at the European Institute of the London School of Economics. Her research interests are European monetary integration, public finances, economic growth and governance in the EU. She conducted research projects for the European Commission, the German Ministry of Labour and Ministry of Finance as well as the World Economic Forum. Her current research is on structural change and growth in EU countries.

Michael H. Stierle is Economist at the European Commission, Directorate General Economic and Financial Affairs. He studied economics at Trier University and UNAM, Mexico City and holds a PhD from Speyer University. He has worked in economic departments in the private financial sector as well as in academic research. He is a founding member and Chairman of the International Network for Economic Research (INFER) since 1998. His policy-oriented research is mostly concentrated on international economics, financial markets, growth and business cycles as well as regional economics.

Ulrike Stierle-von Schütz holds a Diploma in Economics from Trier University. Currently she is working as research assistant at the RWTH Aachen University, Department of Public Economics. Her main fields of expertise are economic integration, regional economics and fiscal federalism. She is co-ordinator of the INFER Working Group Growth and Business Cycles and elected INFER board member.

Iulia Traistaru is Senior Researcher at the Center for European Integration Studies (ZEI) of the University of Bonn. Her key areas of expertise include the economics of European integration, international trade, open economy macroeconomics, intra-national macroeconomics, and applied econometrics. She is currently scientific co-ordinator of the research program at ZEI on 'European Integration, Structural Change and Adjustment to Shocks' which includes research projects, policy advice and the co-ordination of a European network of researchers and policy makers. She has been a consultant to the European Commission, European Central Bank, World Bank, Inter-American Development Bank, and the World Economic Forum.

Contributors

Marc Baudry, University of Rennes 1 and CREM
Volker Caspari, Darmstadt University of Technology
Henri L.F. de Groot, Free University Amsterdam, CPB Netherlands Bureau for Economic Policy Analysis and Tinbergen Institute
Adriaan Dierx, European Commission
Christian Dreger, Halle Institute for Economic Research
Béatrice Dumont, University of Rennes 1, CREM-CNRS and College of Europe
John Fitz Gerald, The Economic and Social Research Institute, Dublin
Fabienne Ilzkovitz, European Commission, ULB and ICHEC
Christoph Meister, ECIS, Eindhoven University of Technology
Susanne Mundschenk, ZEI, University of Bonn and LSE
Richard Nahuis[†], CPB Netherlands Bureau for Economic Policy Analysis and Utrecht School of Economics
Peter Nijkamp, Free University Amsterdam
Günther Rehme, Darmstadt University of Technology
Jens Rubart, Darmstadt University of Technology and Center for Empirical Macroeconomics, University of Bielefeld
Michael H. Stierle, European Commission and INFER
Ulrike Stierle-von Schütz, RWTH Aachen University and INFER
Paul J.G. Tang, CPB Netherlands Bureau for Economic Policy Analysis
Iulia Traistaru, ZEI, University of Bonn and INFER
Bart van Ark, Groningen Growth and Development Centre, University of Groningen
Bart Verspagen, ECIS, Eindhoven University of Technology and TIK, University of Oslo
Guntram B. Wolff, Deutsche Bundesbank, ZEI, University of Bonn, UCIS-University of Pittsburgh

[†] The editors and contributors of this book regret deeply the sudden and tragic death of Richard. He will be remembered by us all as an excellent economist and talented researcher.

Preface

This book contributes fresh theoretical and empirical evidence on competitiveness and growth in the context of the commitment made in Lisbon in March 2000 by the heads of state and government to 'make the European Union the most competitive and dynamic knowledge based economy in the world by 2010, capable of sustainable economic growth, with more and better jobs and greater social cohesion'. This commitment, known as the 'Lisbon strategy', is clearly a very ambitious one. The progress up to now is slow and a lot remains to be done to meet the targets.

The Lisbon Strategy started as a political initiative with no coherent economic framework or intellectual underpinning. There has been very little in-depth economic analysis of the objectives and policy implementations of the Lisbon strategy. This book aims at filling this gap by contributing to a better and deeper understanding of the challenges and opportunities of the Lisbon Strategy.

The contributions in this book are the results of a workshop organized jointly by the Center for European Integration Studies (ZEI) of the University of Bonn and the International Network for Economic Research (INFER). This workshop, held in Bonn at ZEI in September 2004, brought together researchers and policy makers to discuss the growth potential of the Lisbon strategy and how to achieve better progress.

The focus of this book is on revealing patterns of growth and cohesion, productivity and competitiveness as well as innovation and knowledge spillovers. The novelty of this book consists of presenting, in a coherent framework, policy relevant research on: determinants of growth, cohesion strategies and the role of institutions, education, R&D and technological progress in economic performance.

This book will be of particular interest to researchers and policy makers working in the fields of competitiveness and growth in the context of economic and monetary integration.

We gratefully acknowledge the financial support from the Center for European Integration Studies of the University of Bonn. In particular, we wish to thank Jürgen von Hagen for many inspiring discussions and support for this book project. We thank the contributing authors for following our editorial guidelines and tight deadlines. We are indebted to John Ryan and

James McKenna for their editorial support. Finally, we thank Hadya Eisfeld
for her excellent editorial assistance.

Susanne Mundschenk, ZEI, University of Bonn and LSE
Michael H. Stierle,* European Commission and INFER
Ulrike Stierle-von Schütz, RWTH Aachen University and INFER
Iulia Traistaru, ZEI, University of Bonn and INFER

NOTE

*   Opinions expressed here are exclusively those of the author and do not necessarily reflect
    those of the European Commission, DG Economic and Financial Affairs.

PART I

OVERVIEW

1. Competitiveness and Growth in Europe: An Overview

Susanne Mundschenk, Michael H. Stierle,*
Ulrike Stierle-von Schütz and Iulia Traistaru

At the Lisbon Summit in March 2000, Europe's heads of state and government declared their ambition to make the European Union (EU)'the most competitive and dynamic knowledge-based economy in the world by 2010, capable of sustainable economic growth, with more and better jobs and greater social cohesion'. This broad objective includes an increase in the employment rate from an average of 61% in the EU to 70% by 2010, or 20 million additional jobs, and an EU average annual real growth rate of 3%, considerably higher than the average of 2.1% over the past ten years. To achieve this, the European Council adopted the Lisbon Strategy, an agenda consisting of short-term political initiatives as well as medium and long-term economic reforms aimed at achieving higher economic growth and employment, better environmental protection and increasing social cohesion. These measures aim for an increase in education levels and total spending in research and development from 2% to 3% of GDP as well as the completion of the single market with liberalization of telecommunications and electricity markets, as well as financial services.

Recent growth theories suggest that government policies may play a role in fostering efficiency and growth. According to endogenous growth models government intervention can raise the level of efficiency in the economy by addressing market failures, externalities and spillovers that prevent optimal allocation of resources. In particular, these models uncover the role of positive externalities associated with public investment that can generate benefits to the productive capacity of the economy (Romer, 1986, 1990, Aghion and Howitt, 1998). Schumpeterian type models of creative destruction (Aghion and Howitt, 1992) emphasise the innovation process leading to economic growth with implications for competition and patent policies. Governmental intervention may be justified when the socially desired level of R&D activity is higher than the level enterprises wish to engage in. This is due to the non-rival nature of technological knowledge and the trade-off faced by the enterprise between the positive effects of competition on its motivation to innovate and the potentially negative effects of strong competition on its ability to appropriate adequate returns to its R&D investment. In evolutionary theories (Nelson and Winter 1982, Nelson 1993) where enterprises seek profits under non-quantifiable uncertainty the aim of government policies is to provide conditions that support innovations by facilitating the distribution of knowledge. The existence of general-purpose technologies, where sector specific technological improvements find applications in other industries, could suggest that policies should be targeted at particular sectors. One note of caution, emphasized by the evolutionary theory, is that government failures in design and implementation of growth enhancing policies might prove to be counterproductive given insufficient information, thus compounding existing market failures.

The Lisbon Strategy is an ongoing process where the main responsibility for the reform process lies with the Member States. Yet, even if Member States had the political backing and were willing to reform, there is no simple recipe to achieve the targets. EU governments can promote and support faster growth by encouraging enterprises either directly through altering their incentives for investment or indirectly through improving the business environment. Direct influence on investment is exerted via taxes, subsidies or legislation while the environment in which firms operate is determined by institutions such as national education and training systems, product market regulations, transport and infrastructure as well as labour and financial market regulations.

The launch of the Lisbon Strategy was mainly a political achievement, without prior academic involvement or a coherent economic underpinning. It still remains a challenge to frame the debate about the Lisbon Strategy coherently, at least from an economic point of view. The Sapir Report (2004) was the first to do so. This book contributes added value to this debate by bringing together recent policy relevant research results on patterns of growth and cohesion, productivity and competitiveness as well as innovation and knowledge spillovers. The presented papers focus on areas where EU governments should take actions in order to (1) speed up convergence of the least developed Member States; (2) increase productivity through improved operation of markets; (3) strengthen the innovation process and its diffusion. Part II includes four keynote papers on the Lisbon Strategy, its main challenges and achievements to date. Part III provides lessons to learn from current research about Lisbon relevant topics on the role of institutions, education, R&D and technological progress on economic performance.

Adriaan Dierx and Fabienne Ilzkovitz discuss the rationale behind the Lisbon Strategy in chapter 2. EU GDP per capita has been stagnating at 70% of the US levels since the 1970s. This is the result not only of shorter working hours but also of much lower employment rates and lower productivity per hour. Given the implementation record so far, there are considerable doubts whether the three pillars of the Lisbon Strategy – economic growth, social cohesion and environmental sustainability – can be achieved simultaneously. Recent experience confirms these fears as productivity increases have been nearly offset by low employment rates. Thus instead of improvement of both employment rates and productivity, the recent record suggests a trade-off between employment creation and productivity gains, a chain the Lisbon Strategy had intended to break. Progress has been hampered first and foremost by the lack of implementation as identified by the High Level Group chaired by Wim Kok. The authors examine different reasons for the poor implementation record, highlight the benefits of the 'open method of co-ordination' and put forward possible improvements. To avoid that conflicting goals paralyse policy making, they propose a stronger focus on the growth objective. They also recommend that the current lack of ownership of the Lisbon strategy and the currently poor functioning of the idea of peer pressure should be overcome through the introduction of national Lisbon action programmes, involving parliaments, social partners and the public at large, as also suggested by the High Level Group.

The lessons and policy implications for the European knowledge society and innovation system form the focus of Peter Nijkamp's keynote paper in chapter 3. He argues that public expenditures and institutional reforms are crucial for creating and advancing a European knowledge society, the goals envisioned by the Lisbon Strategy and the 2002 Barcelona Summit . Meta analysis on the empirical evidence suggests a stable positive effect of education and research expenditures. He strongly recommends increased public expenditure in order to meet the Lisbon and Barcelona goals. But he also requires an institutional innovation in the European science policy as institutional ramifications in the European research landscape are considered a major obstacle to efficient use of the knowledge potential. In particular he identifies six challenges, where efficiency benefits can be gained through better linkages between science and industry and an improved research infrastructure across Europe, through a more open and more competitive process to attract the best people and to foster research excellence as well as to offer equal opportunities for new EU Member States. He pleads for a more flexible handling of the existing framework programmes, new joint initiatives by the European Commission, national governments and the Council of Ministers to overcome national fragmentation, the establishment of a European Research Infrastructure Fund and the installation of an independent European Research Council. The success of a European Research Council depends on its recognition by policy makers and the research community but, if warranted, it would assure the efficient use of scarce resources, create more flexible research careers, improve cooperation and stimulate new research endeavours.

Integration fosters the transfer of technology via trade and foreign direct investment between countries with different productivity levels, eliminates firms' incentives for duplication of innovation and increases market size for successful researchers and innovations. Ambiguous effects are to be expected from product market competition. While more product market competition raises the incentive for a firm to innovate, it eventually also lowers the expected return of the innovation. Integration allows the Member States to share the technological progress equally and hence they may under certain conditions exhibit the same growth rate in the steady state. Applying additional assumptions like identical aggregate production functions for all Member States, they also share the same steady state income level. Against this background what are the driving forces of real convergence within the EU? What policy lessons can be drawn from the catching-up experience of the cohesion countries?

In chapter 4, John Fitz Gerald's keynote paper compares the different EU integration experiences and policies of Ireland, Spain, Portugal and Greece over the last 20 years. Productivity gain has been the key convergence factor in the cases of Ireland, Spain and Portugal. However, he warns that this success could be jeopardized if wage rates grow faster than productivity. Also the tax wedge has become increasingly important for earnings in the context of EU integration. This suggests that a rapid rise in the additional provision of public services adversely impacts the convergence process. According to his analysis the driving force behind the high productivity increases has been investment in human capital. Returns on education increased remarkably in the cohesion countries for the last 30 years but high unemployment among low skilled workers suggests that further investment is required to improve the standard of living. The shortage of physical infrastructure was a significant constraint on growth and convergence and may remain so in the near future. Higher public and private investment means that consumption levels in the cohesion countries lag further behind the rest of the EU compared to output. The EU Structural Funds were important in that they reconciled higher investment needs and fiscal borrowing constraints under the Stability and Growth Pact. They also improved administrative investment procedures. Fitz Gerald draws attention to the fact that human capital could be sidelined since returns on infrastructure investments in the cohesion countries are high.

Among nations, competitiveness is a difficult concept as it suggests a false analogy between enterprises and countries. A meaningful concept of competitiveness at the national level defines a competitive country as one that can maintain high rates of growth and employment. Competitiveness in this sense depends on the quality of a country's economic and political institutions and the extent to which they are supportive of employment, productivity growth, innovation and the ability to adjust to changing circumstances (Mundschenk et al. 2002).

Under the Lisbon strategy one indicator of competitiveness is labour productivity measured as GDP per hour. According to this indicator, the EU, with higher growth rates in labour productivity, showed signs of catching up with the US since the 1960s. In 1995 the catching up process came to an end as US labour productivity accelerated while EU growth figures declined.

Exploring the factors behind accelerating US labour productivity since 1995 and the slowdown in the EU over the same period is the subject of chapter 5 by Bart van Ark, who asks whether the EU needs to revive productivity growth. His data show that faster productivity growth in the US was driven by information and communication technology (ICT) used in services, in particular retailing, wholesaling and financial services. He argues that the European slowdown in productivity growth was the consequence of an adjustment process that has developed more slowly in Europe than in the US. But with some delay, the diffusion of new technologies will ultimately lead to faster growth in Europe as well. To facilitate this development, governments can employ four policy mechanisms. The first concerns macroeconomic management. Wage moderation has lowered the price of labour relative to capital in Europe. The decline in the growth of the capital/labour ratio is an important source for the slower growth in labour productivity. The second policy mechanism is directed towards technological change and innovation in response to the recent decline in total factor productivity. The third mechanism relates to market institutions, such as the regulatory environment, consumer protection, and so on. The fourth mechanism refers to human capital, training, and education. Van Ark acknowledges that it is not always easy to find the right mix between these four mechanisms. He concludes that a more flexible market environment facilitates the restructuring of industry, and thus helps exploit the potential for growth.

In chapter 6, Henri de Groot, Richard Nahuis and Paul J.G. Tang question whether the American model is 'Miss World'. While the extent of the GDP per capita difference between the US and the EU average gives reasons for concern, a statistical decomposition shows that this difference is mainly due to the number of hours worked per employee. Consequently, the difference in income does not necessarily reflect differences in welfare since the value of leisure and household production are ignored in the income statistics. By contrast, in terms of productivity per hour worked and employment per inhabitant, several countries such as Norway, Denmark and the Netherlands score equally well or even better than the US. Therefore, an analysis of the EU average only is to some extent misleading. Moreover, EU countries generally outperform the US almost without exception in terms of a more equal secondary income distribution. Thus, economies scoring well in all three aspects – productivity, employment and income equality – are seen as the benchmark model, not the US.

In a second step, the authors shed more light on the trade-off between macroeconomic efficiency and social-economic equality by focusing on the impact of labour market institutions on economic performance, including inequality. Based on an OECD-wide econometric analysis exploiting both cross-sectional and time-series variations, they argue, in contrast to frequently expressed views, that income redistribution policies do not necessarily lead to lower participation and higher unemployment, as long as countries supplement it with active labour market policies. Furthermore, their results suggest that generous unemployment benefits of short duration contribute to employment without widening the income distribution.

From a different perspective, in chapter 7, Christian Dreger analyses a closely related issue, namely, the impact of institutions on the employment threshold in European labour markets over the period 1979–2001. In line with the Lisbon objective to increase the participation rate, here, in contrast to most previous studies, the focus is on employment rather than unemployment. In this paper, the employment record is measured in different dimensions in order to get statistically robust results. In particular, employment and participation rates, the threshold of output growth for additional employment and the intensity of employment growth relative to output growth are considered to be endogenous. The empirical analysis uses different econometric techniques, several institutional variables like employment protection legislation, strength of trade unions, measures in favour of the unemployed (unemployment benefits and active labour market policies) and taxes on labour.

Christian Dreger's empirical findings support the mainstream view that more flexibility on labour markets would improve the employment situation in Europe. Compared to the current institutional setting, greater flexibility and higher incentives to work appear to be appropriate strategies to improve the employment record. This includes changes to employment protection legislation, social security benefits, labour taxes and the wage bargaining power of unions. On the latter, he finds that higher levels of coordination in wage negotiations tend to increase employment. While acknowledging that the employment record cannot exclusively be explained by the institutional setting, his findings support the view that the progress achieved in recent years in some aspects of labour market institutions is not sufficient. In contrast, a comprehensive liberalisation strategy taking into account interactions between different institutions is needed.

The following three papers focus mainly on the role of innovation in fostering economic performance. In many theoretical and empirical models innovation is defined as a linear process where scientific research leads to technological developments and new technologies that satisfy market needs. Although innovation surveys exist, the number of patents most commonly approximates innovation. The process is thereby biased towards the manufacturing sector while recent studies also suggest the importance of innovations in services.

A second definition provided by evolutionary theory suggests a more complex concept, known as national innovations systems, as a network of public and private sector institutions whose activity and interactions initiate, import, modify and diffuse new technologies through sectors, space and time. Therefore, the number of patents falls short in describing the characteristics of an innovation process. Another important difference is that innovation policy is input-oriented under the first definition while under the second definition policies that support networks and collaborations are at the core. Many public policies are already in place at EU and Member State levels that seek to promote a two-way knowledge transfer between firms and academic institutions and to encourage enterprises to build collaborative R&D networks. National institutions and cultures are then considered to be determinants for the efficiency of growth-enhancing policies, such as R&D and education.

Depending on which analytical framework is used, the way innovation occurs differs, as does the recommendation of what determines a successful strategy for a region or a country. The common ingredients are knowledge creation and diffusion.

In chapter 8, Christoph Meister and Bart Verspagen concentrate on the 3% R&D intensity target for Europe formulated at the 2002 Barcelona Summit and investigate the potential productivity impact of increased R&D in manufacturing industries. In a first step Meister and Verspagen show the development of the total factor productivity gap in manufacturing of four EU-Member States (Germany, France, Italy and United Kingdom) relative to the United States between 1973 and 1997 and provide the background of the ambitious Barcelona R&D target. In a second step, the authors assess the potential success of the Barcelona target on productivity gaps by focussing on business R&D. Since the inclusion of R&D spillovers in the empirical analysis is an important issue in order to measure the net effect of R&D expenditure, the authors include the concept of direct and domestically and internationally indirect R&D stocks. For their simulation experiments Meister and Verspagen assume that a successful implementation of an increase of European R&D intensity by one third is possible. By increasing R&D stocks following the Barcelona target they obtain a substantial positive effect on total factor productivity. This translates into a clear reduction of the productivity gap with the United States, but this uniform R&D impulse may not put European industry in a leadership position. In order to illustrate the sectoral impact of an increased R&D expenditure the authors apply their simulations to 21 sectors divided into high-tech, medium-tech and low-tech sectors. Their results indicate that a focused R&D impulse in low-tech industries may have the strongest effect on the reduction of the productivity gap followed by medium-tech sectors. However, according to the authors, this result in particular should be taken with caution when it comes to policy conclusions, since the required and assumed increases in R&D expenditure are enormously high in the case of low-tech industries, so focusing on these sectors alone may not be appropriate to realize the Barcelona target. Even if other important factors for successful implementation such as absorption capacity, functioning networks of researchers, institutional and even cultural factors, and so on. have not explicitly been analysed, the authors argue that these seem to be important in order to close the productivity gap.

In chapter 9, Marc Baudry and Béatrice Dumont analyse unobserved effects (institutional, cultural etc.) as well as allocative efficiency of R&D spending to see whether they are partly responsible for different levels of performance in terms of innovation in various OECD countries over the period 1994–2000. In order to make their results internationally comparable they use triadic patent families as a measure of innovative performance. Moreover, by using this definition they concentrate on high value patents. The authors can show in their descriptive analysis that the United States are outperformed by most northern European countries and Japan in terms of average productivity of total R&D expenditure although their effort level in business and public R&D expenditure per capita does not differ from, or is even higher than, in the more productive countries.

In their econometric analysis, Baudry and Dumont estimate innovation production functions of the Poisson type and use their results to assess the fixed effects by computing a relative index of efficiency which reflects influences of non observed factors on innovation in a given country with the United States as reference country and the allocation efficiency of R&D spending between the private and public sector. According to the authors, an optimal allocation of expenditure contributes about 71.5% of total spending to business R&D, which is nearly the EU target agreed upon at the Barcelona summit. Their findings show that EU Member States differ quite largely in their innovation performance and allocative efficiency. Regarding the fixed effects, Baudry and Dumont can show that northern and core countries of the EU perform significantly better in terms of efficiency scores than the United

States while southern Member States and New Member States are less efficient. Regarding allocative efficiency the gap of Member States is less obvious. A mixed picture for certain countries concerning both measures might indicate that less well performing Member States with a weak influence of non observed factors benefit from an appropriate allocation of R&D expenditures while a misallocation between public and private spending may, to a certain degree, offset the positive impact of the non observable factors on the innovation process. Thus both non-observed factors and allocative efficiency seem to be important when improving the conditions for efficient R&D expenditure by focussing on just one part of the Lisbon Strategy.

In chapter 10, Volker Caspari, Jens Rubart and Günther Rehme focus on the relationship between education as a driving force for a successful innovation process and growth by undertaking a descriptive and empirical analysis on the productivity of the German and the US education and research systems. The declining growth trend of the German economy is their main motivation for a time series investigation of both education and research systems between the 1960s and the 1990s. In their descriptive part, they show that the US system, with a higher ratio of educational expenditures per GDP on average, produces more students at colleges and universities relative to employment but also relatively more doctorates in science and engineering leading to activities responsible for advances in the technological progress. In contrast, the German system is rather focused on educating on a skill specific basis up to master's level.

Concerning the empirical analysis the authors compare several input and output indicators in order to investigate the efficiency and productivity of both systems. Here they found very different results for Germany and the US For example, higher efforts in education measured as educational spending per GDP neither lead to an increase of the wage spread, indicating a higher value of productivity due to higher education, nor to a higher participation rate in education in the German system while the opposite is true for the US. Regarding the productivity of the educational systems it turns out that Germany performed on average better in the last decades but the US system was more successful in producing more high potentials in science and engineering. Another picture can be drawn for the research system. Quantifying the production of knowledge with national patent applications the authors show that Germany suffers from a large decline of research productivity although recovering slightly in the 1990s. However, the US system demonstrates a much better performance in efficiency terms compared to the German system. Collecting all these first tests and measures, the authors argue for a more in-depth analysis of national educational and research systems as growth driving factors.

NOTE

*   Opinions expressed here are exclusively those of the author and do not necessarily reflect
     those of the European Commission, DG Economic and Financial Affairs.

REFERENCES

Aghion, P. and P. Howitt (1992), 'A model of growth through creative destruction',
     Econometrica, **60** (2), pp. 323–351.
Aghion, P. and P. Howitt (1998), *Endogenous Growth Theory*, Cambridge (MA):
     MIT Press.
Mundschenk, S., J. von Hagen, P. Cornelius, J. Blanke, F. Paua and A. Mettler
     (2002), 'The Lisbon review 2002–2003, An assessment of policies and reforms in
     Europe', Geneva: World Economic Forum.
Nelson, R. and S. Winter (1982), *An Evolutionary Theory of Economic Change*,
     Cambridge: Harvard University Press.
Nelson, R. (1993) *National Innovation Systems*, Oxford and New York: Oxford
     University Press.
Romer, P.M. (1986), 'Increasing returns and endogenous growth', *Journal of Political
     Economy*, **94** (5), pp. 1002–37.
Romer, P.M. (1990), 'Endogenous technological change', *Journal of Political
     Economy*, **98**, pp. 71–102.
Sapir, A. (2004), 'An agenda for a growing Europe; The Sapir Report', Oxford:
     Oxford University Press.

PART II

THE LISBON STRATEGY:
MAIN CHALLENGES AND ACHIEVEMENTS

2. Economic Growth in Europe: Pursuing the Lisbon Strategy

Adriaan Dierx and Fabienne Ilzkovitz*

2.1 INTRODUCTION

The European Union witnessed a slowdown in its real growth from mid-2000 onwards. The main feature of this economic slowdown was not its sharpness but its duration. There was a gradual but steady widening of the output gap over the four years from 2000 to 2004. In contrast, over the same period the US saw a sharp deterioration in the output gap for the first two years but an improvement thereafter. This discrepancy suggests that the European Union's relatively weak growth performance is not solely attributable to cyclical factors but that supply factors have played an important role as well. From this perspective, making a success of the Lisbon strategy, which aims to transform the European Union into the most competitive and dynamic knowledge-based economy in the world while preserving the European social model, becomes all the more important. The aim of this chapter is to assess whether the Lisbon strategy is an effective tool to revive economic growth in the European Union.

The chapter first examines the rationale for the Lisbon strategy, which is to increase population welfare by raising the growth potential of the European economy in a sustainable way. The next section explains how a comprehensive strategy of structural reforms can contribute to stimulating growth but why possible tensions may exist between the economic, social and environmental objectives of this strategy. Section 2.4 addresses the question of how to best implement such a strategy of structural reforms. This touches on sensitive areas of national competence, such as taxation, social benefits and public service provision. Section 2.5 assesses the progress made towards the main Lisbon targets and concludes that it has been impossible for the European Union to make simultaneous progress in raising productivity and employment. This analysis focuses on the fifteen 'old' Member States because the ten 'new' Members have only been involved in the Lisbon strategy from 2004 onwards.[1] Section 2.6 takes a step back, and wonders whether this assessment of the EU situation is too negative, considering that the productivity growth slowdown may only be a temporary phenomenon. Section 2.7 provides an overall assessment of the success of the Lisbon strategy, highlighting its main achievements and failures at mid-term, and Section 2.8 concludes.

2.2 RATIONALE

The Lisbon strategy was launched in 2000 during a period of optimism about the future of Europe. During this period, economic growth was strong with a real GDP growth of 3.6%, the EMU had been launched and there were great expectations about new opportunities to be opened up by the information society and EU enlargement.

However, the post-war catching-up process of the EU with the US in terms of GDP per capita had come to an end in the mid 1970s (see Figure 2.1). Since then, GDP per capita in the EU has hovered at just above 70% of the US level. During the 1960s and 1970s the average annual growth rate of GDP per capita in the EU exceeded that in the US by 0.8 percentage points but since 1996 the average annual per capita growth rate of the European Union has been 0.4 percentage points below that of the US (see Table 2.1). In order to redress this reversal it seemed appropriate to introduce a comprehensive structural reform agenda such as the Lisbon strategy.

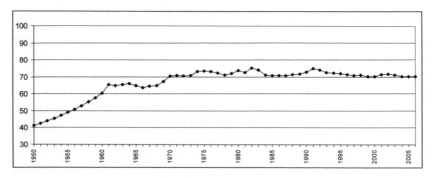

Source: Commission Services; 2004–2005–2006: forecasts.

*Figure 2.1 EU15 real GDP per capita in PPS (at 1995 prices) (US=100),
       1950–2006*

Table 2.1   GDP per capita growth rates in the EU15 and the US, 1961–2006

Annual % change of real GDP per capita	EU 15	US
1961–1980	3.3	2.5
1981–1990	2.1	2.2
1991–1995	2.2	2.2
1996–2000	2.4	2.9
2001–2006	2.3	2.7

Source: Ameco Autum 2004 forecasts.

The observation that the EU was unable to match the US performance in terms of GDP per capita and that the catching-up process with the US in this respect had come to an end, was a main reason for the Lisbon strategy. According to the data available at the March 2000 Lisbon summit, GDP per capita in the EU was 30% below that of the US. The heads of state and government therefore identified the closure of the gap in per capita income between the EU and the US as one of the main goals of the Lisbon strategy.

What were the underlying causes of the 30% gap in per capita GDP between the EU and the US? Figure 2.2 illustrates that on the basis of 1999 data (the data available at the time of the Lisbon Summit), this gap could be explained by lower EU employment rates (87.4% of the US level in 1999), number of hours worked (in 1999, Europeans worked 87.5% of the number of hours that Americans worked), and productivity per hour (91.9% of that in the US in 1999). In other words, lower productivity per hour contributed to 24% of the per capita GDP gap between the EU and the US, while the remainder of the gap was due to Europeans working fewer hours than Americans (38%), and to lower employment rates in the EU (38%).

The main conclusion that can be drawn from this is that the EU needs to increase both its employment rate and labour productivity if it wants to catch up with the US. Raising the employment rate would require addressing the still relatively low participation by women and older workers in the labour market as well as the still high structural unemployment rate. The relatively low productivity may be associated with a lack of dynamism of the European economy. Several factors could contribute to explaining this lack of dynamism: markets are still fragmented; business regulations act as a barrier to market entry and make it more difficult for companies to grow; R&D expenditures are insufficient; and it is too difficult to transform European ideas into marketable products and processes. The EU also lags behind in the development and use of new technologies (see also section 2.5).

Making progress on productivity and employment is all the more important given the ageing population in the EU. Demographic changes underway mean that the working-age population in Europe will start to shrink from 2010 onwards (as the post-war baby-boom cohorts reach their retirement ages). The working-age population is projected to decline by 40 million or 18% by 2050. Unless this is offset by increased productivity growth, this decline in the size of the labour force will result in a lower potential growth rate. Projections by the Commission indicate that the pure impact of ageing populations would be to reduce potential growth in the EU from the present rate of 2–2.25% to about 1% by 2040 (see Figure 2.3). This fall in the potential growth rate may at first sight appear small, but its cumulative effect over 50 years would imply a shortfall in GDP per capita of some 20%. This does not imply that living standards in the EU will fall by 20% but rather that they will be lower than what could be expected in the absence of demographic changes.

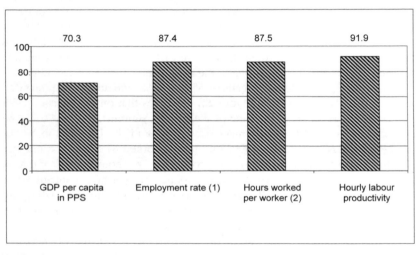

Notes:
(1) Calculated – employment rate = 100* (GDP per capita / labour productivity per person employed)
(2) Calculated – hours worked by worker = 100* (labour productivity per person employed / hourly labour productivity)

Source: DG Ecfin based on structural indicators.

Figure 2.2 EU15 relative performance (US=100), 1999

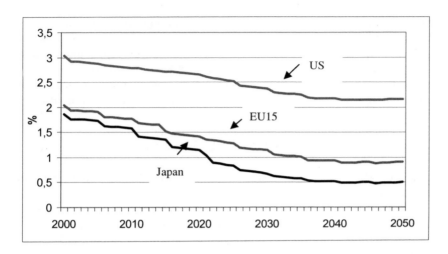

Source: Commission services.

Figure 2.3 Potential GDP growth rates in EU15, US and Japan, 2000–2050

2.3   A COMPREHENSIVE STRATEGY OF STRUCTURAL REFORMS

Based on the analysis above, the Lisbon Summit recognised a need for a comprehensive strategy of structural reforms. It is now widely recognised that structural reforms which contribute to removing barriers to the smooth and efficient functioning of product, capital and labour markets are essential for increasing the growth potential in the medium and longer term. In this section, we will first discuss the relationship between structural reforms and growth. Next, we will examine the advantages of having a comprehensive strategy of reforms as well as highlight the difficulties of pursuing a broad policy agenda encompassing economic, social and environmental objectives. Finally, we will briefly discuss the interactions between macroeconomic conditions and reforms.

2.3.1 Structural Reforms and Growth

Structural reforms can affect the potential growth rate of an economy through their influence on the growth of employment and productivity.

The relationship between structural reforms and population welfare
The ultimate objective of economic reforms is an improvement of population
welfare. The latter depends on two factors: first, per capita income and
second, its distribution among individuals. Addressing distribution issues
would bring us to a different strand of the economic literature, which would
go beyond the scope of the present chapter. Focusing on income issues, per
capita income can be decomposed as follows:

$$GDP/Pop = (GDP/Emp)*(Emp/Pact)*(Pact/Pop) \qquad (2.1)$$

where *GDP* is the Gross Domestic Product, *Pop* is population, *Emp* is
employment and *Pact* is the active population.

The third term in this equation is generally considered as exogenous (at
least in the medium-run). In contrast, the first two terms (labour productivity
and the employment rate) will be affected by reforms on labour, product and
capital markets.

The effect of structural reforms on productivity and the employment rate is
through their impact on the better functioning of markets. Labour market
reforms tend to focus on creating incentives for employers to hire workers
and for workers to become or remain active participants in the labour market.
Moreover, efforts to lower the mark-up of wages over the reservation wage
are aimed at lowering insider-outsider barriers, thus helping to bring down
the rate of structural unemployment. Finally, better working labour markets
allow for an efficient (re-)allocation of labour and encourage investment in
human capital thus raising productivity.

The structural impact of product market reforms as well can be split into
three categories:

- Restoring allocative efficiency: when producers have market power,
  prices deviate substantially and persistently from marginal costs.
  Thus the structure of consumption is distorted and total output is
  kept below its socially optimal level;
- restoring productive efficiency: while firms produce at lowest cost
  under conditions of competition, they begin to operate inefficiently
  (through overstaffing, higher wages, lack of response to new
  opportunities, poor management) in situations of poor competition;
  and,
- fostering dynamic efficiency. This is an extension of productive
  efficiency and concerns product and process innovations. It speeds
  up the move to the technology frontier, which is a major source of
  growth.

The immediate impact of reforms is on allocative efficiency. In a given market, increased competition reduces monopoly rents, which translates into lower prices (close to marginal costs). Even with unchanged nominal incomes, the outcome is higher demand and output in real terms. At a more aggregate level, when all markets are more competitive, production and employment (through labour demand) increase as does income.

However, allocative efficiency gains are neither the only nor the most important outcome of reforms. Pelkmans (1984) and Geroski and Jacquemin (1985) argue that productive and dynamic efficiency effects are far more important than allocative ones. To shed light on the impact of reforms on productive and dynamic efficiency, the developments in the new growth theory and their relation to market functioning provide a very useful framework.

The new growth theory extended the neo-classical analysis of growth initiated by Solow in various ways. While keeping labour, capital and technological progress as the main sources of growth, it makes the rate of technological progress endogenous, relaxes the assumption of constant return to scale in production and emphasises the quality (in addition to the quantity) of labour and capital. To make the rate of technological progress endogenous, the theory uses dynamic models of oligopolistic firm behaviour that incorporate the Schumpeterian incentives for research and development. Relaxing the assumption of constant returns to scale drives the permanent effects of factor accumulation on growth. Finally, the introduction of the notion of human capital instead of labour quantity points to the importance of knowledge, education and health as engines of sustained growth.

Structural reforms in the European Union have been targeted at creating better functioning markets. Labour market reforms aim to improve the functioning of labour markets, a key condition to increasing employment and decreasing unemployment. For example, changes in tax and benefits systems could help to increase the employment rate. Other measures, such as more flexible work contract arrangements, better targeted active labour policies and reform of wage bargaining systems which reflect productivity differentials, could also contribute to improving labour market functioning. Product market reforms could increase productivity growth by increasing competition and stimulating business investment and innovation. Such reforms aim to eliminate the remaining barriers to cross-border trade and market entry, creating a supportive environment for entrepreneurship, increasing competition in previously monopolistic sectors, such as electricity and gas, and developing framework conditions supportive to R&D, innovation and the diffusion of ICT. Structural reforms on financial markets could also raise output and employment by creating an integrated financial market. This should allow capital to flow where the returns are the highest and should create better financing conditions for business.

By improving the functioning of markets, structural reforms could also increase the ability of countries to adjust to country-specific shocks. This is particularly important in the euro area because the loss of the exchange rate instrument for participating countries requires the use of alternative adjustment mechanisms. Effectively functioning product, labour and capital markets increase the ability of an economy to adapt smoothly to changing economic circumstances.

A number of studies provide empirical support for the argument that market reforms have positive effects on economic performance. Some of these studies investigated the impact of trade liberalisation, others focused on competition and regulation and attempts were made to consider different types of reforms simultaneously (for a survey of these studies, see Dierx, Ilzkovitz and Sekkat 2002). The European Commission (2002) provides estimates of the macroeconomic impact of market reforms in the second half of the 90s, using its macro-econometric model QUEST. The conclusions of this study were that product and labour market reforms over the period 1996–2001 led to a medium term increase in GDP relative to its baseline level of about 3–4%. This corresponds to an acceleration of output growth by almost half of a percentage point annually over that period. Without reforms, average growth would have been 2.2% instead of 2.6% over the period 1996–2002. This would have translated into 5–6 million fewer jobs in the EU and unemployment would have been higher by 2 million. If the effects of the increased knowledge instruments foreseen within the Lisbon strategy were added in, the increase in EU GDP growth rate could reach three-quarters of a percentage point annually over the medium term (European Commission 2003).

2.3.2 A Comprehensive Strategy of Reforms

The Lisbon strategy is more than a series of market reforms that are limited to the economic domain. Rather, the Lisbon agenda foresees structural reforms in the economic, social and environmental policy domains. This raises the question of whether the Lisbon objectives of economic growth, social cohesion and environmental sustainability can be attained at the same time or to the same degree, or whether there would be trade-offs.

While the Lisbon Strategy intends to be a comprehensive set of reforms that are mutually reinforcing, the potential trade-offs between its three pillars are impossible to ignore. For example, by calling for higher growth but greater social cohesion, the Lisbon Strategy recognises that policies to promote higher rates of growth could produce rising social inequalities unless they are accompanied by the appropriate employment and social policies. Similarly, there are possible short-term trade-offs between growth and environmental policy if the costs of reducing pollution are too high relative to the gains in other parts of the economy, such as in industries that produce pollution abatement equipment. Such trade-offs could only be resolved by a thorough consideration of the costs and benefits of alternative courses of action, while taking account of the fact that economic growth is a pre-condition for progress to be made in terms of social and environmental objectives. A better exploitation of the potential complementarities between the three pillars would imply that the growth objective be placed more clearly at the centre of the Lisbon strategy. This does not mean that the social and environmental objectives should be abandoned but rather that the reforms should be better organised in order to maximise synergies.

The coherence and comprehensiveness of economic reform effort are a key characteristic of the Lisbon strategy. The reason is that, for maximum effectiveness, product, labour and capital market reforms need to be introduced jointly. Without better functioning labour markets, conducive to resource re-allocation across firms and sectors, employment and growth opportunities created by freeing highly regulated sectors and opening up new markets would not be seized. This would lead to a shrinking of the constituency in favour of reform and even entail risks of reversibility of the on-going reforms. On the other hand, a failure to liberalise product markets when introducing labour market reforms would continue to leave prices at high levels, resulting in losses of competitiveness and jobs. Coherence of reforms on product markets is also crucial. For example, increases in state aids could be counterproductive to a further integration of product markets and could lead to a reduction in the degree of competition in these markets.

2.3.3 Macroeconomic Conditions and Structural Reforms

The interactions between market reforms and macro-economic conditions are also worthwhile to discuss. Structural reforms could contribute to improving the macroeconomic environment. Well-functioning markets are essential to create the conditions for non-inflationary growth. For example, structural reforms that improve market functioning raise the potential output level that is compatible with price stability. This would facilitate the conduct of monetary policy by reducing inflationary pressures. By reducing market rigidities, structural reforms can also reduce the burden on macroeconomic policies in the event of shocks. Finally, confidence in the economic situation may be jeopardised if poorly functioning markets contribute to high and persistent unemployment or social exclusion.

There are two opposite views on the macroeconomic conditions that are conducive to reforms. On the one hand, a sound macro-economic environment can facilitate the introduction of reforms since the costs of these reforms are generally less painful and distributional effects are less visible. For example, Lisbon was launched during a period of strong economic growth in the EU. On the other hand, difficult economic conditions could foster support for reforms because the costs of maintaining the status quo become too high. However, the two views are not necessarily contradictory. Evidence provided by the IMF (2004) shows that the period of recovery after a prolonged period of weak growth is the most conducive to an acceleration in structural reforms.

2.4 IMPLEMENTATION

The implementation of the Lisbon strategy requires governance instruments to push the strategy forward (Rodrigues 2001). Three main decisions have been taken to improve the instruments of governance at the European and at the national level. First, an 'open method of coordination' (OMC) has been adopted to develop the European dimension and to promote co-operation between Member States in different policy fields. Second, the Spring European Council has received a stronger role as a co-ordinator of the strategy. Third, an annual policy cycle has been established to monitor progress on Lisbon.

The reforms required in order to achieve the Lisbon objectives touch on sensitive areas of national competence, such as education and training, social benefits and public service provision. Therefore, in accordance with the principle of subsidiarity, national governments retain the prime responsibility in these areas. This explains why a soft form of co-ordination is generally used in the area of structural reforms. The Lisbon European Council called this the 'open method of co-ordination'.

This method of economic governance has been designed in such a way that it enables, in principle, the combination of the benefits of partial centralisation through agreements on targets, timetables, benchmarks and indicators with the degree of decentralisation that is required by the differing economic structures and preferences of the Member States. For example, achieving the objective of increasing the European research effort to 3% of the EU's GDP by 2010 requires, on the one hand, the integration of research efforts at the European level with a view to establishing a 'critical mass' of resources. On the other hand, it requires an improvement of the framework conditions at the national level that are conducive to R&D, such as access to risk capital, good science–industry links and an ample supply of well-educated researchers.

In the aftermath of the Lisbon European Council of March 2000, the OMC has been established in a number of areas including R&D, innovation, enterprise policy, social inclusion, pensions, education, and vocational training. The application of the OMC varies quite substantially between these areas, reflecting the different policy priorities. Nevertheless, the OMC can be considered as a useful tool to finding consensus at the EU level on common goals and on how to achieve these goals. It is also a helpful tool to exchange best practice and improve policy coordination between EU Member States. However, the OMC also has limitations as an instrument of peer pressure and as a tool to bring forward structural reforms at the national level. The method is not armed with any formal instruments to foster compliance with agreed policy orientations, and on sensitive issues, the Member States remain quite reluctant to commit themselves to the objectives agreed and to be subject to the peer-review process, which is a central element of the OMC.

The implementation of the Lisbon reform agenda also builds on a stronger guiding and coordinating role of the European Council and on an annual policy cycle established to monitor progress on Lisbon goals at a European and national level. This cycle consists of three steps:

First, a policy impulse is given each year by the Spring Report, which presents to the Spring European Council the Commission's priorities for action. Although the Commission is only responsible for Community actions, the proposals address both the European and the national levels. The Spring Report is complemented by 'conclusions' prepared by different Council formations, which highlight areas where further progress needs to be made (also reflecting the outcome of the open methods of coordination, where applicable).

Second, on the basis of this information the Spring European Council identifies its policy priorities. These priorities are reflected in three main instruments of economic and social policy coordination: the Broad Economic Policy Guidelines, the Employment Guidelines and the Internal Market Strategy, which provide recommendations to the Member States on what actions to take. In particular, the Broad Economic Policy Guidelines are a key mechanism in implementing the Lisbon strategy as they bring together the EU's macroeconomic and structural policies coherently. The recommendations in the guidelines Package are orientated towards medium term objectives and are in principle fully reviewed only once every three years.

Third, these policy actions have to be implemented by the Member States, who then report on progress made during the autumn. The Commission's assessment of progress made by the Member States in implementing the different recommendations is presented in the so-called 'Implementation Package' that accompanies the Spring Report. In addition, the Spring Report gives an assessment of performance levels and progress made by the different Member States towards achieving the Lisbon objectives.

The question remains whether these instruments of governance are sufficiently effective in delivering results or whether we need stronger methods of coordination to drive forward the implementation of reforms. Deroose and Langedijk (2002) argue that stronger forms of coordination are necessary in order to overcome the political resistance to reforms due to time inconsistencies and asymmetric benefits. Collignon (2003) and Coeuré and Pisani-Ferry (2003) make the case as well that hard forms of policy coordination need to be introduced in order to achieve the Lisbon goals, particularly in light of the increased number of EU Member States post enlargement. Collignon shows that the soft forms of policy coordination such as the OMC will be ineffective when it is difficult to exclude non-participating countries from the benefits of the common policy and when there is a degree of rivalry amongst participants regarding the benefits that they can draw from their participation. In practice, however, stronger forms of co-ordination are politically not realistic in the near future as far as many sensitive issues in capital, labour and product markets are concerned. As a consequence, structural policy co-ordination has to rely on exchange of best practices, benchmarking, peer pressure and policy competition.

2.5 PROGRESS ON THE MAIN LISBON TARGETS

The European Commission's assessment of progress made towards the Lisbon objectives is based on a set of structural indicators agreed between the Commission and the Council. A distinction is made between 14 headline indicators reflecting key objectives, which are attached to the Spring Report in the form of illustrative graphs and a database of over 100 (sub-)indicators used by the Commission in drafting the Report. This database is publicly accessible via a Eurostat website.[2] The description below of progress made on the main Lisbon targets is largely based on this database as well.

One of the main goals of the Lisbon strategy launched in 2000 was to close the gap in living standards between the EU and the US by implementing a comprehensive set of reforms which would allow the European Union to better face the new challenges of globalisation, the knowledge economy and an ageing population. Four years later, the picture is a mixed one. The growth performance of the EU15 has been rather disappointing over the recent years, with real GDP growth declining from 3.6% in 2000 to 0.8% in 2003 and recovering to 2.2% in 2004. Clearly, potential growth remains well short of the 3% anticipated in 2000 at the time of the Lisbon summit. This section aims to identify the main factors underlying the disappointing growth performance of the fifteen 'old' Member States. Developments in the ten 'new' Member States are not considered here as they were not yet members of the EU for most of time period covered (that is, 1999–2004).

2.5.1. Short-term (Macroeconomic) Factors

Unfavourable short-term macroeconomic developments have not helped the Union to make progress towards the main Lisbon economic targets and partly explain Europe's disappointing economic performance. External shocks and demand factors have contributed to keep growth below its potential in the EU over the period 1999–2004. Adverse shocks, such as the stock market collapse in early 2001, the September 11 terrorist attacks, the SARS epidemic and the war in Iraq have hit the EU during the last four years. These shocks have contributed to a prolonged period of subdued demand over the period 2001–2003, mainly related to weak household consumption (see Table 2.2) but also to a contraction in investment spending (see Figure 2.4). There is a debate among economists regarding the role of macroeconomic policy in explaining the prolonged period of sluggish growth in the EU. This question is not discussed here.

*Table 2.2   Growth rates of private consumption in the EU15,
the US and Japan, 2000–2004*

Annual % change of private consumption	EU 15	US	Japan
2000	3.0	4.7	2.0
2001	2.0	2.5	2.7
2002	2.1	3.1	0.5
2003	2.3	3.3	2.2
2004	2.8	3.5	3.1

Source: European Commission, Ameco, Autumn forecasts, 2004.

The slow growth of consumption is in marked contrast with developments in some of the EU's main trading partners. Indications are that the weakness of consumption can be associated with an increase in the saving rate. The latter may be related to such issues as the ageing population, uncertainty about the sustainability of social security systems and/or public deficits and debt levels. To the extent that individuals perceive these changes as leading to a fall in permanent income, the effects on the saving ratio would be longer lasting.

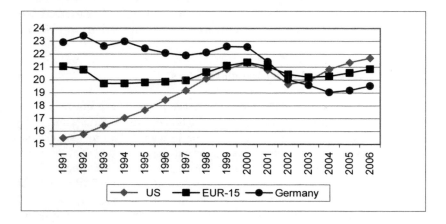

Source: AMECO autumn 2004 forecasts; 2004 2005 2006: forecasts.

Figure 2.4 Investment ratios (as % of GDP), 1991–2006

In 2001 and 2002, both the EU and the US experienced a contraction in capital spending, but while investment growth returned to positive territory in the US in 2003, in the EU (and Germany in particular) the recovery came later and was much weaker. Moreover, the contraction in the US may be viewed as an unavoidable adjustment following the investment boom of the period 1993–2000, when the investment to GDP ratio increased by more than five percentage points. There is no evidence of an investment boom in the euro area on the same scale as in the US. It appears that structural factors have played a role in explaining these different trends. These factors are discussed in the next section.

2.5.2 Longer-term (Structural) Perspective for the EU15

As a result of the poor growth performance, EU15 living standards as measured by GDP per capita, remained pretty much unchanged at around 70%[3] of that of the US. As explained in Section 2, the 30% gap in GDP per capita could be attributed to a lower productivity per hour and to a lower total number of hours worked in the EU. Since the launch of the Lisbon strategy, it has proved impossible to make simultaneous progress on these two fronts. The increased contribution of employment to EU GDP growth (both in number of hours worked per worker and in terms of the employment rate relative to that in the US) has been almost completely offset by a reduction in the contribution from labour productivity (see Figure 2.5). Therefore, improving the productivity performance and raising its employment rate are both essential to increase the long-term growth potential of the EU economy.

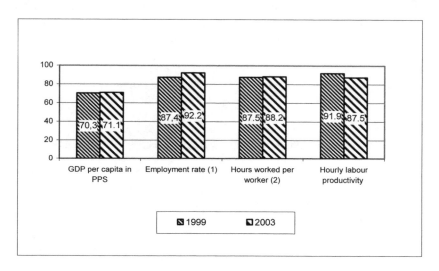

Notes:
(1) Calculated - Employment rate = 100 * (GDP per capita / Labour productivity per person employed)
(2) Calculated - Hours worked per worker =100 * (Labour productivity per person employed / Hourly labour productivity)

Source: Eurostat Structural Indicators.

Figure 2.5 EU15 performance (US=100), 1999 and 2003

Between 1999 and 2003, the number of employed persons in the EU15 increased by some 6.5 million people, including 4 million women and 2.5 million older workers. However, this growth trend is not adequate and there is a great risk of missing the Lisbon employment targets for 2010. The EU25 should create some 21 million new jobs by 2010 if it is to succeed in meeting its overall employment target of 70%. Of these jobs, around 8 million should be filled by women and roughly 6 million by older workers if the targets of the employment rates for women and older workers are also to be met. The required annual growth in the overall employment rate would be of the same order of magnitude as the employment increase during the best years in the late 1990s. The target for the female employment rate seems to be somewhat easier to achieve because the younger female age cohorts entering the labour market during this decade will have higher participation rates than those leaving the labour market.

While the employment gap has narrowed, the productivity gap with the US has widened. For the first time in decades, the labour productivity in the EU is on a trend growth path which is lower than that of the US. Over the period 1996–2003, the EU15 productivity growth rate[4] averaged 2.4%, as opposed to 2.2% recorded for the US (see Table 2.3).

Table 2.3 Contributions of hourly productivity and hours worked to GDP growth, EU15 and US, 1966–2003 (annual percentage growth rates)

	Labour productivity per hour		Hours worked		GDP	
	EU15	US	EU15	US	EU15	US
1966–1970	5.6	2.8	−0.6	2.6	5	3.4
1971–1980	3.8	2.6	−0.6	2.6	3.2	3.2
1981–1990	2.2	2.4	0.2	2.7	2.4	3.1
1991–1995	2.4	1	−0.7	2.4	2.7	2.4
1996–2003	2.4	2.2	0.8	1	2.2	3.2

Source: Commission services.

The decline in EU labour productivity growth rates in the mid-1990s can be attributed in equal parts to a lower investment per employee and a slowdown in the rate of technological progress, as measured by total factor productivity (see Figure 2.6).

The former can be partially explained by a higher rate of job creation, the argument being that the newly created jobs tend to be low-productivity jobs, while the latter has been associated with insufficient investment in R&D and education; an insufficient capacity to transform research into marketable products and processes; and the lower productivity performance in ICT producing industries (including office equipment and semiconductors) and in ICT using services (such as wholesale and retail trade, financial service) due to a slower ICT diffusion. As a result, the contribution of ICT to growth was half that observed in the US.

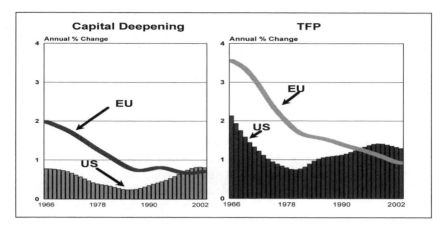

Source: European Commission (2004a).

Figure 2.6 Capital deepening and total factor productivity growth in
the EU15 and the US, 1966–2003

While the absorption of new technologies is a fundamental element which contributes to explaining the EU's relatively poor productivity performance, this performance is also linked to its industrial structure, which is based on more low and medium-tech industries, and to its difficulty in reorienting its specialisation towards sectors with high productivity growth prospects. In this respect, a study of the European Commission (2004a) shows that the US is more specialised in those high-tech sectors which contribute the most to the overall productivity growth. All this indicates that it is crucial for the EU to increase its innovative capacity and to foster entrepreneurial dynamism allowing it to better adapt its specialisation pattern towards new activities.

2.5.3 Longer-term (Structural) Perspectives for the Individual Member States

Improving the EU's productivity performance and raising its employment rate are both essential to increase the long-term growth potential of the economy. However, the key challenges are different among Member States.

Over the period 1999–2003 Denmark, Germany, France[5] and Ireland have improved on their already relatively high hourly productivity levels. Above average productivity gains were also recorded by Greece, Sweden, Finland and the UK, albeit from lower starting levels. These productivity gains could be associated either with the privatization or deregulation of industries leading to productive and allocative efficiency gains (in Germany and the UK for example) or with policies aimed at advancing the knowledge economy (in the Nordic countries in particular). Productivity growth in Italy and the Benelux was below average over this period, although productivity levels in 2003 in the Benelux countries remained well above that of the EU as a whole. The relative productivity levels in Spain and Portugal, on the other hand, deteriorated from what were already low levels. In the case of Spain, most of the productivity slowdown could be explained by rapid job creation (see below). This was not the case, however, for Portugal.

There appears to have been a convergence of employment rates amongst EU Member States, with those countries already having a relatively high employment rate (such as Austria, Finland, Sweden and the UK) recording relatively small increases or even a decline in employment (in the case of Denmark, Germany and Portugal). With the exception of Belgium, countries with a relatively low rate of employment (Belgium, Greece, Italy and Spain) raised their employment rates quite substantially. For the other EU Member States, the percentage increase in the employment rate was close to the EU average.

A joint analysis of hourly productivity and employment tendencies over the past four to five years (see Figures 2.7a and 2.7b) shows Greece to be the only country that has managed to make substantial progress on both fronts, albeit from below average levels. In Belgium and Portugal, on the other hand, both the productivity and the employment rate have increased substantially less than the EU average.

As already mentioned in section 2.3.2, the Lisbon strategy includes not only economic, but also social and environmental objectives. The list of structural indicators used to assess progress on the Lisbon strategy reflects this, as it includes not only indicators of productivity and employment and their determinants (such as R&D spending, youth educational attainment) but also indicators of social cohesion (the at-risk-of-poverty rate, the regional dispersion of employment rates) and environmental quality (greenhouse gas emissions). The Commission's annual Spring Report provides an overall assessment of performance levels and progress on the Lisbon objectives based on this wider set of indicators.

The 2004 Spring Report (European Commission, 2004b, p. 21) shows that performance levels for the small Northern countries (Denmark, Luxemburg, the Netherlands, Sweden), Austria and the United Kingdom are relatively high, while the Southern Member States (Greece, Spain, Italy and Portugal) are performing relatively poorly. In addition, the Report makes a distinction between countries that have made rather good progress overall (Belgium, France and Greece) – albeit from different starting levels – and others (Germany, Luxembourg, Austria and Portugal) where progress has been rather disappointing. However, this overall assessment tends to hide progress made in specific areas by different countries. Spain and Greece, for example, recorded a relatively strong improvement according to the social cohesion indicators, while Belgium – contrary to Austria and Spain – has made good progress in the environmental domain.

2.6   IS THIS ASSESSMENT OF THE EU SITUATION NOT TOO PESSIMISTIC?

At this stage, it is worthwhile to raise two issues which are presently being debated among economists and which tend to give a less pessimistic picture of the economic situation in the EU. The first issue concerns the preference of Europeans for leisure and the second question relates to the temporary or permanent character of the labour productivity slowdown in Europe. Two prominent economists have been in the forefront of these discussions: Gordon and Blanchard.

2.6.1 The Preference of Europeans for Leisure

The view of Gordon (2003) is that the gap in terms of GDP per capita between the EU and the US is overestimated, because Europeans freely choose to work a lower number of hours. The GDP per capita gap between the EU and the US is therefore mainly due to a different model of society and only partly due to government regulation and a lack of labour market flexibility. Gordon also considers that GDP comparisons tend to overestimate living standards in the US and understate the European standard of living as a result of measurement problems.[6] Taking into account these measurement problems and differences in preferences for leisure between Europeans and Americans, the EU GDP per capita would be only 8% lower than that of the US.

A similar position is defended by Blanchard (2004) who observes a decline in hours worked per person in the EU and argues that this decline can be explained by a decrease in the number of hours worked by full-time workers rather than by an increase in unemployment or an increase in working hours of part-time workers. While this decline in working hours of full-time workers is partly due to larger increases in labour taxes in Europe than in the US, it is essentially a voluntary choice of Europeans towards more leisure.

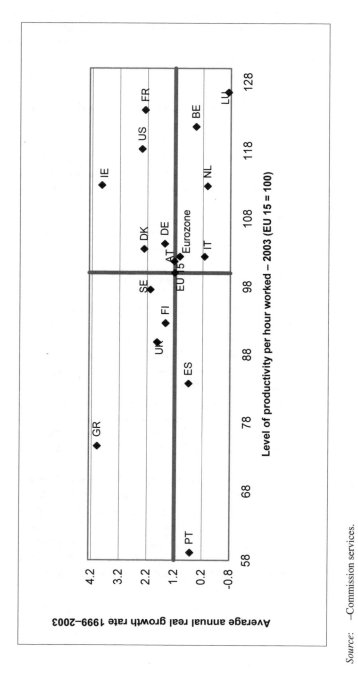

Source: –Commission services.

Figure 2.7a Evolution of hourly productivity in EU Member States, 2003

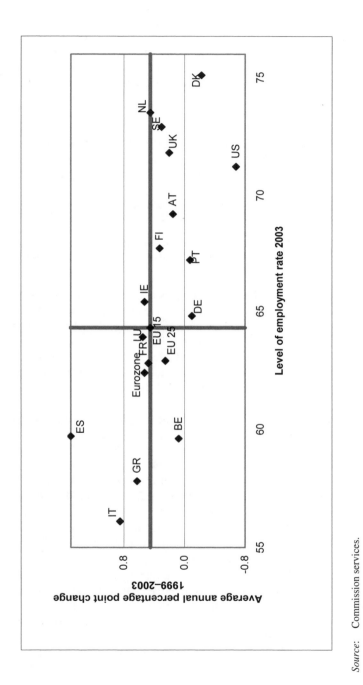

Source: Commission services.

Figure 2.7b Evolution of employment rate in EU Member States, 2003

However, one can argue that this choice would also, to a large extent, be influenced by disincentives to work resulting from early retirement schemes or reductions in working time. In addition, given demographic challenges, it would be difficult to continue to finance the social security and pension systems without more growth and modernisation of the welfare state.

2.6.2 The EU Productivity Setback

Both Gordon and Blanchard argue that the hourly labour productivity gap between the EU and the US is not very large and that the slowdown in productivity growth in Europe is transitory. To quote Gordon:

> Over the five years 1995–2000 the US briefly caught up to the European rate of productivity growth, but over any longer period, e.g., 1990–2000 or 1973–2000, the US growth rate lagged behind. As one European nation after another overtakes and moves past the US level of productivity, one might conjecture that in ten years conferences will be organised at American universities on 'the sources of European advantage'.

Similarly, Blanchard considers that EU productivity growth is simply experiencing a temporary setback and that the US leadership in terms of ICT production is not that significant. The main reason for the slowdown in labour productivity per hour is the decline in the EU's capital–labour ratio, which is the result of labour market reforms that have led to the reintegration of less qualified unemployed in the labour market. In other words, the productivity slowdown is just the reverse side of the medal of employment growth.

However, even allowing for the fact that employment and labour productivity trends in the EU may be negatively correlated, the reversal of past productivity patterns in the 1990s relative to the US has been striking. As illustrated in section 2.5, for the first time in decades, the labour productivity growth in the EU is on a trend productivity growth path which is lower than that of the US. Since the mid-1990s, the EU has proved incapable of arresting the long-run decline in its productivity performance, whereas the US has enjoyed a notable recovery in its secular trend. Results from the Commission's Quest model suggest that about 30% of the reduction in productivity growth in the EU can be explained by the increased employment of less skilled people (see European Commission (2003)).[7] A recent update of this study (European Commission (2004a)) concludes that the decline in the EU's productivity is to a large extent structural in nature and results from the EU's inability to absorb and produce new technologies and to transform its industrial structure. Finally, it should be recalled that the acceleration of US productivity growth is taking place in an economy with an overall employment rate that is almost 9 percentage points higher than that in the euro area and with – one would expect – a higher share of workers with low productivity.

2.6.3 Any Implications for the Lisbon Strategy?

It is probably right to explain at least a part of the GDP per capita gap between the EU and the US by different social preferences. Should we therefore conclude that there is a trade-off between growth and leisure and that the Europeans should not attempt to catch up with the US because they have a different model of society? We do not think so. Structural reforms remain the most effective tool for closing the gap and improving the growth potential of the EU economy.

Similarly, if we were to accept the argument that the productivity slow-down is only temporary, could we then conclude that we should not worry about productivity developments and focus – perhaps exclusively – on labour market reforms in the Lisbon strategy? Again, we would disagree. Improving the euro area's productivity performance and raising employment are both essential to increasing the EU's growth potential. Product, capital and labour market reforms are complementary in this respect. As product market reforms erode firms' monopoly rents, the incentives for workers to fight for a share of these rents and to oppose labour market reforms would be less. Therefore, successful reforms on product markets can be expected to put pressure for continued reforms on the labour market. Similarly, the full benefits of increased product market competition will only materialise when labour market functioning permits a smooth reallocation of labour in case of economic restructuring. Moreover, it is easier to offer an integrated strategy of reforms offering benefits for all, as potential losses associated with one element of the reform package could be offset by gains elsewhere.

Even accepting that the EU productivity slowdown is associated with the increase in employment, efforts to improve the EU's productivity performance in the medium term are essential for increasing the long-term growth potential of the EU economy. This is all the more true, as the ageing population might have a negative impact on productivity growth because an older labour force is less likely to use new technologies. Raising investment in both human and physical capital, developing the innovation potential of the EU economy and pursuing the integration of product and financial markets are thus essential. These are some of the objectives pursued by the Lisbon strategy. However, over the past few years, progress on this strategy has been relatively limited. The next section discusses the reasons explaining this poor performance but also highlights positive elements of the strategy.

2.7 STRENGTHS AND WEAKNESSES

So far, the progress made towards the main Lisbon objectives has been disappointing. This is the reason why the 2004 Spring European Council invited the Commission to establish a high-level group to prepare an independent contribution to the 2005 midterm review of the Lisbon strategy. The main objective of this midterm review is to give a fresh stimulus to the Lisbon strategy and to improve the implementation record of the strategy by involving more closely the Member States and the stakeholders.

According to the Spring Council conclusions, the mandate of this group was to be first, to assess the progress made towards the agreed targets (including a review of the structural indicators used to measure the level and dynamism of Member States, and EU performance, also in the global context); second, to identify the measures necessary to increase the level of growth and to achieve the Lisbon goal set in 2000; third, to evaluate governance and other instruments available to Member States and the EU to attain the Lisbon goal; and fourth, to improve the mechanisms for communicating the objectives of Lisbon as well as best practices among Member States. The High Level Group chaired by Wim Kok published its findings in November 2004.

Taking these findings as a point of reference, this section provides our assessment of the appropriateness of the Lisbon strategy and highlights its main strengths and weaknesses.

2.7.1 Positive Elements of the Lisbon Strategy

The main achievements of the Lisbon strategy are twofold: first, it has contributed to giving a greater emphasis to the main challenges facing the European Union and the need for structural reforms; and second, it has established a comprehensive agenda of reforms. In addition, simple statistical tools, such as the structural indicators, have been agreed to monitor the progress made in the different areas of reforms and in the different Member States and a streamlining of the policy coordination cycle has been initiated.

Greater emphasis on structural reforms

The Lisbon strategy has contributed to focusing attention on the main challenges of the European Union, bringing the need for structural reforms more into the limelight. Some political momentum in favour of structural reforms has been created and this might have contributed to gradually changing the philosophies underlying various countries' approaches. However, it has to be recognised that the Lisbon strategy has also built on the on-going effort of reforms in Europe, such as the internal market, financial market integration, the opening up of network industries to competition, and the employment strategy. This has put these reforms into a context of raising growth, while maintaining macro-economic stability and social cohesion and improving the sustainability of the environment.

A comprehensive reform agenda

The Lisbon strategy established a comprehensive reform agenda. A comprehensive strategy of reforms permits the exploitation of the complementarities between different structural reform policies, which is essential for their maximum effectiveness. While the Lisbon strategy has contributed to launching a collective effort of reforms in the various Member States and may have to some extent reduced the resistance against unpopular measures (for example, the liberalisation of the energy sector or pension reforms), it is clear that the scope and speed of reforms has continued to differ widely across countries and sectors. For example, progress in the area of labour market reforms has been more limited than progress in product market reforms and financial market integration.

Better tools to monitor progress made in the area of structural reforms

In order to maintain the momentum in favour of reforms and to encourage peer pressure, it is crucial that progress is systematically monitored and evaluated. This is the reason why the Lisbon European Council requested the Commission and the Council to agree on a set of structural indicators to be used in the 'Spring report'. These indicators are relatively simple and easy to understand instruments, which are used to monitor the progress made towards the targets. The High Level Group recommends using these indicators as a tool to praise countries that have performed well and castigate those that have done badly, thus increasing political pressure for reform. However, as a tool the structural indicators are rather blunt. It is therefore important to further develop analytical tools to better understand the effects of reforms and the interactions between the different areas of reforms.

Streamlining the EU economic policy coordination framework

The organisation of the annual Spring Council devoted to structural reforms has been a catalyst for some streamlining of the policy coordination framework. The two main building blocks of this policy coordination cycle are on one hand the Spring Report and the 'Implementation Package' and, on the other hand the 'Guidelines Package'. The Spring Report contains a detailed assessment of the measures implemented in the various policy areas and, on the basis of this assessment, it defines the new priorities for structural reforms. The Guidelines Package translates the general political orientations of the Spring European Council into recommendations for further action in the various policy areas, while keeping in mind that the Guidelines have been framed for the medium term and should only be varied in intermediate years in case of major changes. This streamlining has introduced a stronger orientation towards medium term goals and has improved the timing of the different policy processes. However, it has only partially succeeded in simplifying the different policy processes and in improving the coherence and complementarities of the different elements contained in the 'Guidelines Package'.

2.7.2 Weaknesses of the Lisbon Strategy

Over the past years, progress on the Lisbon strategy has been relatively limited and it has been hampered by a lack of implementation of the measures agreed by the different Spring European Councils. This section attempts to identify the reasons that explain this poor record of implementation and makes proposals on how to address the weaknesses of the Lisbon Strategy.

Too many priorities
One of the problems of the Lisbon strategy is the proliferation of sectoral targets and policy measures, which tend to distract attention and resources from the main objectives of the Lisbon strategy. For the next five years, it is essential to identify a shortlist of key targets that are essential to attaining the Lisbon objective. Action over the second half of the decade could then be focused on achieving these key targets.

Priorities for action should be identified on the basis of sound analysis, fully taking into account the economic, social and environmental elements of the Lisbon strategy. The full set of structural indicators should contribute to this effort. Appropriate analysis should also be used to assess the link between reforms and economic performance and to highlight interdependencies, synergies and trade-offs in the different areas of the Lisbon strategy. Indeed, it is important to accept that there are not only complementarities but also trade-offs between the economic, social and environmental objectives of the Lisbon strategy. Economic and social cohesion has been central to the process of the construction of Europe, but specific policies aimed at greater cohesion may have had negative effects on productive efficiency and growth. As a result, the sustainability of the European welfare state in a low growth context is being called into question more and more.

Greater emphasis should be given to reforms which contribute the most to increasing the growth potential of the EU economy when choosing the priorities for structural reforms. Moving to a higher growth trajectory is necessary for the other elements of the Lisbon strategy to fall into place. Higher competitiveness, leading to more economic growth, creates jobs. Getting a job is one of the most effective ways of increasing social inclusion. Similarly, competitiveness and growth can contribute to the resources needed to deliver higher environmental and social standards. Competitiveness and growth should thus be put at the centre of the Lisbon strategy. This conclusion appears to be very much in line with the advice of the High Level Group, chaired by Wim Kok to focus on 'growth and employment in order to underpin social cohesion and sustainable development': see box on page 39 in the report of the High Level Group (2004).

Insufficient drivers of reforms and lack of ownership by the Member States

The Lisbon strategy seems overambitious. Checks should be made as to whether the different targets are realistic, and more importantly whether the measures taken to achieve the Lisbon targets are the most appropriate ones, and whether the necessary instruments are available. For example, the Single Market Programme was based on the transposition of a number of specific Community Directives, and the entry into EMU was based on the fulfilment of well-defined convergence criteria. In this respect, it is important to identify the main bottlenecks in achieving the Lisbon targets.

The simple fact that a policy objective is (over)ambitious does not necessarily imply that the policy will fail to take off or be abandoned. Using a case study approach, Castanheira et al. (2004) identify three 'drivers of reform' that determine the success of a reform attempt. First, there may be a strong need to correct large inefficiencies that emerge in specific markets or economies, for instance when the current legislation is no longer consistent with the current economic environment due to technological developments or trade liberalisation. A second driver of reform is ideology, which was at the basis of the reduction in the degree of state intervention in the UK under the Thatcher governments. Finally, external constraints, such as the conditions for entry into the WTO or the euro area, are very powerful instruments to initiate a process of reforms. Within the context of the Lisbon strategy, the argument could be made that the first 'driver' is clearly present, but that the two other drivers are largely missing. Peer pressure is only a weak substitute for hard external constraints, while ideology tends to be diluted by the need for compromise to reach decisions at the EU level. There is a lack of 'ownership' of the Lisbon strategy by politicians, whose political support is mainly determined by their actions at the national level. In order to increase ownership, the High Level Group recommends that governments present national Lisbon action programmes that should be subject to debate with national parliaments and social partners.

A lack of peer pressure at the level of the Member States
Peer pressure is a central element in the Lisbon strategy via the Guidelines Package and the Open Method of Coordination (OMC). It may help Member States to overcome vested interests at the national level. The pressures to adopt common statistical tools and to use benchmarking to measure the progress made could also improve national monitoring and offer elements of comparison with other Member States. Despite the absence of formal sanctions against Member States that do not conform to the guidelines, non-compliance with agreed targets or guidelines should expose the Member States to the cost of losing credibility and reputation. In this respect, the monitoring of targets and of the implementation of guidelines is crucial. However, despite the fact that the performance of the Member States is regularly exposed and compared in public reports, there is still currently insufficient pressure put on governments to match best performance. In particular, there is the question of how to strengthen the incentives for reforms and to improve the level of accountability of Member States for implementing reform. At the very least, this would imply a reinforcement of the OMC process as an instrument for pushing ahead with domestic structural reforms. A greater involvement of parliaments and social partners at the national level would seem to be a useful first step, a point also made by the High Level Group.

At the Community level, the Commission proposed a shortlist of 14 headline indicators that were used in the 2004 Spring Report to compare the performance of the Member States with respect to the most important Lisbon targets. This type of comparison has however been contested by some Member States (including large ones); not surprisingly these are among the worst performers. Ultimately, stronger peer pressure and a more effective open method of coordination can only be achieved through a greater involvement of national public opinion. The High Level Group proposed to strengthen the central elements of the OMC – peer pressure and benchmarking – through the annual publication of a country ranking that would use the structural indicators to illustrate progress made towards achieving the main Lisbon targets. However, this proposal encountered strong opposition from Member States.

Deficiencies in economic governance
A first issue to consider is whether the OMC is an effective tool to promote structural reforms. Some authors have argued that this development was a second-best option after the failure to adopt common targets and policies. As we have seen, some economists also consider that this soft instrument of governance is insufficient to boost reforms. One should reflect whether a carrot and stick approach might be useful in this respect. Such an approach

could imply rewarding actions that go in the right direction. For example, the Commission has proposed to link the next financial perspectives (2007–2013) to the Lisbon objectives. This is also in line with the proposals of the High Level Group to bring the EU budget more in line with the Lisbon priorities and to consider the introduction of budgetary incentives encouraging Member States to make progress towards the Lisbon targets.

The streamlining of the various economic policy coordination processes, which has been initiated by the Commission, should be further pursued and should also be implemented at the level of the Member States. Furthermore, there should be a strengthened effort to coordinate the different Commission policies in the light of the Lisbon objectives. The contents of the different reports produced by the Commission and the Member States need to be examined to assess their respective roles and usefulness, to avoid overlap between procedures and to prevent conflicting messages. In addition, the effectiveness of the BEPGs as the central and overarching policy instrument for implementing the Lisbon strategy should be increased as one single economic policy coordination instrument is needed more than ever.

At the national level, the information coming from the Member States should be better organised. A single national reporting mechanism on policy intentions and implementation would allow a better follow-up, help to improve the coherence between reforms in the different policy areas and reduce the burden on the Member States. Member States should also put in place institutional frameworks that ensure an effective coordination of reform efforts at the national level. Finally, the federal organisation of some Member States might create additional coordination problems at the national level and these Member States should ensure full cooperation of appropriate actors (for example, the regions).

Poor communication about the benefits of reforms

Structural reforms are not an end in themselves but are part of an overall strategy aimed at improving the standard of living and the welfare of European citizens. However, the macro-economic payoffs of structural reforms materialise with a significant time lag and are difficult to measure. Therefore, politicians who face re-election and members of pressure groups are often tempted to settle for second best solutions that promise a payoff within the electoral cycle. In order to counter the temptation to avoid politically sensitive reforms that have medium-term benefits but short-term adjustment costs, it is crucial to highlight the positive effects of such reforms. Measuring the effects of reforms can also help to better define priorities for further policy actions. More analysis is necessary to determine the effects of reforms in terms of employment, innovation and growth. Moreover, the results of the reforms undertaken should be better communicated to the public at large in order to increase their public acceptability and political support. Better analysis could certainly contribute to a more convincing communication strategy.

2.8 CONCLUSION

The Lisbon strategy directly addresses the structural weaknesses of the EU economy that would seem to explain the disappointing economic performance of the past decade. Nevertheless, at midterm there appears to be a broad agreement that the Lisbon strategy has failed to deliver. The increased contribution of employment to EU GDP growth has been almost completely offset by a reduction in the contribution from labour productivity. The arguments by Gordon and Blanchard that the thirty percent gap in GDP per capita between the EU and the US is simply a reflection of different social preferences and that the EU productivity slowdown is only temporary, are not entirely convincing.

The Lisbon European Council was right to place the need for structural reform at the top of the policy agenda. As a result, a comprehensive agenda of reform has been established, tools for assessing progress on Lisbon have been developed, and the policy coordination framework has been streamlined.

However, a number of weaknesses have appeared as well. This is the reason why the 2004 Spring European Council invited the High Level Group chaired by Wim Kok to make proposals on how to give a fresh stimulus to the Lisbon strategy. The report of the High Level Group concludes that progress on the Lisbon strategy has been hampered first and foremost by a lack of implementation of the measures agreed by the different Spring European Councils. Our chapter has focused on the different reasons that might explain this poor record of implementation and has made some suggestions on how to address a number of the current weaknesses of the Lisbon strategy. For example, one of the problems of the Lisbon strategy is the proliferation of targets, which tends to distract attention and resources from the main objectives of the Lisbon strategy. A stronger focus on economic growth would help to put the strategy back on track. The chapter also reflected on ways to improve the credibility of the Lisbon strategy and on underlying drivers of reform. National politicians should be encouraged to take 'ownership' of the Lisbon strategy by increased peer pressure and involvement of national public opinion. Finally, a number of remaining deficiencies in economic governance need to be addressed, in particular through better use of the tools of EU multilateral surveillance. Better communication of the results of the reforms undertaken should be organised to increase their public acceptability and political support.

NOTES

* The opinions expressed by the authors are their own and do not reflect in any way the position of the European Commission on the issues discussed.
1. However, the process of structural reforms is already well underway in the new Member States and they are already integrated in the Lisbon strategy. In particular, they have been included in the analysis of the Spring Report since 2003, data for most of the structural indicators are available and they already integrated in the Community's economic policy coordination procedures.
2. http://europa.eu.int/comm/eurostat/structuralindicators
3. If the new Member States are taken into account the average level of GDP per capita drops to 65% of the US level.
4. Given the generally higher dynamics of the new Member States, the EU25 average productivity growth was slightly higher over this period at 1% but still far behind that in the US.
5. The introduction of the 35-hour workweek in France led to a one-off increase in hourly labour productivity reflected in the productivity graph, but also to a decline in working hours not shown here.
6. For example, America's climate is more extreme than western Europe's, so more has to be spent on air conditioning and heating. This extra spending boosts GDP but does not enhance welfare. More of US GDP is also spent on security and the huge cost of keeping 2 m people in prisons also increases US GDP but not its welfare. On the other hand, a greater variety of products is available in Europe and this improves welfare, but GDP ignores such welfare effects.
7. However, using other methods (VAR analysis), only 10% of the reduction in productivity growth is explained by increased employment (see European Commission (2004)).

REFERENCES

Blanchard, O. (2004), 'The economic future of Europe', *Journal of Economic Perspectives*, forthcoming.
Castanheira, M., V. Galasso, S. Carcillo, G. Nicoletti, E. Perotti and L. Tsyganok (2004), 'How to gain political support for reforms', paper prepared for the 6th Conference of the Fondazione Rodolfo Debenedetti.
Coeuré, B. and J. Pisani-Ferry (2003), 'Autour de l'euro et au-delà: l'UEM et les coopérations renforcées', report of a working group of the Commissariat au Plan, Paris.
Collignon, S. (2003), 'Is Europe going far enough? Reflections on the EU's economic governance', EI Working paper, December, available at: http://www.lse.ac.uk/collections/europeanInstitute/pdfs/EIworkingpaper2003–03.pdf
Deroose, S. and S. Langedijk (2002), 'Economic policy in EMU: accomplishments and challenges', in M. Buti and A. Sapir (eds), *EMU and Economic Policy in Europe: The Challenges of the Early Years*, Cheltenham, UK: Edward Elgar, pp. 205–27.

Dierx, A., F. Ilzkovitz and K. Sekkat (2002), 'Structural reforms on European product markets: the Cardiff process', mimeo European Commission.

European Commission (2002), 'Structural reforms in labour and product markets and macroeconomic performance in the EU', *The EU Economy: 2002 Review*, *European Economy*, No. 6, pp. 171–210.

European Commission (2003), 'Drivers of productivity growth – an economy wide and industry-level perspective', *The EU Economy: 2003 Review*, *European Economy*, No. 6, pp. 95–158.

European Commission (2004a), 'The Lisbon strategy and the EU's structural productivity problem', *The EU Economy: 2004 Review*, *European Economy*, No. 6, pp. 163–96.

European Commission (2004b), 'Delivering Lisbon: reforms for the enlarged Union', Report from the Commission to the Spring European Council of 26 March 2004, COM(2004)29.

Geroski, P. and A. Jacquemin (1985), 'Industrial change, barriers to mobility and European industrial policy', *Economic Policy*, **1** (1), pp. 170–218.

Gordon, R.J. (2003), 'Two Centuries of Economic Growth: Europe Chasing the American Frontier', available at:

http://faculty-web.at.northwestern.edu/economics/gordon/researchhome.html

High Level Group chaired by Wim Kok (2004), *Facing the challenge: The Lisbon strategy for growth and employment*, Luxembourg: Office for Official Publications of the European Communities.

IMF (2004), 'Fostering structural reforms in industrial countries', *World Economic Outlook*, pp. 103–146.

Pelkmans, J. (1984), *Market Integration in the European Community*, The Hague: Nijhoff.

Rodrigues, M.J. (2001), 'The open method of coordination as a new governance tool', in M. Telo (ed.), *L'evoluzione della governance europea*, special issue of 'Europa/Europe'.

3. Elements and Determinants of Economic Growth – Lessons and Policy Implications for the European Knowledge Society and Innovation System

Peter Nijkamp

3.1 CHALLENGES FOR EUROPE

The history of European culture has been decisively influenced by a strong science orientation, which has created progress and prosperity. Europe has become one of the leading world regions in terms of innovative capability and there are highly skilled human resources in many European countries. Science-driven research – ranging from fundamental to applied research – has created a wealth of innovations, which have laid the foundation for a modern knowledge-based society that is predominantly characterised by strong international ties.

Modern science is increasingly characterised by a strong internationalisation process, as is, for instance, witnessed by a multiplicity of cooperative agreements between research institutions in various countries and by multi-country authorships of scientific publications. The rising cross–border orientation of scientific research prompts various challenging questions: Is Europe able to keep pace with the unprecedented dynamics in scientific development in our globalising world? Are the national and European research (funding) systems sufficiently and effectively addressing the far-reaching challenges of the emerging European knowledge economy? Is the result of national funding mechanisms for science-driven research in Europe comparable to that of competing regions like the USA?

Whilst Europe has moved in recent decades to a common market for goods, services, people and capital, the market for scientific research is still mainly nationally oriented. Despite the plethora of advances in the European knowledge-based society, two significant challenges have to be recognised.

In the first place, the demand and user side of R&D is often insufficiently addressed in Europe. Secondly, efforts outside the Framework Programme (FP) of the European Commission (EC) to invest in science-driven research in European countries lack focus and critical mass in many cases, with the consequence that the fragmented national funding schemes in Europe do not generate the maximum possible revenues and the high-quality knowledge intensity that is required to keep European industry internationally competitive. European policy-makers have fortunately reached an agreement on the ambitions of and clear commitments to the European knowledge economy as well as on the amount of R&D spending in Europe, as laid down in the Lisbon and Barcelona agreements which act as milestones of the European Research Area (ERA). From the side of both the science community and policy-making bodies awareness is growing that new institutional constellations may be necessary to reinforce the position of science-driven research in European countries in association with the ERA.

Clearly, the European knowledge society is suffering from several flaws which preclude an optimal use of its resources and its scientific talents. The most prominent weaknesses of the knowledge system in Europe are:

- a systematic and structural underinvestment in scientific research (including R&D), in both the private and the public sector;
- a lack of focus and mass in world-class research, caused by fragmented research strategies and funding mechanisms in Europe;
- the co-existence of various research funding mechanisms (both private and public), which lead to overlap and duplication in research efforts (leave aside financial inefficiencies);
- the absence of benchmarking systems through which the highest quality European scientific research can be identified.

The question has to be raised: is Europe taking its mission as a generator of world-class research and innovation endeavours seriously? Is there sufficient awareness that science is taking place in an open international (that is, global) market and that Europe cannot afford the luxury of leaning back and relying on its glorious past?

Clearly, in recent years the scene of science policy in Europe has changed, but whether Europe has managed to create effective new structures for growth and innovation that will lead to a promising future remains to be seen. A major advantage compared to the past is certainly the broad willingness for research cooperation in Europe.

Scientific cooperation among European countries already has a long history; it has adopted different forms ranging from bilateral covenants and intergovernmental agreements to EU-instigated framework programmes.

With the advent of the ERA a much discussed issue recently has been whether the national markets for science-driven research should be opened up to all European countries. An open research market would have many advantages, in particular:

- significant enhancement of the quality of scientific research (for example, through more competitive bids and strict benchmarks of evaluation standards and procedures);
- stimulation of research mobility in all academic ranks within the EU countries;
- more efficient use of large-scale research infrastructures among EU countries;
- high international research standards resulting from trans-national scientific cooperation and networking and from open access to research programmes.

The widely accepted policy goal to establish a European knowledge society which would be internationally competitive and even at the forefront of science development in our world has prompted a vivid debate on the question whether a European Research Council (ERC) would be instrumental – or even necessary – to meet the high knowledge and science ambitions of Europe. Clearly, an ERC would only be meaningful, if it created an added value compared to existing institutional research ramifications in Europe. What is this added value and how can it be achieved? Can added value be created without a significant rise in expenditures for scientific research? We will first address some of the financial necessities and then move on to the need for institutional reform.

3.2 R&D, ECONOMIC GROWTH AND INNOVATION

Science has always been the trademark of Europe. In the ancient Greek period, the statesman, scientist and writer Euripides stated, 'knowledge is more important than a strong arm.' This has been confirmed in the long history of Europe. The message – today more relevant than ever before – is that the best way to serve society is to invest in education and research; in European history we can find thousands of examples confirming this claim. For example, what would have been the position of Europe in international trade in the past centuries, if Europe had not invested in cartography as a leading scientific discipline in the 17th century? Investment in knowledge (education, R&D) is of critical importance for economic progress and prosperity.

Science used to be an individual knowledge activity, but the functioning of modern societies is so much determined by the pervasive nature of scientific knowledge that we speak nowadays of the knowledge economy. And indeed, modern economic development is to an important extent determined and driven by the fruits of this knowledge economy.

As a consequence knowledge has in recent years become a key driver for growth of cities, regions and nations. Access to knowledge is, therefore, generally recognised as a key condition for innovative activities in our modern society. Consequently, the creation and dissemination of new knowledge may also act as a critical success factor for urban, regional and national growth (Shane, 2004). Knowledge has, however, important characteristics of a fluid good, which easily becomes obsolete. It also has various features of both public and private goods. These characteristics of knowledge prompt a wide range of questions regarding knowledge, research and science policy in Europe.

The central importance of science – and more specifically scientific research (including R&D) – was also recognized in a study by the Science and Policy Research Unit, Sussex, UK (SPRU, 2001), where broadly the following expected benefits of expenditures and investments in science and technology were distinguished:

- production of new scientific information and of relevant insights for society;
- better education and training of students;
- construction and use of new scientific networks and international cooperation;
- improvement and extension of problem-solving capacities in our society;
- creation of innovative business life;
- generation of scientific knowledge in favour of culture and society.

It is an intriguing question whether different R&D efforts in different countries have led to contrasting patterns. We present here data derived from the European Report on Science and Technology Indicators (EU, 2003) (see Appendix, Figures 3.3 to 3.6). The following conclusions can be drawn from these figures:

- there is significant variety in R&D spending patterns,
- the same applies to other input measures, such as knowledge workers,

- there is a global association between R&D growth and scientific and economic performance, but this does not necessarily hold for each individual country.

Consequently, there is a need to address more specifically the impact of R&D expenditures.

3.3 THE SIGNIFICANCE OF PUBLIC EXPENDITURES IN SCIENCE, TECHNOLOGY AND EDUCATION

Do public expenditures on knowledge creation and dissemination matter? This question has intrigued many policy-workers and researchers. They often refer to Silicon Valley types of development, to North Carolina, to Finland, to Taiwan or Singapore, where research has created an avalanche of spinoffs in the form of innovations, new start–ups, licenses and patents, and so forth.

It is undoubtedly true that such regions with a research-benign climate tend to grow faster than others (Acs, 2002, Bertuglia et al., 1997, Suarez–Villa, 2000). Clearly, public expenditures in science and technology are not the only critical success factors for accelerated economic development. Other factors, such as the development of timely niche markets (such as ICT and biotechnology) are important as well. For example, Roller and Waverman (2001) demonstrate that there is a significant positive causal link between telecommunications infrastructure and economic growth for 21 OECD countries over 20 years. Responsive governments may see it as their task to orient their R&D expenditures towards promising new market niches.

This message is also reflected in the new growth theory which stipulates that public policy is not only driven by demand stimuli, but also by endogenously determined factors such as infrastructure, education, innovation and the like (see Romer, 1986, Nijkamp and Poot, 1997, and Acs et al., 2003). Several explanatory paradigms have been put in place in recent years, with a view to the identification of successful regions or sectors that might be further stimulated by public policy. Some of these paradigms are the new economic geography (Fujita et al., 1999), the endogenous growth theory (Aghion and Howitt, 1998), and the new economics of innovation (Acs, 2002). The diversity in all these explanatory frameworks has, however, one element in common, the importance of knowledge availability and access. Knowledge creation and diffusion are to a large extent a mission of academic research and education institutions (universities, research laboratories, colleges, high schools and so on), so that governments are not a neutral actor in this context. The size and direction of public expenditures on science and education may exert a decisive impact on the prosperity and well-being of nations or regions. But how significant is this premise in a real-world setting?

The question whether public sector expenditures – in general or for specific policy domains – enhance or retard economic development has been the subject of heated debates in the past, with an interesting mix of scientific and policy arguments. A recent study by Nijkamp and Poot (2004) tries to avoid various traps in this debate by presenting the results of 123 empirical and officially published studies on (categories of) public expenditures and economic growth for a great variety of countries and for different time periods. Meta-analysis is deployed in the study to test the robustness of the evidence regarding the effect of fiscal policy on economic growth. Five fiscal policy areas are distinguished and analysed in their large sample of studies: general government consumption, tax rates, education expenditure, defence and public infrastructure. Based on an extensive data set, several meta-analytical methods were applied, including descriptive statistics, contingency table analysis and rough set analysis. Clearly, the outcomes of each individual study are dependent on various research design parameters, such as the type and quality of data, the model specification and the statistical–econometric techniques used in the study. In addition, the level of scientific quality of the publication channel of any particular study is taken into consideration. On balance, the empirical evidence for a convincingly positive impact of conventional fiscal measures and instruments on long-run economic growth is in many cases not strong. But the meta-analysis clearly pinpoints two categories of fiscal expenditure that in general have a positive effect, namely expenditures for education and research and for infrastructure. These findings can concisely and schematically be summarized in the following table (see Table 3.1). The conclusion is clear: public expenditures do matter. More precisely: Europe will not be able to reach the Barcelona and Lisbon ambitions, if public expenditures on R&D are not significantly increased. Private R&D expenditures are equally critical. After this policy-analytical and financial analysis we will in the next section address institutional ramifications in the European research landscape.

Table 3.1   Impact of government expenditure on economic growth

Education and research	++
Infrastructure	++
Taxation pressure	–
Defence	–
Government consumption	?

3.4 AN EXPLORATION OF THE EUROPEAN RESEARCH LANDSCAPE

Europe was in past centuries the home of science and a source of innovation in many fields of industrial and economic activity, exemplified in the Industrial Revolution some 200 years ago. At present, the scientific position of Europe is less firm and even slightly hesitant. Nowadays, Europe sometimes tends to be a follower – fortunately, not in all respects – and sometimes more a science consumer than a science producer. Hence, there is a danger that Europe may be losing momentum. Clearly, there are also good elements, signposts for hope, such as the Lisbon Declaration, the Barcelona Agreement, and more recently the communication by Commissioner Busquin on 'Europe and Basic Research'. Increasingly we are facing in Europe the intriguing question: Do we have sufficient scope for an open market for research in Europe? This question is in fact not new; it has been discussed already several decades ago by important policy-makers such as Spinelli and Dahrendorf, but politically this issue has never materialised in the form of a common market for research (see also Nijkamp, 2003). Fortunately, we have at least various good examples of research cooperation all over Europe, bilateral, trilateral or multilateral agreements; we have also inter-governmental arrangements, and furthermore we have network arrangements put forward by the European Commission. All of them have their own merits. Nevertheless, the bitter reality is that nowadays we still have, to a large extent, closed national research markets.

The benefits of a more open market, however, are rather evident from an economic trade perspective. We would be able to achieve much higher scientific quality through competition. We also would be able to stimulate a better flow of researchers all over Europe and maybe also from outside of Europe. And we would certainly also be able to put in place high standard review protocols, which perhaps do exist in individual countries, but are not commonly shared with other countries, so that we do not know exactly how research performance in a given country compares to other European countries. In addition, we might have a more efficient use of and better access to large-scale research facilities. An important element – especially in view of the demographic cycle in European universities where in ten years' time some 40% of the existing staff will retire – is of course the question of the next generation: how do we get the next generation incorporated into our educational and research systems? It would be a major benefit, if that could be achieved. And finally, we would have in place better benchmarks for funding agencies. These issues have been discussed rather intensively in recent years. The question is how much time we have.

It is timely here to make a reference to a recent interview with Commissioner Busquin, which is included in Cordis Focus, 15 December 2003, where he comes up with the alarming message that the statistics confirm a decline in EU research investment and performance. His closing sentence in this interview is, 'Progress is being made at the level of words but we must now take action.' The scene in Europe is certainly not overall negative; we can be proud of many scientific highlights that have been achieved, but we are no longer on a rising edge.

I would like to distinguish and to present now six challenges which ought to be addressed and recognized in Europe. The first one is capacity building vis-à-vis industry, or vis-à-vis the public sector. This leads to the need for proper applied science to overcome the knowledge paradox in Europe, where we have sometimes excellent research results with an enormous number of international publications in the most prestigious journals, but low application rates in industry and in government. Apparently, at present, European competitiveness is not always leading to the best results.

A second challenge which ought to be addressed is talent scouting, especially the younger generation, in the light of the demographic cycle referred to above. The next generation ought to be addressed more explicitly in research education. International mobility should be favoured, including non-Europeans who might be willing to come to Europe. I found it rather stunning on a recent tour through Asia to see that almost automatically in countries like Japan, Taiwan, China, Korea or Singapore, most of the universities would send their PhD students to the United States. They would not even think of Europe. Why not? We are convinced that the research climate can be very interesting in Europe, but the mindset in many non-European countries is oriented towards other parts of the world. Consequently, we need a dedicated policy to attract young people toward Europe. It is of critical importance that Europe is a learning house for scientific development and training for scientific talent all over the world.

The third challenge to be addressed is the need to further research excellence. I would not argue that research in Europe is not excellent, but I am convinced that we could do much better. Europe should go for world-class leadership and also create excellent targets out of Europe. We also need better benchmarks in terms of scientific quality, and new review mechanisms would have to be put in place; this is also the responsibility of research councils in Europe. And finally, we have to address the question of focus and critical mass for very promising world-class teams in Europe.

The fourth challenge to be addressed is fragmentation. This is a different challenge compared to research excellence. Fragmentation has to do with lack of co-operation inside Europe and sometimes also with a feeble, uncoordinated innovation potential within our European countries. Often, we concentrate on intra-European competition, that is, competition between countries in Europe, rather than putting our efforts together at a global level. It ought to be recognized that essentially the playing field of scientific research is not exclusively Europe; it is the world as a whole. The fragmentation in Europe may sometimes also lead to duplication of research efforts in different countries. This is supported by various OECD studies which have clearly spelt out that in many countries almost all research groups tend to do the same things. It may be questioned whether duplication is a good way of spending public money.

A fifth challenge is the national bias in large-scale research facilities. This is a domain where Europe certainly should improve its performance. There are questions of open access, but also of co-ordination of decision–making in view of a better profile of Europe. If we do not have the most sophisticated research facilities in Europe, we will not be able to keep the young generation inside Europe. This means that the strategic needs for Europe have to be mapped out more precisely on a long-term basis.

Finally, there are important questions about equal long-term opportunities for new EU member states, accession countries and pre-accession countries. Such countries have great potential, because in many – though not all – we find indeed intellectual magnets with a great scientific performance and hence we need to develop a pathway toward equity conditions from a longer–term perspective. But it would not help very much if we created a situation of positive discrimination.

In summary, the concept of an ERA leads to the formulation of six challenges in research policy. These are concisely mapped in the 'ERA-circle' (see Figure 3.1). What actions are needed to meet these six challenges?

The first challenge identified above was capacity building. Capacity building is very important for industry, but also for governments in Europe. We might need perhaps a slightly more focused Framework Programme system, but it would be unwise to destroy the existing system, as it is still functioning rather well. It could be more demand-driven, though it ought to be perhaps less bureaucratic and more flexible. The newly proposed system of Technology Platforms might help to address the needs of European industries, to get them at the forefront.

The second task is talent scouting with a view to the next generation. Here we have already several things in place, like Marie Curie and other mobility and human resource programmes; open access is important, not only within Europe but all over the world, because we should be able to attract young researchers from all over the world.

There are also complementary initiatives from the EUROHORCs, for instance: the EURYI-scheme, money for scientists, money for cooperation and related initiatives. Care for the needs of the accession countries is certainly an important topic.

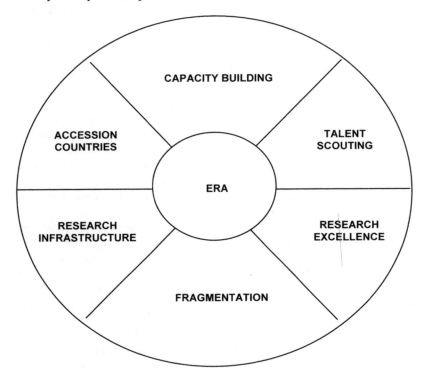

Figure 3.1 The European Research Area (ERA) circle

The third challenge is to improve European excellence in science. This is a different type of challenge. An ERC could play an important role in realizing this specific challenge in Europe, leading to innovative and top quality scientific research on a world-wide scale. Only merit–based research via strict competition and highly exclusive scientific quality standards and only the best teams with a clear critical mass might be seen as candidates for this new type of institutional funding arrangement.

Fourth, collaborative programmes between Research Councils in Europe are a mechanism for coping with the issue of fragmentation. On this issue the Commission, individual countries, Council of Ministers, and Research Councils would have to work as partners to develop new models and flexible institutional arrangements. Articles 169 and 171, which specify the conditions under which the Commission, together with governments and

Council, can organize a modus operandi, is very promising and could be extremely important. It would also put the Research Councils and European Science Foundation as partners together on the same platform, provided that additional money for research – and not only for overhead costs – would be available; this constellation would be based on a strong partnership between all the players in the field, the Council and the Commission.

Number five is a European Research Infrastructure Fund. As argued above, this is one of the weaker points in Europe. Parallel to the principles of the Trans European Network (TEN) policy, a similar type of arrangement might be developed for international research facilities, leading to a large research infrastructure fund with an international flavour, with international aspirations for recruiting and attracting people from inside and outside Europe. This would require a new system dealing with major types of strategic decisions and joint financing schemes.

Finally, for the accession countries – apart from being involved in regular cooperative schemes described before – there might be new mechanisms to be incorporated in the Cohesion Funds, like the European Regional Development Fund and the European Social Fund, so as to address questions of research infrastructure, training, mobility and educational schemes in these countries. The funds might, in principle, be allocated in part for these purposes, but everything would of course in the end be based on research partnership in Europe.

These tasks and opportunities lead to a simple message depicted in the 'ERA policy-circle' below (see Figure 3.2); there are six challenges (mapped out here in the inner part of the circle) which each need a specific action line. Capacity building, for instance, is more focussed on Framework Programmes; talent scouting and reinforcement of the existing mobility programmes are, for instance, incorporated in Marie Curie; the research excellence challenge is to be solved by the ERC; the fragmentation issue is to be addressed by new forms of partnership; the research infrastructure challenge may be solved by creating a European Research Infrastructure Fund; and the accession countries may temporarily be assisted by new types of partnerships.

In conclusion, we need a portfolio of complementary actions. In the next section, we address one of the proposed institutional constellations which has received much attention in Europe, the ERC.

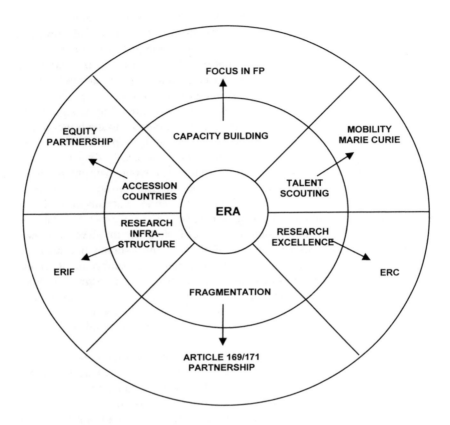

Figure 3.2 The European Research Area (ERA) policy–circle

3.5.　OPPORTUNITIES OF A EUROPEAN RESEARCH COUNCIL

The task of the ERC would be to favour European research excellence. It should be clear at the outset that the ERC complements and completes the European research architecture and would by no means replace existing research councils, but rather build on them and even reinforce them. A truly European research body would not only act as a funding agency for science driven research in the ERA, but would also create the necessary and facilitating conditions for a significant upgrading of the European research landscape. An important guiding question would always have to be: what are 'the costs of non-Europe' in the research field?

Thus, the ERC will only be a meaningful institution, if it is able to create scientific synergy on the basis of existing strong national research councils. Consequently, an ERC would have to avoid an unnecessary duplication of national research endeavours (institutions and programmes), and would have to focus on complementary or cooperative initiatives (ranging from small-scale projects to large thematic programmes), while respecting the subsidiarity principle. It is evident, that an ERC would have to operate under low transaction costs and would have to avoid any increase in bureaucratic burden (see EUROHORCs, 2004).

The main test is whether an ERC would contribute evidently and significantly to an improvement of the innovative capability of the ERA. Clearly, the benefits of an ERC cannot be unambiguously measured in advance, but in the light of the current fragmented and sub-optimal functioning of the European research system, a decisive improvement may be expected from an ERC. From this perspective, the development of a convincing joint learning trajectory seems to be a wise strategy to ensure the momentum. The following positive socio-economic advantages of an ERC for enhancing research quality in the ERA may be assumed to emerge for all participating European countries:

- more efficient quality control and more ambitious review procedures and protocols through the use of commonly shared, Europe-wide referee panels;
- better use of existing scientific talents of both young and established researchers by introducing open access to national programmes for researchers from other participating European countries;
- free mobility of all researchers in European countries who have received a research grant from a participating national research council ('money follows people');
- better economic spending of research money in Europe with a view to the achievement of internationally accepted, top quality research in Europe.

Clearly, an ERC would have to avoid both an overlap of research in individual countries and a violation of the subsidiarity principle, while it would certainly not replace existing successful national funding schemes. Its main task would be to offer a convincing, visible and innovative contribution to European research quality, based on both competition and co-operation in research.

A sine qua non for the success of an ERC is the fulfilment of three conditions:

- it would have to be recognised by the established research community as a major tool for favouring excellence in research in European countries (using merit-based peer review systems and avoiding 'juste retour' mechanisms);
- it would have to be accepted and supported by policy-makers (at both the national and the EU level) as a prominent vehicle for reaching the goal of the world's leading knowledge economy;
- it would have to generate additional ('fresh') research money for high quality research in Europe, mainly from EU funds.

Under these conditions, an ERC, once put in operation as a prestigious research council for European scientists, would generate a multitude of appealing scientific benefits to the research community in Europe:

- efficient use of scarce resources by avoiding fragmentation and duplication in scientific research in European countries;
- avoidance of support for non-superior research projects, through a system of European competition based on transparent peer review systems;
- encouragement of best practices in evaluation through the introduction of European benchmarks;
- open access to research participation in individual countries' research programmes (of course, on the basis of symmetric arrangements);
- creation of more flexible career paths for young researchers in Europe in order to induce a favourable research climate that would retain researchers in Europe (or attract researchers to Europe) and avoid brain drain;
- development of joint research training programmes for promising young researchers;
- protection of the viability and vitality of 'small disciplines' through the creation of a broader critical research mass among European countries;
- efficient co-operation in the use of large research facilities, as well as visible participation in global or international research programmes;
- stimulation of new research endeavours (for example, multidisciplinary initiatives) by linking knowledge and research from different countries, for instance via large-scale technology programmes;
- open flexible research networks with funding access possibilities for new participants at any convenient time.

The prospects of an ERC to favour excellence in European research are promising. This new concept has generally been well received by the research community, but the main question is how to get there and under which conditions. It is clear that Europe needs another state of mind, with due emphasis on a proper blend of basic research (curiosity-driven) and focussed research (solution-driven). This is not only a matter of scientific and industrial innovation, but also of institutional innovation in European science policy.

REFERENCES

Acs, Z. (2002), *Innovation and the Growth of Cities*, Cheltenham, UK: Edward Elgar,.

Acs, Z., H. de Groot and P. Nijkamp (eds) (2003), *The Emergence of the Knowledge Economy*, Berlin: Springer–Verlag.

Aghion, P. and P. Howitt (1998), *Endogenous Growth Theory*, Cambridge, MA: MIT Press.

Bertuglia, C.S., S. Lombardo and P. Nijkamp (eds) (1997), *Innovative Behavior in Space and Time*, Berlin: Springer–Verlag.

EU (2003), *Third European Report on Science and Technology Indicators*, Brussels.

EUROHORCs (2004), 'Letter to European Commission on a European funding mechanism for basic research', Bonn: DFG.

Fujita, M., P. Krugman and A. Venables (1999), *The Spatial Economy*, Cambridge, MA: MIT Press.

Nijkamp, P. and J. Poot (1997), 'Endogenous technological change, long term growth and spatial interdependence', in C. Bertuglia, S. Lambardo and P. Nijkamp (eds) *Innovative Behavior in Space and Time*, Berlin: Springer–Verlag, pp. 213–38.

Nijkamp, P. (2003), 'The European Research Council – a point of no return', *Innovation*, **16** (1), pp. 79–85.

Nijkamp, P., and J. Poot (2004), 'Meta–analysis of the effect of fiscal policies on long–term growth', *European Journal of Political Economy*, **20**, pp. 91–124.

Roller, L. and L. Waverman (2001), 'Telecommunications, infrastructure and economic development', *American Economic Review*, **91**, pp. 909–23.

Romer, P. (1986), 'Increasing returns and long run growth', *Journal of Political Economy*, **94**, pp. 1002–37.

Shane, S. (2004), *Academic Entrepreneurship*, Cheltenham, UK: Edward Elgar.

SPRU (Science and Policy Research Unit) (2001), 'The economic returns to basic research and the benefits of university–industry relationships', report, University of Sussex, Brighton, UK: Falmer.

Suarez-Villa, L. (2000), *Invention and the Rise of Technocapitalism*, Landham, New York and Oxford: Rowman and Littlefield.

APPENDIX

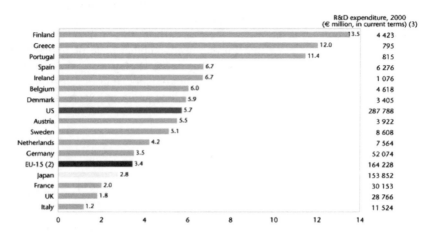

Notes:
(1) FIN, UK, US, EU–15: 1995–2000; JP: 1996–2000; D, E, A: 1995–2001; I: 1997–1999; F: 1997–2000; all other countries: 1995–1999.
(2) L data are not included in EU–15 average.
(3) B, DK, EL, IRL, I, NL, P, S: 1999; D, E, A: 2001.

Sources: OECD MSTI database and European Commision (2003)

*Figure 3.3 R&D expenditure – average annual real growth (%), 1995 to
          latest available year (1)*

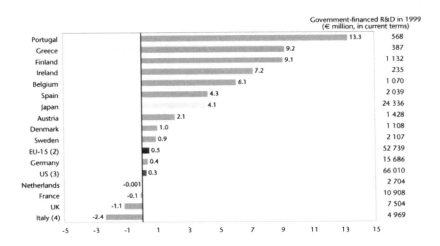

Government-financed R&D in 1999
(€ million, in current terms)

Country	Growth (%)	€ million
Portugal	13.3	568
Greece	9.2	387
Finland	9.1	1 132
Ireland	7.2	235
Belgium	6.1	1 070
Spain	4.3	2 039
Japan	4.1	24 336
Austria	2.1	1 428
Denmark	1.0	1 108
Sweden	0.9	2 107
EU-15 (2)	0.5	52 739
Germany	0.4	15 686
US (3)	0.3	66 010
Netherlands	-0.001	2 704
France	-0.1	10 908
UK	-1.1	7 504
Italy (4)	-2.4	4 969

Notes:
(1) I: 1995–96; JP: 1996–97; F: 1997–99.
(2) L data are not included in EU–15 average.
(3) US: excludes most or all capital expenditure. (4) I: 1996.

Sources: OECD MSTI database and European Commission (2003)

Figure 3.4 Government–financed R&D – average annual real growth (%), 1995–1999 (1)

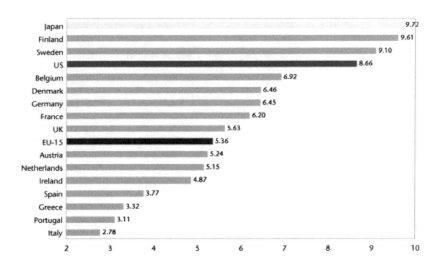

Note: Total numbers are in FTE; data for labour force are HC. No data for L, which is not included in the EU average.

Sources: OECD MSTI database, Eurostat and European Commission (2003)

Figure 3.5 Researchers per 1000 labour force, 1999

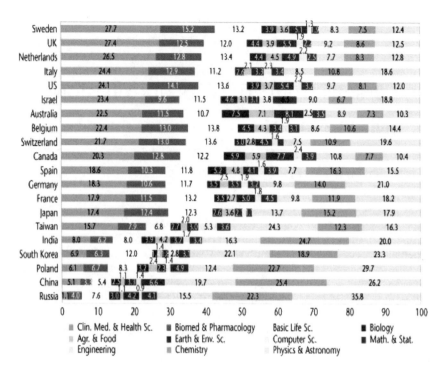

0   10   20   30   40   50   60   70   80   90   100

■ Clin. Med. & Health Sc.   ■ Biomed & Pharmacology   Basic Life Sc.   ■ Biology
■ Agr. & Food   ■ Earth & Env. Sc.   Computer Sc.   ■ Math. & Stat.
Engineering   ■ Chemistry   Physics & Astronomy

Note: Countries are listed according to decreasing share in the life sciences, especially clinical medicine and health sciences. The field 'Multidisciplinary' has been omitted.

Source: European Commission (2003)

Figure 3.6 The 20 largest scientific producers: publications (%) by main fields, 1995–1999

4. Lessons from 20 Years of Cohesion

John Fitz Gerald

4.1 INTRODUCTION

Over the last twenty years the four poorest states in the EU 15 have experienced very significant benefits as a consequence of their membership of the EU. Ireland became a member of the then EEC as early as 1973, whereas Greece became a member in 1980 and Spain and Portugal in the middle of the 1980s. These four 'cohesion' states have pursued rather different policies over the past twenty years and have undergone rather different experiences of integration into the EU economy. For three of the four countries the last twenty years have seen a significant convergence in living standards towards the EU average. For Ireland the period of convergence in the 1990s was quite dramatic in terms of its speed. However, the progress in Spain and Portugal was also notable over the same period. It is only in the case of Greece that the progress has been less marked over the same period.

These differing experiences of integration into the EU economy carry some lessons. It is clear from the sheer diversity of the policies pursued and the differing pace of adjustment that there is not a single 'model' of convergence. There are many different possible paths for states to promote economic development and no single strategy dominates the other possible strategies. Nonetheless, out of this diversity there are a number of common themes which may prove useful to the ten new member states, which are already well down the path to integration into the wider EU economy.

Economic development is a long-term process – there is no simple instrument that can painlessly transform an economy overnight. Much public discourse ignores this fact, seeking immediate solutions to what is inevitably a long-term problem of underdevelopment. Research into the process of catching up (economic convergence) must take this into account. It makes the identification of the role of the different economic processes in promoting convergence no simple task. However, it is clear from the huge experience built up over the last half century that certain key elements are essential to economic prosperity: free trade and an open and competitive economy, investment in human capital, and adequate infrastructure.

Free trade is sometimes sold as a simple and speedy medicine that will rapidly transform an economy from poverty to wealth. In fact it is a far from simple process, operating through many different channels simultaneously. Even if the process of adjustment to free trade is properly managed it will take some considerable time to produce its full benefits. The process of adjustment from a regime of autarchy to a regime of free trade will also involve considerable adjustment costs. However, the experience of the existing four cohesion countries, Greece, Ireland, Portugal and Spain, suggests that even during the adjustment to free trade, the costs are offset by benefits, and the long-term effects are hugely beneficial.

Membership of the European Union is more than just membership of a free trade zone. It enshrines the free movement of labour and capital as well as goods. The completion of the internal market in 1992 completed this process of integration for the existing EU members. The success of the Single Market programme has been very important, not just for the richer members of the EU, but also for the existing four cohesion countries. While the manifesto of the Single Market, the Cecchini report (1988), raised the possibility that some of the more peripheral countries might lose out as a result of the completion of the market, the opposite has proved to be the case. As is discussed below, the 1990s saw considerable success in the process of convergence, as the cohesion countries narrowed the gap in living standards between them and the richer members of the EU.

The Structural Funds support for the cohesion countries was increased in the late 1980s in anticipation that these countries would face problems of adjustment. While this additional support contributed to the process of convergence, it is clear that market forces played a much more important role in promoting cohesion within the wider EU. It is also clear that the completion of the internal market was generally good for promoting convergence rather than the reverse (ESRI, 1997). It is the strength of the market forces promoting cohesion among the fifteen 'old' members which is the key message for the 'new' members who joined on the first of May 2004.

For the new members, the way forward was clear from the fall of the iron curtain. The process of adjustment to free trade and preparation for EU membership began immediately on the change of political regime. All these countries have undergone a very painful process of adjustment, with much of the existing business base closing and gradually being replaced by new businesses. There have been considerable social costs to this adjustment, with continuing high levels of unemployment in many of these countries. However, the experience of the existing four cohesion countries indicates that such a painful process will be rewarded by more rapid growth within an enlarged EU market.

While the four existing cohesion countries had an easier transition to full EU membership than has been the case for those who joined earlier this year, it was by no means easy. Many of the same problems, of industrial decline and social dislocation, have been experienced in the process of convergence, albeit on a somewhat smaller scale. The reassuring feature of this story is that the strength of the forces driving convergence has been sufficient to overcome the many policy mistakes that have been made along the way in the four cohesion countries.

This chapter considers some of the lessons that can be learned from the experience of the existing cohesion countries – how to do it better. The chapter first considers the record on convergence and the role of the single market and the domestic policy environment in bringing it about. It then considers the significance in this process of convergence of flexible labour markets, of investment in human capital, and investment in infrastructure.

4.2 THE RECORD

The process of convergence has not been straightforward, with each of the four countries pursuing rather different paths. Taking output per capita, adjusted for PPS, as the measure of convergence, Figure 4.1 shows the contrasting paths of the four cohesion countries over the last 20 years.

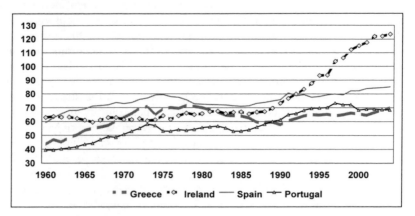

Figure 4.1 Cohesion countries' GDP per capita in PPS (relative to EU average), 1960–2003

In the case of Ireland there was little change over the period 1960 to 1990. However, over the course of the 1990s Irish GDP per head moved from about 60% of the EU average in 1990 to over 120% of the EU average today. In terms of GNP per head, a more appropriate measure of standard of living for Ireland, the Irish position today is just over 100% of the EU average, still a notable rate of convergence over a short period of time.[1] A number of studies have argued that the exceptionally rapid Irish convergence to the EU average should be seen as a belated convergence, one that would have occurred more gradually over the previous twenty years if more appropriate domestic policies had been pursued (Fitz Gerald, 2000 and Honohan and Walsh, 2002).

In the case of Spain there has also been notable progress, moving from a GDP per head of 70% of the EU average at the time of accession to the EU in the mid-1980s to around 85% today. Beginning from a lower base at the time of EU membership, at 53% of the EU average, Portugal has moved to around 68% of the EU average to date, a rather similar speed of convergence to that of Spain. Greece is the exception among the four cohesion countries with a GDP per head of around 70% of the EU average, roughly the position it was in at the time of membership in 1980.

To better understand the factors driving convergence it is useful to decompose the change in living standards into a number of components, as shown in Figure 4.2. Probably the key factor in the long-term convergence process is the growth in productivity. The growth in productivity can be affected by supply side policies in a number of different ways. However, public policy and the effects of EU integration can also affect the employment rate (the inverse of the unemployment rate) and the participation rate. While also affected by policy in the very long-term, the age dependency ratio was largely predetermined within the period of EU integration considered here: the effects of the fall in the birth rate in earlier decades take some considerable time to affect this ratio.

$$\underbrace{\frac{GDP}{Pop}}_{\substack{\text{GDP per} \\ \text{capita}}} = \underbrace{\frac{GDP}{Emp}}_{\text{Productivity}} \cdot \underbrace{\frac{Emp}{LForce}}_{\substack{\text{Employment} \\ \text{Rate}}} \cdot \underbrace{\frac{LForce}{Pop15-64}}_{\substack{\text{Participation} \\ \text{Rate}}} \cdot \underbrace{\frac{Pop15-64}{Pop}}_{\substack{\text{Dependency} \\ \text{Ratio (inverse)}}}$$

Figure 4.2 Decomposition of measure of GDP per capita

Figure 4.3 shows a decomposition of the growth in GDP per capita over the period 1980–2000 for the four cohesion countries. For comparative purposes a similar decomposition is shown for the EU as a whole and also for the US for the same period. (For Ireland the decomposition is made in terms of GNP/head, a better measure of standard of living than GDP/head.)

This Figure shows that an important factor in the convergence of Portugal and Ireland was that the growth in productivity was significantly greater than the EU average (or than in the US). For Spain the rate of growth of productivity was also slightly greater than for the EU as a whole. In the case of Greece the growth in productivity was notably slower than for the rest of the EU. It is this more rapid growth in productivity in Ireland and Portugal that is likely to be crucial for the accession countries if they are to show a rapid convergence to the EU average over the coming decade. In subsequent sections, this chapter concentrates on the factors affecting the growth in productivity and on how public policy can accelerate the growth in this vital factor.

The rise in the participation rate was fairly general across the four cohesion countries and was broadly in line with the experience of the rest of the EU and of the US over the same period. The biggest contribution of rising participation rates to growth in GDP per head was that in Spain of 0.7% a year compared to an EU average of 0.6% a year and 0.3% a year for Portugal.

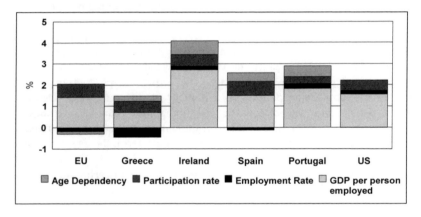

Figure 4.3 Decomposition of growth in GDP per capita, 1980–2000

The other major factor contributing to convergence was the growth in GDP per head arising from the fall in the rate of age dependency. This reflects the fact that the birth rate fell rather later in the four cohesion countries than in the EU as a whole. In Ireland the fall in the birth rate, which began in 1980, was compounded by the effects of past emigration. The very high rate of emigration in the 1930s, 1940s and the 1950s has the effect of reducing the numbers aged over 65 in the population today.

This benefit from the fall in age-dependency is an exceptional factor, which will be reversed in the very long run. It is also unlikely to be relevant for most of the accession countries, which have a demographic profile closer to that of the richer members of the EU 15, who are now suffering from the problems associated with rising age dependency.

4.3 EU INTEGRATION, THE SINGLE MARKET AND A COMPETITIVE ECONOMY

The single most important factor in promoting convergence between the four existing cohesion countries and the rest of the existing EU has been free trade. For much of Western Europe the period after the Second World War saw an immediate recognition of the importance of free trade in promoting growth. The foundation of the EEC in 1956 was the most obvious manifestation of this policy. However, it was also central to the economic policies of the bulk of the non-EEC members in Western Europe and to the United States. The foundation of EFTA further strengthened this commitment to free trade.

The fruits of the commitment to free trade can be seen in the rapid growth of most of the economies in Western Europe. The exceptions to this widespread adoption of a policy of openness and free trade were the four existing cohesion countries, which together lagged behind the rapid progress in the rest of Western Europe.

In the case of Ireland the rapid growth of the 1990s is often portrayed as a success story that could be repeated in other countries. However, it is better understood as belated progress, progress that would almost certainly have occurred much earlier if Ireland had pursued a more enlightened policy in the years immediately following the Second World War. Unlike much of the rest of Western Europe, Ireland continued to pursue a policy of self-development, closed to the outside world, for much of the 1950s. It was only towards the end of that decade that it began to dawn on Irish policy-makers that they had 'missed the boat' of free trade.

In the case of Spain and Portugal the obstacles to free trade were compounded by the undemocratic nature of the political regimes, which continued until the 1970s. The problems of Greece were also compounded by the political difficulties of the country in the late 1960s and the 1970s.

While economic theory has long taught the central importance of free trade, it does not mean that adjusting to such a regime is an easy process. In the case of Ireland, because the process was long drawn out the costs and benefits of the change in regime are difficult to disentangle from the policy mistakes that overlay the process. These issues are discussed in detail in Fitz Gerald, 2000, and Honohan and Walsh, 2002. These included the continuation of a policy of economic autarchy through the 1950s; a failure to invest in human capital when the rest of Northern Europe from the Urals in

Russia to Snowdonia in the United Kingdom realised its importance; and the serious mistakes in fiscal policy in the late 1970s and the early 1980s. Without these mistakes the process of economic convergence would almost certainly have occurred much sooner in Ireland.

The public finance crisis of Ireland in the 1980s was a self-inflicted wound. The serious delays in undertaking the necessary adjustment in the early years of the 1980s compounded these problems. By reducing the resources available for investment in human capital and infrastructure the crisis had a serious medium-term impact on the economy's potential growth rate. In addition, in the early years of adjustment the focus was more on raising taxation than on cutting current expenditure. As Alesina and Perotti (1995) indicate, fiscal adjustments are more successful when they rely on cutting current expenditure. The Finnish experience of the early 1990s shows that a short sharp adjustment process, while painful, can minimise the long-term damage to an economy.

A second aspect of the experience of the four cohesion countries relevant to the new members of the EU is the importance of embracing the opportunities that EU membership offers, rather than fighting a rearguard action to preserve businesses and sectors that are in decline. Letting firms die through the operation of market forces is very painful socially and politically. However, the desperate fiscal position faced by many of the accession states in the early years of the 1990s left them with little choice but to pursue such a policy. A fiscal crisis in Ireland in the early 1980s also forced the abolition of the agency that was targeted at supporting domestic firms facing major difficulties from the transition process. At the time it was painful but it helped to force a change in the focus of economic policy directed at sectors of the economy likely to grow in the future. Indirectly this involved seeking to promote business that provided skilled jobs, likely to be competitive in the long term, rather than attracting low-skilled employment, which was likely to have a shorter 'shelf life'.

A key positive factor in promoting the transformation of the economies of some of the existing cohesion countries has been the process of Foreign Direct Investment (FDI). In Ireland it played a central role in policy over the last forty years. It was adopted at the beginning of the process of opening the economy to free trade in the late 1950s, and it has been pursued with consistency by all governments since then. The importance of the consistency with which this policy was pursued in establishing credibility with potential investors has been emphasised by Ruane and Görg (1997). Multinational investors are cautious and they require proof that the legal, regulatory and tax framework in the countries where they are considering investing is stable and is unlikely to change in an unfavourable way. Establishing such a track record takes time and many accession countries have not yet seen the full benefits of the reforms undertaken over the last decade in the form of increased investment.

The most important factor in attracting foreign direct investment has been the guarantee of ready access to the huge EU market. Once it became clear that Spain would definitely join the EU it began to see a significant flow of foreign investment. So too, once it became certain that countries such as Hungary and Poland would join the EU investors were reassured and moved accordingly. Thus 1 May 2004 was not the key date for foreign investors; they were already treating the accession countries as EU members in making their investment decisions.

Foreign direct investment has played a wider role in promoting development in the cohesion countries than would be accounted for by its direct share of output in the economy. It has helped to bring in new skills and so to expand the human capital of the work force. For economies with little experience of trading in a wider European market, the management skills and the ready access to markets abroad which foreign investors bring has expanded the vision of business throughout the economies of the countries where they operate. This has been particularly important in Ireland, but it has also played an important role in Spain. Greece has proved to be a less attractive market for foreign direct investment than the other cohesion countries.

Creating a competitive economy is not just about eliminating barriers to trade. It is also very important to tackle the barriers to competition within individual economies. The 'Lisbon Strategy' was important long before its name was coined. In the case of each of the cohesion economies internal barriers to trade and efficiency were important factors in the relatively underdeveloped nature of their economies. The success or otherwise in tackling these problems has affected the speed with which these economies have converged to the EU average standard of living.

4.4 THE LABOUR MARKET

The behaviour of the labour market has been of crucial importance in the process of convergence in each of the cohesion countries. Inflexibility in the labour markets of the different countries has posed obstacles for the convergence process. Too rapid a convergence in wage rates, with a resulting loss of competitiveness could slow or halt the convergence process, while a slow adjustment of wage rates to rising productivity levels could hasten convergence. The experience of the four cohesion economies, where market forces have played an important role in the speed of adjustment of wage rates, can be contrasted with that of East Germany where the convergence in wage rates was determined institutionally.

Each of the cohesion countries has undergone a process of transition, including freeing of trade and EU membership, affecting both the demand for labour and the supply of labour. In the case of labour supply the role of trade unions has changed, with direct implications for the wage bargaining process itself. EU membership has also opened up the possibility of migration affecting labour supply. On the demand side, membership of the EU and the completion of the Single Market have changed the focus for many of the firms operating in these previously rather closed economies. Today firms producing tradable goods, and increasingly tradable services, are competing in a global market and this has important implications for the factors driving their demand for labour.

The Irish labour market has a unique structure, having been so closely integrated with that of the UK in the past, and having a very elastic supply of labour through short-term migration. There are many similarities in the structure of the Iberian labour markets, such as relatively high levels of employment protection (see OECD, 1999), apparently similar architecture of wage bargaining, and comparable generosity of unemployment insurance systems since 1989 (Bover et al., 2000). However, these similarities mask significantly different labour market outcomes, with Portugal enjoying one of the lowest unemployment rates in the EU (4.1% in 2001) while Spain suffered the highest (13% in 2001).

In looking at Ireland, Spain and Portugal we are considering three very different economies that have shown significant convergence towards the EU average standard of living over the last thirty years (see Fitz Gerald and Hore 2002 for a fuller discussion). All three have undergone radical transformation in that period and all three have become members of the EU since 1970. This process of convergence has affected the process of wage determination.

In a standard neo-classical model, if wage rates converge too rapidly towards the EU standard of living, then the incentive for firms to increase production in the converging economy will be reduced. This could slow, or even halt the process of convergence. On the other hand, if wage rates were to lag behind the convergence in living standards (measured in terms of output), then the enhanced profitability of firms could accelerate the convergence process. The rise in output and the rise in productivity will themselves affect the labour market through their effects on the demand for labour. EU membership and the broader process of EU integration could also be expected to affect the supply of labour through enhancing the opportunity for migration and, indirectly, through changing expectations and the regulation of the labour market. Thus the behaviour of the labour market can play a potentially important role in determining the speed and nature of the convergence process.

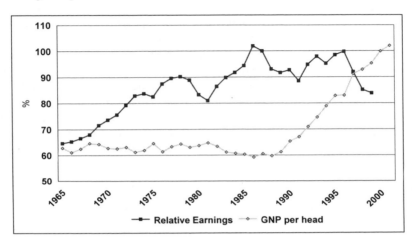

Figure 4.4 Ireland – wage and output convergence (GNP relative to EU, labour costs relative to UK), 1965–2000

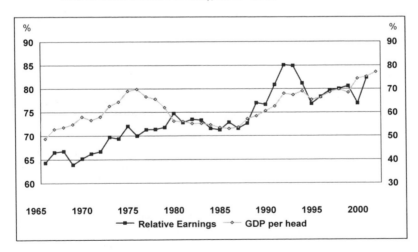

Figure 4.5 Spain – wage and output convergence (GDP relative to EU, labour costs relative to France), 1965–2000

Figure 4.4 shows how Irish labour costs have moved relative to the UK over the 40 years from 1960 to 2000. Between 1960 and the mid-1970s Irish labour costs rose rapidly relative to the UK. However, from the late 1970s to today Irish labour costs have plateaued out, fluctuating around a level of 90 per cent of UK labour costs. Since 1980 such changes as have occurred have arisen from changes in the exchange rate, with no obvious long-term trend in relative wage rates. This convergence in labour costs predates the convergence in living standards to the EU average, as shown in Figure 4.4.

Figure 4.5 shows the path of wage and output convergence in Spain since the mid-1960s. While less dramatic than in the case of Ireland, relatively steady progress is seen in the process of convergence over the full period. In the case of labour costs, they rose much more rapidly in Spain in the early 1990s than in other partner EU countries. However, within a few years there was a major downward adjustment, such that labour costs in Spain fell back below 70 per cent of the French level, while convergence in living standards continued.

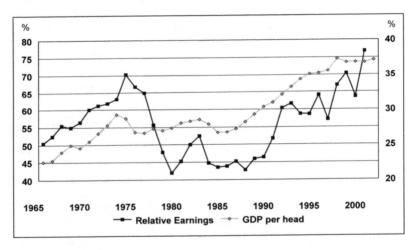

Figure 4.6 Portugal – wage and output convergence (GDP relative to EU, labour costs relative to France), 1965–2000

As shown in Figure 4.6, since joining the EU in the mid-1980s Portugal has made fairly steady progress in terms of convergence in living standards towards the EU average. While still experiencing a significantly lower standard of living than the average, the gap has narrowed dramatically over the last fifteen years. Labour costs began the 1980s very much below labour costs elsewhere in the EU. They began to rise more rapidly than in France in the late 1980s, after the process of convergence in living standards had begun. Since then progress has continued over the 1990s. However, unlike the case of Spain and Ireland, they still remain very far below EU average levels. To some extent this reflects lower price levels in Portugal, so that the purchasing power of a given level of wages (in euros) is higher than in neighbouring countries. However, even allowing for this difference in prices, the figures still reflect the fact that the purchasing power of wage rates in Portugal remains well below that in the rest of the EU.

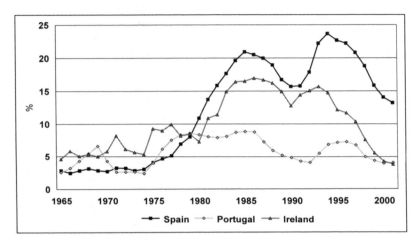

Figure 4.7 Unemployment rates, Ireland, Spain and Portugal, 1965–2000

If the labour market cleared instantly then the explanation for the path of wage rates would be found through modelling labour demand and labour supply; the wage determination equation would just be a reduced form of the simple underlying structural model. However, as shown in Figure 4.7, the path of unemployment in Spain and Ireland indicates that the labour market has been very slow to clear. In Portugal, by contrast, unemployment never rose above 9 per cent of the labour force and the labour market has shown more rapid adjustment to the state of the economic cycle.

In the case of Ireland, unemployment rose rapidly in the early 1980s. While there was certainly evidence that it was affected by the state of the economic cycle, there was also extensive evidence of hysteresis. However, the late 1990s and the early years of this decade witnessed a phenomenal reduction in the unemployment rate, as the domestic economy boomed, resulting in a record rate of employment growth. The unemployment rate reached a historic low of 3.8% in 2001.

For Spain, the pattern of the unemployment rate mirrored that in Ireland in the 1980s, with little evidence that the labour market cleared in the short term. However, the rate rose further in the early 1990s, reaching a much higher level, and still remains high relative to the rest of the EU, even given a phase of rapid economic growth throughout the late 1990s. This contrasts sharply with the Portuguese unemployment rate, which has remained lower than most EU countries throughout the period under consideration. It seems that the explanation for such different performance lies in differing labour market institutions and wage adjustment processes between Spain and Portugal. Demand- or supply-side shocks are unlikely to hold the key to explaining the differing performances, as both Spain and Portugal have been exposed to similar shocks since the 1970s. However, when different labour market institutions are exposed to similar shocks, this can lead to significantly different outcomes (Blanchard and Wolfers, 2000).

Blanchard and Jimeno (1995) identify the unemployment benefit system as one of the key differences between the countries, with a generous system in operation in Spain whereas benefits were virtually non-existent in Portugal before 1986. Throughout the 1990s replacement ratios and benefit coverage have converged between the two countries, although the system still remains more generous in Spain. Another similarity between the countries is the existence of minimum wage laws set each year, including collective bargaining agreements that set wage floors for the different occupation categories. However, these wage floors are set at a relatively lower level in Portugal, thus giving the employer more scope for manoeuvre. This results in actual wages exceeding the agreed minimum levels in Portugal (by about 10% for unskilled workers), but not in Spain (see Bover et al., 2000).

These data suggest that the Portuguese labour market has been more flexible than that of Spain and Ireland, with wage rates adjusting to clear the labour market over a relatively short space of time. However, labour market reforms in Spain gradually reduced employment protection since the late 1980s (by narrowing the definition of an 'unfair' dismissal) and also increased the number of workers on fixed term contracts, thus adding more flexibility to the system. Nevertheless, a more generous benefit system combined with less flexibility in wages helps to explain the large unemployment differential between Spain and Portugal.

The data shown above for relative labour costs include both wage costs and social insurance contributions paid by employers. The after-tax wages received by individual workers are significantly different from the cost to employers, due to the operation of the tax (including social insurance) system. For employees what concerns them in the long run is the development of real after tax wage rates. For employers it is the cost of employing a unit of labour relative to the price they get for their output. The 'wedge' between these two prices is accounted for by changes in tax rates and changes in output prices relative to consumer prices.

The rise in tax rates, especially when the rise was quite rapid, may have had an impact on wage determination. The evidence in Drèze and Bean (1990) using data for an earlier period, found that the tax wedge did not have a significant effect on wage determination in many of the countries they considered. However, they did find a significant effect on Spanish wage rates (they did not consider Ireland). Anderton and Barrell (1995) did not find any long run effect of the tax wedge for Spain, but did find a significant effect for Ireland, consistent with Bradley and Fitz Gerald (Bradley et al., 1993). Fitz Gerald and Hore (2002) using more recent data find a significant tax wedge effect for the three countries Ireland, Spain and Portugal. As a result, the rise in taxes to fund enhanced public services on joining the EU had a knock-on effect on domestic wage rates and labour cost competitiveness.

The ratio of personal taxation to personal income for Ireland, Spain and Portugal rose fairly steadily up to the 1980s. In the case of Ireland it peaked in 1987 and fell back by 1990, remaining relatively unchanged thereafter. In the case of Spain it continued to increase until the early 1990s, showing some small reduction in 1995. In Portugal, while showing a fairly continuous increase over the thirty years, it grew particularly rapidly in the second half of the 1980s. The effect of this rise in tax rates was to put upward pressure on wage rates, adversely affecting the competitiveness of these economies.

The final factor that potentially affects labour supply in a global economy is migration and its related effect on employees' expectations. While in a closed economy, labour is assumed to choose between employment in the domestic economy and leisure (unemployment), in an open economy migration presents a third possibility. In a fully integrated market, labour in one country or region can choose between the after tax wage rate available in the home country or region and the after tax wage rate in other countries or regions. Obviously there are costs to migration so that the rate of return in the foreign country must significantly exceed that in the home country to adequately reward migration. The broad process of European integration improves information on living standards in neighbouring countries (or regions), and this may give rise to pressures for similar conditions domestically, even if the costs of migration prevent the bulk of the labour force from moving.

While in the case of Ireland, migration to the UK has been unrestricted for the last two centuries, the same was not true for emigration from Spain and Portugal. In the latter two countries full free movement of labour only became possible with EU entry in 1986. However, even with the possibility of free movement of labour after EU entry, Blanchard and Jimeno (1995) find that migration has not played a major role in balancing the labour markets in Spain and Portugal. While migration is not a major determinant of labour supply in Spain, there may be some role for migration in the wage determination process in Portugal. In 1999, over half a million Portuguese were living in France, representing 5% of the total Portuguese population. In 1982, there were over three-quarters of a million Portuguese living in France, almost 8% of the total population (see OECD, 2001). Although the number living in France has declined, the number living in Belgium, Germany and Luxembourg has doubled over the same period.

A succession of papers highlights the importance for Ireland of substantial migration flows relative to the size of the labour force. These flows are driven by changes in both unemployment and wages relative to the UK (see Barrett, 1998, Kearney, 1998, and O'Grada and Walsh, 1994). While changes in unemployment may exert a negative effect on wage rates in the short run, emigration will reduce unemployment in the long run, eliminating any downward pressure on wage rates. The converse will be true for falls in unemployment that will attract immigration.

As discussed above, while migration has had a significant effect on wage determination in Ireland, this was not the case for Spain and the Portuguese case requires further investigation. However, it played a significant role in the post-unification German labour market and, with EU enlargement, there remains the possibility that it could play an important role in the convergence process for the new EU member states.

In addition to the factors considered above, a range of institutional factors might have affected wage determination in the three countries examined. In Ireland, the advent of what is referred to as the 'partnership process', beginning in 1987, introduced institutionalised wage bargaining between the government, employers and trade unions (Sexton and O'Connell, 1996). The process involves an explicit trade off of tax-cuts for wage moderation. This arrangement has persisted up to and including the present.

Unionisation may also have played a significant role in affecting the wage bargaining process, changing the shape of the supply curve of labour. The evidence suggests that for Ireland, union density did play a significant role (Curtis and Fitz Gerald, 1994). However, unionisation was itself endogenous, and it may have picked up other aspects of structural change occurring in the economy. In the case of Spain unions only became legal in 1977, which means that any effect that unionisation could have is limited to the post-1980 period. Nevertheless, Blanchard and Portugal (2001) mention differences in union power as a principal factor behind longer unemployment duration in Spain than other countries.

The opening up of the cohesion economies as part of the EU integration process changed the factors that affect the price they are prepared to pay for their factor inputs, including the price of labour. To remain competitive they have to consider the global demand for their product and their competitiveness compared to foreign producers.

In the case of labour supply, the potential to choose employment in different labour markets can directly affect expectations of individual workers. Even if the extent of migration is low, the potential for migration (the option value of a job abroad) affects wage expectations of individual employees. In turn this can affect the domestic supply of labour.

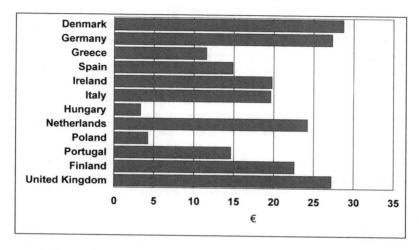

Figure 4.8 Relative skilled wage rates, 2000

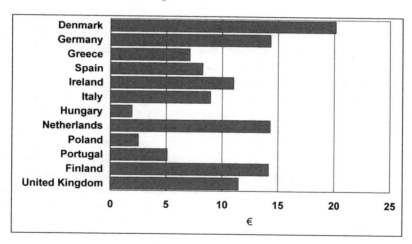

Figure 4.9 Relative unskilled wage rates, 2000

The analysis in Fitz Gerald and Hore (2002) shows that integration into the European Union has significantly affected the wage determination process in Ireland, Portugal and Spain. In each of these three countries there is evidence of a change in wage formation behaviour because of the process of EU integration. As a result, labour market conditions elsewhere in the EU now directly affect domestic wages in these cohesion economies. Ireland has the most open labour market, with a lower degree of openness for Spain and Portugal. This reflects the fact that Irish labour supply is much more sensitive to labour market conditions abroad through migration, than is the case for the other two countries. For all three countries the bargaining behaviour of firms was affected by the process of EU integration.

The higher mobility of skilled labour within the EU could be expected to result in a narrower dispersion of skilled wage rates across the EU than for unskilled wage rates. Figures 4.8 and 4.9 give estimates for the dispersion of skilled and unskilled wage rates across most of the 15 EU members in 2000.[2] In the case of unskilled wage rates, the Portuguese and Spanish rates are around €5 and €8 an hour respectively whereas rates in Germany, the Netherlands and Finland are around €14 an hour – between twice and three times the Iberian rates. However, as shown in Figure 4.9, for skilled rates the German, Netherlands and Finish rates of around €25 an hour are less than twice the Portuguese and Spanish rates.

For employers, because of the wedge represented by payroll taxes, the dispersion of skilled wage rates is even narrower than it is for employees, with the cost lying between €20 and €30 an hour for most of the EU member states.

The Figures also show estimated skilled and unskilled rates for Hungary and Poland. In the case of these two countries there is, not surprisingly, a very big gap between their wage rates and even those of the poorest EU countries. This applies to both skilled and unskilled rates.

For the EU accession countries undergoing a fast-track accession process these results have important implications. The research that predicts major migration flows as a result of enlargement (Boeri and Brucker, 2000, and Sinn and Werding, 2001) fails to adequately take account of the likely impact of EU membership on the labour markets of the new members. The experience of Ireland, Portugal and Spain suggests that EU integration will cause wages to adjust upwards in the accession countries, as these economies begin the process of convergence. This will reduce the potential for migration flows, since the incentives to emigrate are much lower than a static model would suggest. This is what happened in Portugal when they joined the EU in 1986. However, the potential for migration may still be sufficient in the accession countries to have an appreciable impact on labour supply as people adjust their expectations to the advent of free movement of labour.

A study of wage dispersion in Poland between 1988 and 1996 shows that skilled wage rates rose much more rapidly than unskilled over that period (Keane and Prasad, 2002). At the same time, we know from Boeri and Brucker (2000) that the bulk of the significant emigration from Poland over that period was of skilled labour, substantially tightening domestic supply.

Under these circumstances it is in no way surprising that skilled wage rates rose rapidly. If any of the forecasts for future emigration from these countries in Boeri and Brucker (2000) and Sinn and Werding (2001) were to be realised, there would be a further dramatic tightening of the labour markets for skilled labour in the origin countries. The evidence from Ireland in the late 1990s shows the potential importance of this mechanism in driving changes in skilled wage rates. In the Irish case the immigration of skilled labour resulted in a narrowing in wage dispersion and higher economic growth (Barrett et al., 2002), the opposite of the potential effects of skilled emigration on the new EU members.

Large scale emigration of skilled labour would set off a process driving rapid convergence in skilled wage rates between the new EU members and the existing member states. Even if many of the skilled emigrants initially work in unskilled employment in the destination countries the effect would still be to promote convergence between skilled wage rates in the origin countries and unskilled rates in the destination countries. As there are only around 15 million people aged 20 to 34 in the new member states, emigration on the scale predicted could have very big labour market effects in the origin countries.

4.5 HUMAN CAPITAL

The importance of investment in human capital in promoting growth has long been recognised in economic theory. However, there remains considerable controversy about its practical significance in explaining differentials in realised growth rates. There are difficulties in measurement of the stock of human capital and there have been a wide range of comparative studies that have tried to quantify its role. Nonetheless there is considerable evidence that it plays a very important role in promoting economic growth and hence in underpinning the process of economic convergence (de la Fuente and Ciccone, 2003).

The investment in human capital can affect the economy through a number of different channels: it can increase the productivity of the work force; it can increase labour-force participation, especially by women; and it can reduce the numbers of unskilled at risk of unemployment. There is extensive data for EU countries showing the return to education for the individual. All of them indicate substantial private gains from education. For Portugal those with a third level education earn around 178% of what someone who has only completed their second level education. For Germany the figure is 145% and for Italy it is a low 127%.[3]

While the returns to human capital for the individual may be substantial at a point in time, theoretically this might not be the case over time as the supply of skilled labour rises. There is the potential for 'qualification inflation', with the increase in the supply of skilled labour driving down the price. However, the evidence from a range of studies suggests that this is not necessarily the case. For the United Kingdom and the United States there is extensive evidence that the returns to education have, if anything, risen over time (Harmon, Walker and Westergaard-Nielsen, 2001). The evidence for Ireland indicates that the returns to education rose markedly between 1987 and 1997 and then fell back somewhat to 2000 with a shortage of unskilled labour and an elastic supply of skilled labour (Barrett, Fitz Gerald and Nolan, 2002). For Poland there was a dramatic increase in the returns to education between 1988 and 1996 (Keane and Prasad, 2002).

The differences in the stock of human capital, and more recent trends in investment in human capital, play a significant role in explaining differences in individual economic performance. In the immediate aftermath of the Second World War many countries in Northern Europe invested heavily in the human capital of their young population. This investment in the immediate post-war years produced its maximum rate of return in countries such as Austria and Germany in the 1970s (Koman and Marin, 1997). The investment in human capital made forty years ago is reflected in the stock of human capital of the population aged 55 to 59 in those countries today. Thirty years ago there were major differences in the stock of human capital between the cohesion countries and the rest of Northern Europe. As shown in Figure 4.10, for the existing EU 15, as well as for a number of states in Central Europe, around 80% of this cohort completed second level education. However, for Ireland, Spain, Portugal and Greece the situation was very different. In what can now be referred to as the 'Cohesion' countries only 40% of those aged 55 to 59 today had the benefit of completing second level education.

However, as shown in Figure 4.11, for 25–29 year olds the situation in the cohesion countries is very different today. In the case of both Ireland and Spain 40% of that cohort had completed third level education in 2002, which is above the EU average.

With the exception of Ireland and Greece, there was less progress in increasing the share of the population completing their high school education. For Spain almost 40% of the population aged 25–29 had not completed high school whereas for Portugal the figure was around 60%.

Using these data on educational attainment as weights, it is possible to use the data on the returns to education to generate a human capital index for the 25–29 cohort and the 55–59 cohort in a range of different countries. Figure 4.12 shows the ratio of the index for 25–29 year olds to that for 55–59 year olds, providing a measure of the investment in human capital over the last 30 years in the cohesion countries and a range of other EU and accession countries. This figure shows that the index for countries like Germany, Denmark, Finland and Hungary, which already had good educational systems 30 years ago, increased little over time. However, for Greece, Spain, Portugal, Ireland, which all had relatively poor educational systems a generation ago, there has been considerable progress.[4] Of the richer EU countries there has also been significant additional investment in education in Italy and the UK over the last 30 years.

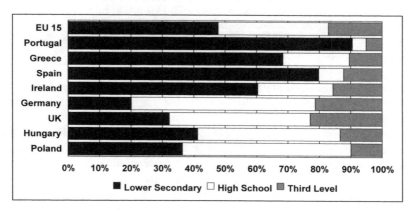

Figure 4.10   Educational attainment of population aged 55–59, 2002

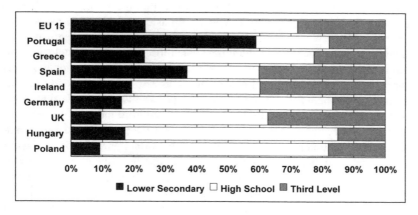

Figure 4.11   Educational attainment of population aged 25–29, 2002

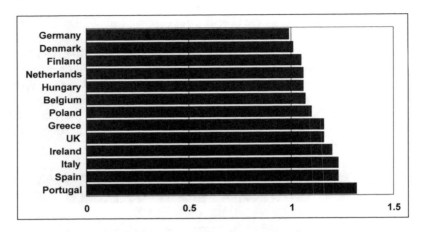

Figure 4.12   Investment in human capital; ratio of human capital index
for 25–29s/55–59s, 2002

In spite of the major improvement in educational attainment, Portugal still has a low level of attainment as shown in Figure 4.11. The very high proportion of the population who have not completed high school in Portugal has serious implications for productivity and, therefore, for convergence in that economy. For Spain, while there has been major progress in the proportion of the population going on to third level, the proportion not completing high school is very high.

De la Fuente and Ciccone (2003) comment that the returns to additional education for those with a very low level of basic attainment are particularly high. A study by Breen and Shortall (1992) for Ireland, showed that upgrading the educational attainment of those leaving school with no qualifications to at least the most basic level of qualification would greatly reduce the level of unemployment, and of state expenditure on unemployment benefits. This suggests the possibility of significant further gains to investment in education in both Spain and Portugal.

The evidence discussed in de la Fuente and Ciccone (2003) shows that investment in human capital can play an important direct role in raising productivity and hence promoting convergence. It is clear from the data shown above that there has been a very significant upgrading of educational attainment in the cohesion countries over the last 30 years. This investment in human capital is a very important factor in explaining the more rapid growth in productivity that has contributed to the convergence in living standards.

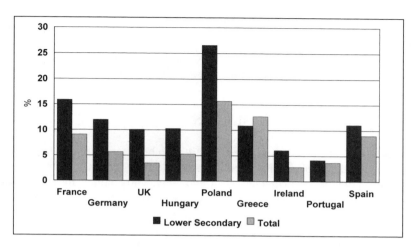

*Figure 4.13   Unemployment rates by educational attainment, 25–29 year
            olds, 2002*

In addition to its effects on enhancing productivity, investment in human capital also helps reduce unemployment by reducing the supply of unskilled labour by turning the unskilled into skilled workers. As shown in Figure 4.13, those with the lowest level of educational attainment have significantly higher rates of unemployment in Ireland and Spain (as in France, Germany and the UK). While the Lisbon Strategy addresses the need to increase the number of unskilled jobs in the EU to address this problem, probably a more effective long-term solution is to reduce the supply of unskilled labour by investment in education. This approach is consistent with the evidence presented in de la Fuente and Ciccone (2003).

Finally, the investment in human capital also has the effect of raising female labour force participation. This is because the participation rate for women with third level education is much higher than that for women who have completed high school. In turn, participation rates for women who have completed high school are higher than for those with very limited educational attainment. As discussed earlier, the rise in participation rates has played an important role in raising the growth in GDP per head in the cohesion countries. This is an additional channel through which investment in human capital has contributed to the convergence process.

This analysis suggests that investment in human capital has played an important role in promoting convergence by the cohesion countries. For Portugal, in particular, the substantial investment to date still leaves that country with a relatively low stock of human capital. For many of the accession countries the stock of human capital is already quite high.

However, the experience of the cohesion countries suggests that investment in human capital can play an important role in their convergence process. The dislocation involved in the transition process adversely affected the educational systems in some countries leaving room for further improvement.

4.6 DEVELOPMENT POLICIES

While much attention is devoted in all member states to the budgetary process and the stance of fiscal policy, sensible fiscal policy cannot of itself raise the potential growth rate of an economy. Only policy measures that impact on the supply side of the economy can raise the potential growth rate. As discussed above, investment in human capital has an important role to play in raising the productive potential of the accession countries. In addition, the wide range of public policy measures covered by the Lisbon Strategy can play a vital role in making economies more flexible and competitive (Sapir, 2003). In many cases these policies, when considered individually, may appear unexciting and unimportant. However, their cumulative impact can make the difference between convergence and divergence.

Many studies have considered the importance of investment in physical infrastructure in promoting growth. The conclusion of these studies is that, like a child who has outgrown her clothes, a shortage of physical infrastructure can constrain an economy. However, 'too much' infrastructure cannot add to the growth potential of an economy, and could burden a country with unsustainable debts.

It is difficult to measure the stock of public infrastructure. However, there is evidence that a shortage of physical infrastructure has constrained economies from catching up. For example, ESRI (2003) shows that for Ireland the shortage of infrastructure was a particularly serious constraint on growth in 2000, having been largely adequate to the economy's needs in the early 1980s.

Figure 4.14 shows that the level of investment in the cohesion countries is roughly five percentage points of GDP higher than in the richer EU economies. This reflects the deficit in both public and private infrastructure (including private housing) in these economies. For each of these economies the need to devote such a high share of income to investment means that their level of consumption is reduced. As a result, for consumers the rise in living standards has been slower than is suggested by the convergence in GDP per head.

In addition, as shown in Figure 4.15, Ireland, Spain and Portugal have a substantially higher level of public investment, financed partly by the EU Community Support Framework (CSF) and partly by domestic tax revenues.

In the case of the existing EU the major investment in infrastructure in the 1950s and 1960s was partly financed by borrowing. However, under the Stability and Growth Pact (SGP) this is not permitted today for the cohesion countries. However, the significant transfers under the EU CSF partly offset this constraint.

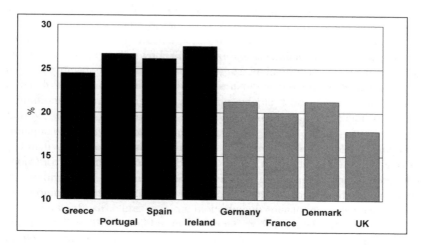

Figure 4.14   Investment ratio (as % of GDP), 2001

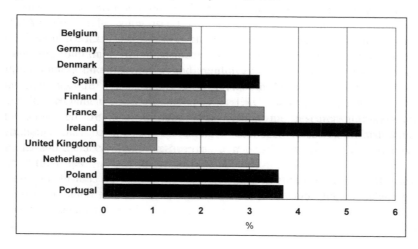

Note: For Ireland investment is expressed as % of GNP.

Figure 4.15   Public investment (as % of GDP), 2001

For the accession countries there is likely to be a continuing need for infrastructural investment over the coming two decades. If the rates of return from such investment are as high as suggested in the studies discussed below, some limited borrowing might be justified to finance it. However, this is not possible under the SGP. Instead, the EU CSF will help relax this constraint, permitting a more rapid deployment of necessary investment.

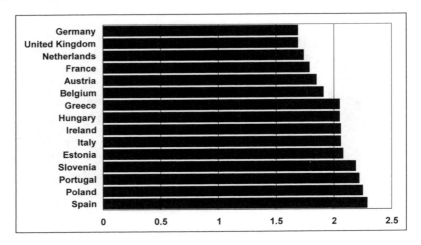

Figure 4.16   Number of adults per independent household, 2001

In addition to the need to provide public infrastructure there is a significant gap in the stock of private infrastructure in the form of dwellings in many of the new member states. Figure 4.16 shows the number of adults per independent household for a range of EU countries. It shows a fairly clear pattern where countries with an ageing population, which have had a high standard of living for a sustained period, have a relatively low number of adults per independent household. Typically countries such as Germany, the UK and France have less than 1.8 adults per household. For countries where the population is still relatively young (Ireland, Spain, and Portugal), with relatively few dwellings being released by the oldest age cohorts, there are significantly more adults per dwelling. In addition, where countries have a standard of living well below the EU average (Slovenia and Poland) they have a very much lower endowment of dwellings relative to the adult population.

For those countries where living standards have shown significant convergence to the EU standard of living (Ireland, Portugal and Spain) the relatively high number of adults per dwelling, combined with increased real incomes could be expected to result in a major increase in investment in dwellings by the household sector.[5] It will take many years of high investment to reduce the number of adults per household in the new member states to close to the rate in the more developed EU members.

The effect of EMU has been to reduce the cost of borrowing for households, increasing the optimal stock of dwellings. Previously households were constrained from rapidly adjusting this stock through investment because of the high and uncertain cost of capital. Even though incomes rose fairly steadily over the last fifteen years it was only with the advent of EMU that there has been a boom in the building of dwellings in Spain, Portugal, and Ireland (Table 4.1). While this boom is not purely attributable to EMU, the advent of EMU has brought about a substantial fall in real interest rates for households through the reduction in the risk premium (Sinn, 2000). This reduction in real interest rates was particularly important for households as while many larger businesses could fund their investment through borrowing in DMs or dollars, benefiting from the lower real rates, this was not possible for households.[6]

Table 4.1 Number of dwellings completed per thousand population, 1992–1993 and 2000–2003

Country	1992–3	2000–3
Denmark	3.1	3.0
Finland	7.3	5.9
Greece	8.3	8.5
Ireland	6.3	17.3
Netherlands	6.0	4.1
Poland	3.5	2.7
Portugal	5.6	10.3
Spain	3.3	10.2
United Kingdom	3.3	3.1
United States	4.5	6.1

Source: United Nations Economic Commission for Europe. UK – UK ONS. US – US Census Bureau New Residential Construction. Spanish data for 1993, all others 1992. Irish data for 2003, Netherlands, Spain, UK and US data for 2002. Greece data for 2000. Rest data for 2001.

In addition to the reduction in real interest rates there was also more variance in the domestic interest rates of the cohesion countries before EMU. Households in those countries now face a more certain environment in which to borrow, one where interest rates are unlikely ever to reach the heights experienced in 1992/3. This greatly reduces the risks for households in borrowing to finance investment in dwellings.

The shortage of dwellings in many of the new EU member states, and the problems with the quality of much of the existing stock, means that there is likely to be a need for major investment by households in dwellings as incomes rise. However, the timing of this investment may be affected by when each of these countries joins EMU. The reduction in real interest rates, consequent on EMU membership, could have significant positive effects on aggregate investment in these new members (Barrell, Holland and Pomerantz, 2004). This could be especially true for investment in dwellings and it may pose issues for each of these new members concerning how best to manage their housing market.

4.7 THE EU STRUCTURAL FUNDS

A range of different studies have looked at the impact of the EU CSF process on the economies of the cohesion countries. Some of these studies have produced quite negative results. These studies with rather negative results have tended to use simple single equation models which relate output to the investment funded under the CSF (Boldrin and Canova, 2003 and Ederveen et al., 2002). However, they have generally taken little account of the fact that the CSF interventions are small in magnitude relative to what is going on elsewhere in the economy. They have failed to take account of the range of other developments and, as de la Fuente (2003) points out, it is not surprising that they have come to a rather negative conclusion.

There are a range of other studies based on more sophisticated models that have identified a significant positive impact from the EU CSF on the cohesion countries. Boeri (2002) and Bradley et al. (2003), summarise a substantial number of studies of the accession countries undertaken using the HERMIN model (Bradley et al., 1995). Table 4.2 summarises these results from HERMIN for the second CSF period, 1994–1999, using two different measures of the long-term impact of the CSF. In the multiplier measure the cumulative impact on GDP over a fifteen-year period is divided by the total expenditure under the CSF. This shows a very substantial payback for Ireland and Portugal, as well as a favourable result for Spain. The second measure is a 'rate of return' where the permanent increase in GDP is measured relative to the cumulated expenditure under the CSF. This measure underestimates the rate of return because it takes no account of the very substantial, but temporary, demand side effects as the CSF money is spent.

Table 4.2 also shows the estimated impact of the CSF in Ireland for the first years of the current planning period. This study (ESRI, 2003) benefited from a range of microeconomic evidence permitting a more precise quantification of the effects of the CSF within the model context. It suggested a rather similar result to that found in previous studies using the HERMIN model.

Table 4.2   Measures of the impact of CSF expenditure

Impact of CSF 1994–2010, Bradley et al. 2003			
Greece	Ireland	Portugal	Spain
Cumulative Multiplier			
1.07	2.83	2.55	1.77
Crude Rate of Return:			
3.67	10.47	11.37	8.13
Impact of CSF: 2000–2002, Fitz Gerald et al. 2003			
Cumulative Multiplier			
3.0			
Crude Rate of Return:			
18.0			

A rather different model-based approach in a study by de la Fuente (2003), has also produced an estimate of the impact of the CSF for the 1994–99 period for Spain. This study would suggest an even higher impact than the measures shown in Table 4.2.

While there remains considerable uncertainty about the precise quantification of the benefits of the CSF funded investment, these studies indicate substantial economic rates of return for Spain, Ireland and Portugal. However, the magnitude of the CSF interventions is small relative to the size of these economies. In the 1994–99 period the CSF expenditure ranged from under 1.5% of GDP in Spain to something over 4% in Greece (Bradley et al., 2003). In addition, the supply-side benefits of the investment will take some considerable time to mature. Thus even with substantial rates of return, the CSF interventions only account for a minority of the convergence in output per head achieved by Ireland, Spain and Portugal over the 1990s.

Figure 4.17 shows how the four cohesion countries used the EU CSF funding over the course of the 1990s. Spain and Greece devoted a particularly high share to financing investment in physical infrastructure, while Ireland concentrated more on human capital. Portugal devoted a particularly high share to aids to the private sector with Ireland in second place on this count. The recent Mid-Term Evaluation of the CSF for Ireland, ESRI (2003) suggested a high rate of return on investment in human capital and in physical infrastructure. However, it suggested that there was a generally lower rate of return on aids to the private sector, with the exception of support for R&D. This reflected the limited evidence of continuing market failure which would justify such aid. As a result, it was recommended that funding be redirected to human capital and physical infrastructure. With the winding down of CSF support for Ireland this recommendation primarily affects the allocation of Irish tax payers funds.

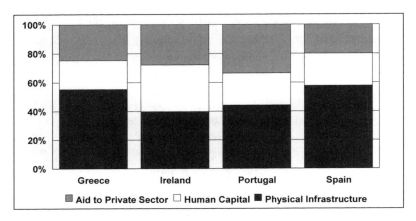

Source: Regional Development Studies No.26.

Figure 4.17   Allocation of EU CSF in the 1990s

The evidence from successive evaluations of the Irish CSF, and also the experience with the CSF in the other cohesion countries, would suggest that future CSF finance for the accession countries may produce greater long-term benefit if it is concentrated on investment in human capital and physical infrastructure. However, the experience of the cohesion countries also indicates that each country's economy has different needs and there is not a simple formula for deciding on national investment priorities.

At least as important as the direct funding provided by the EU has been the effect of the CSF process in introducing an improved methodology for undertaking public investment (Fitz Gerald, 1998). The increase in funding under the EU CSF encouraged the government to raise public investment from its low level in the late 1980s. This was particularly important for Ireland as it emerged from the fiscal crisis of the 1980s. While domestic policy makers lacked faith in the future growth potential of the economy, the ready availability of EU funds leveraged a bigger increase in public investment than would otherwise have occurred. Without such a stimulus Ireland could have found itself suffering from underinvestment in the face of rapid growth in recent years. As such it had a positive influence on the overall stance of public policy.

The CSF process has also encouraged the introduction of effective long-term planning of public investment in the cohesion countries. It is also encouraging such a development in the accession countries, even before membership. In the past, investment projects stopped and started in line with short-term economic pressures on governments, resulting in significant waste of resources. Now the formulation of a national development plan and its subsequent implementation without major interruption leads to a more rational allocation of resources. In addition, the need to satisfy the donor countries, through the EU Commission, that their money is well spent has resulted in the introduction of a set of evaluation procedures which has helped change the way the administration approaches public expenditure. In the past the only question, once money had been voted by parliament, was whether it had been spent in accordance with regulations. Now there is increasing interest in assessing how effective the expenditure has been. In many cases these evaluations have been published and, while not always listened to, they have had a significant influence on policy.

The programme approach to public investment has also tended to focus attention on particular policy problems, making public servants involved in the planning process consider the wider implications of individual measures. For example, each of the so-called operational programmes under the CSF has its own monitoring committee consisting of relevant public servants, representatives of the EU Commission, some representatives of outside interests and, in the case of the major programmes, an independent evaluator reporting to the committee rather than to the government. While ultimate responsibility for spending decisions really rests with the national governments, the involvement of the EU Commission officials has helped nudge domestic decision makers towards measures which are desirable on economic criteria. The long-term involvement of key EU officials in the process also helps provide continuity in decision making.

4.8 CONCLUSIONS

The process of EU integration on its own has played an important role in promoting convergence between the four existing cohesion countries, Ireland, Spain, Portugal and Greece, and the EU average level of output per head. In the case of Ireland and Portugal the higher rate of growth in productivity has been particularly important in bringing about convergence. This has implications for the accession countries: it is important to concentrate on policies that will enhance the growth of productivity in the longer term. However, another important factor in the convergence process was the fall in age dependency. This is not a factor that can be repeated elsewhere.

The way the labour market interacts with the convergence process is important. If wage rates converge to the EU standard of living more rapidly than the rate of productivity, then the convergence process will be interrupted or halted. This suggests the importance of developing flexible labour markets in the accession countries. In addition, because increases in the tax wedge affecting earnings tends to impact on wage formation, an unduly rapid rise in the standard of public services (and hence taxation) could also adversely impact on the convergence process. This was the case in Ireland in the 1980s. It is important that the requirements of accession do not push the accession countries into raising their expenditure on public services more rapidly than their economies can sustain.

The rate of increase in investment in human capital has been higher in the cohesion countries over the last thirty years than in the rest of the EU. This has been an important factor driving the higher rate of productivity growth in these countries. This reflects the fact that these countries had been slow to appreciate the importance of investment in human capital in the 1950s and 1960s and had a major deficit to make up. Even with this investment Portugal still displays a significantly lower stock of human capital than the rest of the EU. While over the last 30 years the accession countries generally had educational systems comparable to those in Western Europe, rather than in the cohesion countries, there is a continuing need to invest in them.

A major factor underlying the high rate of unemployment in the EU and in the accession states is the size of the unskilled labour force relative to demand for unskilled labour. In a global economy the demand for skilled labour is rising rapidly. Unless economies raise the average educational attainment of their labour force in line with the growth in demand for skilled labour, there will either be high levels of unskilled unemployment or else an increase in the dispersion of wage rates. While policy can attempt to stimulate the demand for unskilled labour, it is probably more sustainable to invest through the educational system in turning the unskilled labour of the future into skilled labour. This would greatly enhance the labour force prospects of those involved, increasing welfare, and could significantly reduce future unemployment transfers.

The stock of physical infrastructure in the cohesion countries is still significantly lower than in the rest of the EU. The shortage of physical infrastructure is a significant constraint on future growth and convergence. As a result, the level of both private and public investment in these countries is significantly higher than in the rest of the EU. This greater concentration on investment means that relative consumption levels in the cohesion countries lag further behind the rest of the EU than is the case for output. It will only be when the stock of infrastructure in these countries has reached an acceptable level, probably some time in the next decade, that convergence in living standards can be complete. The EU CSF payments have played a significant role in reconciling this greater need to invest with the constraints on borrowing under the Stability and Growth Pact.

The accession countries have similar needs for accelerated investment and will benefit by a continuation of the EU support for cohesion. The substantial returns to infrastructure investment in the cohesion countries, when properly managed, suggests a significant payback to such investment in the accession countries. Each country will have to determine its own priorities for public investment. There is a danger that the key role of human capital may be undervalued in planning future investment. In addition, the experience of the CSF in Ireland suggests that less emphasis should be put on direct aid to the private sector and a higher proportion of the available resources should be devoted to investment in physical infrastructure and human capital.

Finally, experience in the cohesion countries suggests that the structural funds process brings administrative benefits over and above the direct financial aid. Its emphasis on medium-term planning, consistency between different forms of investment, and evaluation of results can benefit the process of public investment, not just where that investment is funded as part of the EU CSF, but also where it is funded out of domestic taxation.

NOTES

1. GNP excludes profit repatriations by foreign multinationals, which represent a significant share of GDP in Ireland. These repatriations are not available as income for Irish residents and do not contribute directly to enhancing the standard of living.
2. A measure of skilled and unskilled wage rates by country for 2000 was obtained in the following manner. An index of human capital was first derived for each country. This was obtained by weighting the index of returns for each level of education by the proportion of those in employment in that educational category. Then average hourly wage rates (for employees) and labour costs (for employers) in euro were taken from the Eurostat Labour Cost Survey for 2000. The skilled rates are obtained by dividing the average wage rate for all labour by an index of human capital and multiplying by the index of returns for skilled labour. A similar method was used to obtain the measure of unskilled wage rates.
3. These figures are taken from OECD (2003), *Education at a Glance*, Paris: OECD..
4. Data on the returns to education are taken from OECD *Education at a Glance*. For Poland they are taken from Keane and Prasad (2002) and for Greece from Tsakloglou and Cholezas (2000).
5. This assumes that preferences on household formation are similar across EU members. Differences in demographics and family structure could mean that, even with an identical cost of housing and identical incomes, the optimal stock of dwellings would differ.
6. There was no legal restriction but effectively domestic banks were only prepared to lend on mortgages to households in domestic currency.

REFERENCES

Alesina, A. and R. Perotti (1995), 'Fiscal adjustment: fiscal expansions and adjustments in OECD countries', *Economic Policy*, October, pp. 205–248.

Anderton, R. and R. Barrell (1995), 'The ERM and structural change in European labour markets: a study of 10 countries', *Weltwirtschaftliches Archiv*, **131** (1), pp. 47–66.

Barrell, R., D. Holland and O. Pomerantz (2004), 'Integration, accession and expansion', London: National Institute for Economic and Social Research Discussion Paper No. 57.

Barrett, A. (1998), 'European migration: what do we know? The case of Ireland', The Economic and Social Research Institute, mimeo.

Barrett, A., J. Fitz Gerald and B. Nolan (2002), 'Earnings inequality, returns to education and immigration into Ireland', *Labour Economics*, **9** (5), pp. 665–680.

Blanchard, O. and J. Jimeno (1995), 'Structural unemployment: Spain versus Portugal', *American Economic Review*, **85**, pp. 212–18.

Blanchard, O. and J. Wolfers (2000), 'The role of shocks and institutions in the rise of European unemployment: the aggregate evidence', *The Economic Journal*, **110** (462), pp. C1–C33.

Blanchard, O. and P. Portugal (2001), 'What hides behind an unemployment rate: comparing Portuguese and U.S. labor markets', *American Economic Review*, **91** (1), pp. 187–207.

Boeri, T. and H. Brucker (eds) (2000), 'The impact of Eastern enlargement on Employment and labour markets in the EU member states', Berlin and Milano, Report to Employment and Social Affairs Directorate of the European Commission.

Boeri, T. (ed.) (2002), *Who's Afraid of the Big Enlargement?*, London: CEPR Policy Paper No.7.

Boldrin, M. and F. Canova (2003), 'Regional policies and EU enlargement', London: CEPR Discussion Paper No. 3744.

Bover, O., P. Garcia-Perea and P. Portugal (2000), 'Labour market outliers: lessons from Portugal and Spain', *Economic Policy*, **31**, October, pp. 381–428.

Bradley, J., J. Fitz Gerald, D. Hurley, L. O'Sullivan and A. Storey (1993), 'HERMES: a macrosectoral model for the Irish economy', in Commission of the European Communities (ed.), *HERMES: Harmonised Econometric Research for Modelling Systems*, Amsterdam: North Holland, pp. 327–452.

Bradley, J., L. Modesto and S. Sosvilla-Rivero (1995), 'HERMIN. A macroeconometric modelling framework for the EU periphery', *Economic Modelling*, **12**, special issue, pp. 221–47.

Bradley, J., E. Morgenroth and G. Untiedt (2003), 'Macro-regional evaluation of the structural funds using the HERMIN modelling framework', *Italian Journal of Regional Science*, **3** (3), pp. 5–28.

Breen, R. and S. Shortall (1992), 'The exchequer costs of unemployment among unqualified labour market participants', in J. Bradley, J. Fitz Gerald and I. Kearney (eds) *The Role of the Structural Funds: Analysis of Consequences for Ireland in the Context of 1992*, Policy Research Series No. 13. Dublin: The Economic and Social Research Institute, pp. 155–186.

Cecchini, P. (1988), *The European Challenge 1992, The Benefits of a Single Market*, London: Wildwood House.

Curtis, J. and J. Fitz Gerald (1994), 'Real wage convergence in an open labour market', *The Economic and Social Review*, **27** (4), pp. 321–40.

De la Fuente, A. (2003), 'Does cohesion policy work? Some general considerations and evidence from Spain', in B. Funck and L. Pizzati (eds), *European Integration, Regional Policy, and Growth*, Washington: The World Bank.

De la Fuente, A. and A. Ciccone (2003), *Human Capital in a Global and Knowledge-based Economy*, Final report to DG Employment and Social Affairs, May.

Drèze, J. H., and C. R. Bean (1990), *Europe's Unemployment Problem*, Cambridge Mass.: MIT Press.

Ederveen, S., J. Gorter, R. de Mooij and R. Nahuis (2002), *Funds and Games: The Economics of European Cohesion Policy*, The Hague: CPB Netherlands Bureau for Economic Policy Analysis.

ESRI (1997), *Single Market Review 1996: Aggregate and Regional Aspects: the Cases of Greece, Ireland, Portugal and Spain*, London: Kogan Page, in association with the Office for Official Publications of the European Communities, Luxembourg.

ESRI (2003), *The Mid-Term Evaluation of the National Development Plan and Community Support Framework for Ireland, 2000 to 2006*, eds. J. Fitz Gerald, C. McCarthy, E. Morgenroth and P. O'Connell, Dublin: The Economic and Social Research Institute, General Research Series No. 50.

Fitz Gerald, J. (1998), 'An Irish perspective on the structural funds', *European Planning Studies*, **6** (6), pp. 677–94.

Fitz Gerald, J. (2000), 'The story of Ireland's failure – and belated success', in B. Nolan, P.J. O'Connell and C.T. Whelan (eds), *Bust to Boom? The Irish Experience of Growth and Inequality*, Dublin: Institute of Public Administration, pp. 27–57.

Fitz Gerald, J. and J. Hore (2002), 'Wage determination in economies in transition: Ireland, Spain and Portugal', ESRI Working Paper No. 147.

Harmon, C., I. Walker and N. Westergaard-Nielsen (eds) (2001), *Education and Earnings in Europe: A Cross-country Analysis of the Returns to Education*, UK: Edward Elgar Publishing.

Honohan, P. and B. Walsh (2002), 'Catching up with the leaders: the Irish hare', Brookings Papers on Economic Activity, **1**.

Keane, M. and E. Prasad (2002), 'Changes in the structure of earnings during the Polish transition', Washington: IMF Working Paper WP/02/135.

Kearney, I. (1998), 'Is there a stable migration equation for Ireland?', The Economic and Social Research Institute, Working Paper No. 97.

Koman, R. and D. Marin (1997), 'Human capital and macroeconomic growth: Austria and Germany, 1960–92', London: Centre for Economic Policy Research Discussion Paper No. 1551.

OECD (1999), *Employment Outlook*, Paris: OECD.

OECD (2001), *Trends in International Migration*, Paris: OECD.

O'Grada, C. and B. Walsh (1994), 'The economic effects of emigration: Ireland' in B.J. Asch (ed.), *Emigration and its Effects on the Sending Country*, Santa Monica, California: Rand.

Ruane, F. and H. Görg (1997), 'The impact of foreign direct investment on sectoral adjustment in the Irish economy', *National Institute Economic Review*, No. 160, April.

Sapir, A. (2003), *An Agenda for a Growing Europe: Making the EU Economic System Deliver*, Brussels: European Commission.

Sexton, J. and P. O'Connell (1996), *Labour Market Studies: Ireland*, Luxembourg: Directorate General for Employment and Social Affairs, European Commission.

Sinn, H. (2000), 'The euro, interest rates and European economic growth', *CESifo Forum*, autumn.
Sinn, H.-W. and M. Werding (2001), 'Immigration after EU enlargement', *CESifo Forum*, Summer 2001.
Tsakloglou, P.and I. Cholezas (2000), 'Private returns to education in Greece', Athens University of Economics and Business Working Paper.

5. Does the European Union Need to Revive Productivity Growth?

Bart van Ark[1]

5.1 INTRODUCTION

During the second half of the 1990s the comparative growth performance of Europe vis-à-vis the United States has undergone a marked change. For the first time since World War II labour productivity growth in most countries that are now part of the European Union (EU) fell behind the US for a considerable length of time. Until the beginning of the 1970s rapid labour productivity growth in the EU went together with a catching-up in terms of GDP per capita levels on the US. A first break in this pattern occurred in the mid 1970s. While catching-up in terms of labour productivity continued, the gap in GDP per capita levels between the EU and the US did not narrow any further after 1975 (see Figure 5.1). This differential performance reflects the slowdown in the growth of labour input in Europe, which was related to increased unemployment, a decline in the labour force participation rates and a fall in average working hours. The second break, which is the focus of this chapter, occurred in the mid 1990s when the catching up in terms of labour productivity also came to a halt once the average EU level reached the US level. In fact a new productivity gap opened up since 1995. Whereas average annual labour productivity growth in the US accelerated from 1.3% during the period 1980–1995 to 1.9% during 1995–2003, EU productivity growth declined from 2.3% to 1.3%.[2]

The striking acceleration in US output and productivity growth in the mid 1990s has been much discussed in the literature. A consensus has emerged that faster growth can at least in part be traced to the effects of the information and communication technology (ICT) revolution (Oliner and Sichel 2000, 2002; Jorgenson and Stiroh 2000; Jorgenson, Ho and Stiroh, 2003), which in turn has depended on a surge in ICT investment, strong productivity effects from ICT-producing industries and a more productive use of ICT in the rest of the economy. In addition the US economy has also benefited from a greater flexibility of markets in allocating resources to their most productive uses. This is partly realised through the labour market, as the substitution of low-skilled for high-skilled labour has proceeded more smoothly and the restructuring of the economy was not hindered. It has also been realised through product markets, in particular through the creation of new opportunities for productive applications of ICT mainly in service industries and service-related activities in manufacturing. Finally, the combination of reforms and adoption of new technologies has supported creativity of firms and entrepreneurs to develop new products and services and to reshape the organisational and production processes by which these are brought to the market.

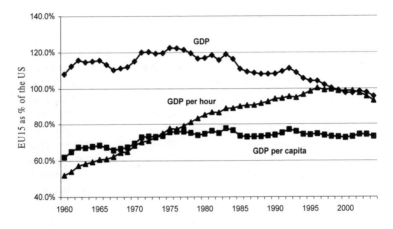

Note: EU refers to EU15 membership as before 1 May 2004.

Source: Groningen Growth and Development Centre and The Conference Board (2004).

Figure 5.1 EU15 GDP, GDP per capita and GDP per hour (US=100), 1960–2004

Unfortunately there is much less consensus on the causes of the slowdown in Europe. Indeed the reasons for the limited impact of technology, innovation and structural reforms on economic growth in Europe are still poorly understood. The urgency to better grasp the causes of the problems is underlined in the recent review by the Kok Commission of the Lisbon agenda for reform in Europe, which aims to improve Europe's competitiveness (European Commission, 2004). Indeed, the Kok report strongly argues for a revival of productivity growth in Europe, in particular in the light of demographic trends towards a smaller labour force relative to the total population in Europe.

At the same time, however, there is also considerable diversity in terms of both productivity growth as well as comparative levels between European countries. Comparative growth rates of labour productivity between 1995 and 2003 differ between –0.2% (for Spain) and 5.4% (for Ireland). And there is a variation of plus 21 percentage points (for Belgium) and minus 47% (for Portugal) in terms of each country's productivity level relative to the US in 2002. Hence although there are also some common traces to the European growth problem, one cannot simply treat the European area as homogeneous.

These developments – the application of ICT and the introduction of modern techniques and innovation more generally, and the structural reforms of the economy – cannot be fully understood without adopting an industry perspective to output, input and productivity performance. Thus there is a need to go beneath the aggregate numbers to ascertain to what extent variations across countries are largely explained by industry structure. In addition it needs to be considered whether these features are common to all or just a subset of EU countries.

This chapter argues that the European slowdown in growth is a reflection of an adjustment process towards a new industrial structure, which has developed more slowly in the EU than in the US. Rapid diffusion of new technology will facilitate the adjustment process in the future. However, an institutional environment that slows down change may hold up the structural adjustment process in Europe and inhibit the reallocation of resources to their most productive uses. The European economic environment creates too little room for good firms to excel and for failing firms to exit the market so as to free up resources for the much needed transition.

This chapter begins with a brief review of the aggregate estimates of productivity and per capita income in order to identify the extent to which labour market developments rather than productivity have impacted on the comparative performance of the EU relative to the US (Section 5.2). I then proceed to examine differential growth performance at industry level (Section 5.3). In particular I distinguish between industry groups that are typically characterized as producers of ICT, intensive users of ICT – measured by their investment intensity – or less intensive ICT users. I identify the specific role of intensive ICT-using industries in services as the key to understanding the productivity differential between the EU and the US. I then focus more specifically on the role of services by identifying the possible reasons for differences in productivity growth rates, namely (1) problems with macro-economic measurement of service performance, (2) a genuine shortfall in innovative capacity of service industries in Europe, and (3) a lack of reforms to exploit the productivity potential of service innovation (Section 5.4). In the final section, I focus on the question whether the European Union needs to change or intensify its strategies to revive productivity growth (Section 5.5). My argument is that a specific productivity agenda is not needed. Instead policy mechanisms, such as macroeconomic management, existing innovation and reform policies and some horizontal policy measures (in particular education policies) should be reconsidered for their effects on the allocation of resources and their effects on productivity at industry and aggregate levels of the economy.

5.2   A TRADE-OFF BETWEEN LABOUR INTENSITY AND PRODUCTIVITY?

Table 5.1 shows the growth rates of per capita income (measured as GDP per capita) and labour productivity (measured as GDP per hour worked) for major regions in the world economy with a breakdown to individual European countries. The table shows a large variation in per capita income and productivity growth rates in European countries. Within the 'old' EU15, the variation of productivity growth is between –0.2% (for Spain) and 5.4% (for Ireland) between 1995 and 2003. Productivity growth in the new member states is higher but also varies between –0.7% (Malta) and 13% (Lithuania) during 1995–2003.

On average EU labour productivity growth is not only slower than in the US, but also compared to Japan and the average of other OECD countries. In terms of GDP per capita growth, the differences are not as big. Between 1995 and 2003 EU-25 per capita income growth was about the same as in the US and substantially higher than in Japan.

GDP per capita growth is driven by an increased input of labour and/or labour productivity growth. Indeed one can simply show that the *difference* in the growth rates of average per capita income and labour productivity can be accounted for by changes in a range of labour market and population indicators (see van Ark and McGuckin, 1999; McGuckin and van Ark, 2004). First, the growth in income per head of the population ($\Delta O/P$) is a function of the change in labour productivity ($\Delta O/H$) and labour intensity, expressed as the number of working hours per head of the population ($\Delta H/P$):

$$\Delta O/P = \Delta O/H * \Delta H/P \qquad (5.1)$$

The change in working hours per person can be decomposed into the change in hours worked per person employed *(H/E)* and the change in the share of employment in the total population *(E/P)*:

$$\Delta H/P = \Delta H/E * \Delta E/P \qquad (5.2)$$

Table 5.1 Growth rates of per capita income and labour productivity growth, 1980–2003

	GDP per capita				GDP per hour worked			
	1980–95	1990–95	1995–2003	of which 2000–03	1980–95	1990–95	1995–2003	of which 2000–03
European Union (EU15, present)[a]	1.7	1.0	1.9	1.0	2.3	2.3	1.5	1.0
Austria	1.8	1.2	1.8	0.8	1.7	1.8	2.5	1.4
Belgium	1.6	1.3	1.8	0.6	2.0	2.3	1.7	0.0
Denmark	1.8	1.6	1.7	0.7	2.5	2.4	1.7	1.2
Finland	1.3	-1.4	3.4	1.5	2.7	2.6	2.8	2.4
France	1.4	0.6	1.7	0.8	2.4	1.4	2.1	1.5
Germany	1.6	1.0	1.1	0.2	2.6	2.7	1.9	1.2
Greece	0.9	0.6	3.5	3.9	0.9	0.6	2.6	2.9
Ireland	3.6	4.1	6.9	4.0	3.7	3.6	5.4	4.6
Italy	1.8	1.1	1.3	0.6	2.1	2.3	0.6	-0.4
Luxembourg	3.5	2.5	3.8	1.0	2.9	2.3	1.2	-1.1
Netherlands	1.8	1.1	1.3	0.6	2.1	2.3	0.6	-0.4
Portugal	2.5	1.6	2.1	-0.2	2.5	3.6	1.6	0.3
Spain	2.3	1.3	3.2	2.3	3.0	2.3	-0.2	-0.1
Sweden	1.2	0.1	2.4	1.3	1.4	2.0	2.3	2.2
UK	2.1	1.3	2.3	1.7	2.4	2.9	2.0	1.9

Table 5.1 Growth rates of per capita income and labour productivity growth, 1980–2003 (cont.)

	GDP per capita				GDP per hour worked			
	1980–95	1990–95	1995–2003	of which 2000–03	1980–95	1990–95	1995–2003	of which 2000–03
European Union (EU10, new)[b]	–	–	3.8	3.1	–	–	4.3	4.8
Cyprus	–	–	2.7	2.1	–	–	1.9	0.9
Czech Republic	–	–	1.8	2.7	–	–	2.9	4.5
Estonia	–	–	6.6	7.0	–	–	7.3	7.1
Hungary	–	–	4.1	3.7	–	–	2.7	3.2
Latvia	–	–	7.0	8.1	–	–	6.1	7.5
Lithuania	–	–	5.6	7.7	–	–	7.7	13.0
Malta	–	–	2.0	-1.0	–	–	1.9	-0.7
Poland	–	–	3.9	2.1	–	–	4.9	4.4
Slovakia	–	–	3.7	3.9	–	–	4.9	6.7
Slovenia	–	–	3.6	2.8	–	–	3.1	2.7
European Union (EU25, enlarged)[c]	–	–	2.1	1.2	–	–	1.9	1.5
US	1.9	1.2	2.2	0.9	1.3	1.1	2.4	2.9
Japan	2.7	1.2	1.0	0.8	2.6	1.9	2.2	2.0

Notes: [a] membership of the European Union until 30 April 2004; [b] new membership of the European Union as of 1 May 2004; [c] all members of the European Union as of 1 May 2004 (see Table 5.2); [d] productivity in China is in terms of GDP per person employed

Source: TCB/GGDC Total Economy Database (www.ggdc.net/dseries), based on OECD National Accounts and Labour Force Statistics.

The change in the employment/population ratio (*E/P*) can be further broken down into the number of persons employed relative to the total labour force (that is employed persons plus registered unemployed persons) (*E/L*), the ratio of the labour force to all persons aged 15 to 64 (that is the working age population) (*L/P1564*) and the share of the working age population in the total population (*P1564/P*):

$$\Delta E/P = \Delta E/L * \Delta L/P1564 * \Delta P1564/P \qquad (5.3)$$

Table 5.2 looks at the breakdown of per capita income into labour market indicators and productivity from the perspective of comparative levels of European countries relative to the United States for 2003. The estimates are converted on the basis of purchasing power parities, which take account of differences in relative price levels across countries.

It is clear from the table that the comparative levels of labour productivity in the 'old' EU15 countries were substantially higher relative to the United States than the relative per capita income levels. This is mainly due to the substantially lower number of working hours per employed person and, in addition, to a lower ratio of employed persons relative to the total population.

The relatively high levels of labour productivity in Europe have been highlighted by various scholars as an indication of a 'European model' that deals differently with the trade-off between labour intensity and productivity than the US model. According to, for example, Blanchard (2004) and Gordon (2004) the European preference for more leisure would be offset against a lower level of per capita income. Moreover, Gordon argues that a significant portion of higher American GDP per capita is required to create decent living conditions in a much harsher natural environment (requiring a greater use of energy for heating and air-conditioning), to fight crime and to travel longer distances across huge metropolitan areas.

Table 5.2 *Labour productivity and income: differences in ranking, 2003*

	Productivity GDP/hour	Productivity % US	Effect of Working Hours (%)	Effect of Employment/ Population Ratio (%)	Per Capita Income GDP/cap	Per Capita Income % US
European Union (EU15, present)[a]	40.2	93	-13.6	-6.6	27546	72
Luxembourg	52.2	121	-17.2	37.5	53958	141
France	50.2	117	-26.9	-13.2	28788	75
Belgium	47.8	111	-15.4	-17.6	29582	77
Ireland	46.5	108	-12.2	-4.5	35035	91
Netherlands	44.7	104	-27.4	3.3	29691	77
Austria	42.8	99	-17.4	-2.2	29991	78
Germany	42.6	99	-20.2	-6.8	26937	70
Denmark	41.1	95	-17.7	3.4	30687	80
Italy	39.7	92	-11.5	-9.3	26721	70
Finland	39.4	92	-11.6	-3.5	29146	76
U.K.	38.6	90	-9.8	-1.2	29935	78
Sweden	37.9	88	-12.3	1.3	29387	77
Spain	32.1	75	-0.7	-9.4	24447	64
Greece	27.3	64	4.4	-12.7	21180	55
Portugal	22.6	53	-3.4	1.8	19017	50

Table 5.2 Labour productivity and income: differences in ranking, 2003 (cont.)

	Productivity		Effect of Working	Effect of Employment/	Per Capita Income	
	GDP/hour	% US	Hours (%)	Population Ratio (%)	GDP/cap	GDP/hour
European Union (EU10, new)[b]	17.5	41	2.6	-8.1	13603	35
Malta	26.8	62	4.4	-18.4	18102	47
Slovenia	24.9	58	4.2	-9.0	20418	53
Cyprus	22.2	52	8.7	-8.3	19692	51
Hungary	21.8	51	-1.1	-9.2	15569	41
Czech Republic	18.4	43	2.1	-1.4	16733	44
Slovakia	17.9	42	-0.1	-6.5	13625	36
Poland	16.7	39	3.0	-10.7	12153	32
Lithuania	12.7	29	5.4	-5.4	11739	31
Estonia	12.5	29	3.5	-3.3	11490	30
Latvia	10.3	24	4.1	-0.5	11065	29
European Union (EU25, enlarged)[c]	36.1	84	-9.7	-7.4	25261	66
USA	43.0	100	0.0	0.0	38324	100
Japan	32.2	75	-2.3	3.6	29193	76
Canada	34.6	80	-2.7	2.1	30197	79
Australia	35.1	82	-2.7	1.2	30440	79

Notes:
[a] membership of the European Union until 30 April 2004 (see Table 5.1). [b] new membership of the European Union as of 1 May 2004 (see Table 5.1). [c] all members of the European Union as of 1 May 2004 (see Table 5.1).

Source: TCB/GGDC Total Economy Database (www.ggdc.net/dseries), based on OECD National Accounts and Labour Force Statistics, with GDP converted to US$ at 2002 EKS PPPs.

While there may be some truth in these arguments, it remains questionable whether the differences between Europe and the US in terms of labour intensity do not also partly reflect differences in incentives for workers to supply their labour and business to demand it. Before jumping to the conclusion that Europeans value leisure more than Americans, it is important to ask the question how Europeans and Americans would allocate labour and leisure under the same set of circumstances. While a complete answer is beyond the scope of this report, it is perhaps useful to refer to Table 5.2 which shows that not all countries in the world make the same trade-off between labour intensity and productivity as the 'old EU15' (for example, Australia, Canada or Japan). The European model is in fact rather an exception than the rule. Moreover, in the light of a downward trend in employment-population ratios due to the relatively rapid greying of the European population, the low labour intensity levels in Europe are unlikely to be viable for much longer. The trade-off between labour intensity and productivity is therefore a false choice and will threaten living standards in the long run.

5.3   AN INDUSTRY PERSPECTIVE ON PRODUCTIVITY GROWTH

In this section we look at the productivity performance from an industry perspective.[3] Although many of the policy issues related to the slowdown of productivity growth in Europe are more of a generic nature rather than industry specific, the sector perspective is useful for several reasons. Firstly, it is important to pinpoint in which industries or industry groups the slowdown occurs and to examine whether it is confined to a few sectors or whether it is more widespread. Secondly, under the influence of both intra-EU economic integration and the on-going globalization of product markets and factor markets, the industry structure is under continuous pressure from competitive forces. It is important to establish how these changes have affected the overall performance of the economy. Finally, the opportunities for new technological applications may have very different implications for industries. Indeed the absorptive capacity for ICT differs highly across industries, and has very different impacts on output, employment and productivity performance.

For the analysis of productivity growth in Europe and the US, the Groningen Growth and Development Centre developed a database, which contains information on value added and employment for 56 industries between 1979 and 2002. On the basis of this data set measures of labour productivity growth and the contribution of individual industries to aggregate productivity growth can be calculated.[4] Table 5.3 summarizes the contributions of the industries with the largest contributions to productivity growth. The table shows that the US is characterized by a much greater contribution from the five largest contributors than the EU. Of the five largest contributors in the US, which account for 61% (1.4%-point) of productivity growth (in gross terms), four are services industries. Together these five industries account for only 30% (0.5%-point) of productivity growth in the EU. The five largest contributors in the EU add only 44% (0.7%-point) to EU productivity growth. In the US these same industries account for 31% (0.7%-point) of productivity growth.

Table 5.3   *Contribution to aggregate labour productivity of 5 industries that contribute most to productivity growth in the US and the EU15, 1995–2002*

	US 1995–2002		EU15 1995–2002	
	%-point contr.	%-contr.	%-point contr.	%-contr.
5 Largest contributors in US				
Wholesale trade and commission trade, except of motor vehicles and motorcycles	**0.36**	15%	0.08	5%
Retail trade, except of motor vehicles and motorcycles; repair of personal and household goods	**0.34**	14%	0.07	4%
Electronic valves and tubes	**0.32**	14%	0.11	7%
Activities auxiliary to financial intermediation	**0.23**	10%	0.02	1%
Communications	**0.18**	8%	0.22	13%
5 Largest contributors in EU				
Communications	0.18	8%	**0.22**	13%
Computer and related activities	0.09	4%	**0.14**	9%
Legal, technical and advertising	0.07	3%	**0.13**	8%
Health and social work	0.06	2%	**0.11**	7%
Electronic valves and tubes	0.32	14%	**0.11**	7%
Aggregate Labour productivity growth	2.37	100%	1.66	100%

Source: Groningen Growth and Development Centre, 60-Industry Database, February 2005, http://www.ggdc.net.

The level of detail in the industry database is sufficient to adequately distinguish between ICT producing industries, ICT using industries and industries that make less intensive use of ICT (Table 5.4). The ICT producing industries include producers of IT hardware, communication equipment, telecommunications and computer services (including software). The distinction is based on an OECD classification (see, for example, OECD 2002). Apart from distinguishing ICT producing industries, we also distinguish between industries that make intensive use of ICT from those that are less intensive users. This is a less straightforward distinction since nearly every part of the economy uses some ICT. As a measure of ICT intensity, we rely on the share of ICT capital in total capital compensation in the United States (van Ark, Inklaar and McGuckin, 2003).[5]

Table 5.4   Average annual growth of GDP per hour worked of ICT-producing, ICT-using and non-ICT industries in the EU15, Germany and the US, 1979–1995 and 1995–2002 (%)

	1979–1995			1995–2002		
	EU15	Germany	US	EU15	Germany	US
Total Economy[a]	2.3	2.1	1.2	1.8	1.9	2.5
ICT Producing Industries	6.8	7.4	7.2	8.6	12.2	9.3
ICT Producing Manufacturing[b]	11.6	10.0	15.1	16.2	14.6	23.5
ICT Producing Services	4.4	5.5	2.4	5.9	10.9	2.7
ICT Using Industries[c]	2.3	2.4	1.6	1.8	1.9	4.9
ICT Using Manufacturing	2.7	1.9	0.8	2.0	1.9	2.6
ICT Using Services	2.0	2.5	1.9	1.7	1.8	5.3
of which:						
Whosale Trade	2.4	2.3	3.5	1.5	1.6	8.1
Retail Trade	1.7	2.0	2.4	1.5	1.3	7.1
Financial Services	1.9	2.7	1.5	2.3	3.4	5.0
ICT-intensive Business Services	0.8	1.6	–0.9	0.6	–0.6	0.7
Non-ICT Industries	1.9	1.5	0.4	1.1	1.0	0.2
Non-ICT Manufacturing	3.2	2.6	2.3	2.1	1.6	1.2
Non-ICT Services[a]	0.8	1.0	–0.3	0.5	0.4	0.2
Non-ICT Other	3.4	1.6	1.4	2.1	2.2	0.4

Notes:
[a] excluding real estate.
[b] based on US hedonic price deflators for ICT production (adjusted for national inflation rates) instead of actual national accounts deflators.
[c] excluding ICT producing.

Industry grouping into ICT-producing industries from OECD; distinction between ICT-using industries and less intensive ICT users is based on share of ICT capital services in total capital services from nonresidential capital; see Van Ark, Inklaar and McGuckin (2003) for exact industry grouping.

Source: Groningen Growth and Development Centre, 60-Industry Database, February 2005, http://www.ggdc.net.

Table 5.4 shows that there is considerable variation in productivity growth across the industry groups. In ICT producing manufacturing, labour productivity growth rates in both the US and the EU15 are considerably higher than for all other sectors and show a similar time pattern with accelerated growth in the late 1990s, although at a higher rate in the US. In contrast, ICT producing service sectors experienced high growth rates in the EU, outperforming the US, in particular during the later period. This is the only ICT industry group for which the EU shows an acceleration from the mid 1990s which is bigger than in the US. The latter is mainly due to the negative productivity growth rates in US computer services. But overall ICT producing services represent only a small share of total economy value added, about 5% in both the US and EU.

The two ICT using sectors generally show considerably lower growth rates than the corresponding ICT producing sectors with the important exception of the ICT using services group in the US which from 1995 onwards shows a sharp acceleration not matched in the EU15. This was mainly due to a major increase in productivity and output growth in distribution (retail and wholesale trade) and financial services in the US as shown in Table 5.4. Equally important in Table 5.4 is the pronounced deceleration of productivity growth in non-ICT industries in the EU, which occurs in all three subcomponents. In non-ICT manufacturing, labour productivity growth decreases in the final period in both the US and the EU15. However the US shows a marginal improvement in non-ICT services, and since this comprises over 60% of the non-ICT group, the overall reduction in US productivity growth in non-ICT industries since 1995 is lower than in the EU. Nevertheless productivity growth rates in the non-ICT sectors are much lower than in ICT using industries in both the US and in the EU.

5.4 WHAT EXPLAINS SLOW PRODUCTIVITY GROWTH IN SERVICES?

The previous section has shown that the productivity slowdown in the EU economy can be largely traced to the service sector of the economy, and in particular those services that are the most intensive users of ICT. Various explanations can be put forward for this phenomenon. Here I address three reasons which have been suggested most frequently, namely (1) problems with macro-economic measurement of service performance, (2) a genuine shortfall in innovative capacity of service industries in Europe, and (3) a lack of reforms to exploit the productivity potential of service innovation.

5.4.1 Measurement Problems in Services

In the past few years there have been increasing concerns about whether the macroeconomic statistics correctly trace the changes at industry level. In practice, the quality of measures of output and productivity differs highly across industries and between countries. Griliches (1994) showed a striking difference between the acceleration of labour productivity growth in 'measurable' sectors of the US economy (agriculture, mining, manufacturing, transport and communication, and public utilities) and the slowdown in 'unmeasurable' sectors (like construction, trade, the financial sector, 'other' market services and government) over past decades. Apart from an increase in measurement error at the aggregate level due to a shift towards the unmeasurable sectors of the economy, one may also observe an increase in measurement problems in the 'unmeasurable' sector itself. This component of the rise in measurement problems may – at least in part – be related to the increased use of ICT.

In practice the largest measurement problems relate to the measurement of output in the service sector. The current methodology of splitting the change in output value into a quantity component and a price component is difficult to apply to many service activities, as often no clear quantity component can be distinguished. Moreover, possible changes in the quality of services are also difficult to measure. These problems are not new, and improvement in measurement of service output has been a topic on the agenda of statisticians and academics for a long time.[6] In many service industries information on inputs (such as labour income) was and still is used as a proxy for output. However, the increased importance of ICT may have accelerated quality changes in services and raised the potential for productivity growth in services which was previously not envisaged.[7] However, to include those quality aspects in the output measure, multiple dimensions of a service need to be taken into account, for example, the service concept, the type of client interface and the service delivery system (den Hertog and Bilderbeek, 1999). This implies that the real output of a particular service cannot be measured on the basis of one single quantity indicator. New measurement methods make use of various volume measures in, for example, financial services in the Netherlands and in the United States, and health services and other government services in the United Kingdom. Even though such changes in measurement methods have not exclusively led to upward adjustments of real output, on balance the bias is probably towards an understatement of the growth in real service output (Triplett and Bosworth, 2004). There is no evidence, however, that this bias is in any way bigger in Europe than in the US.

5.4.2 A Lack of Innovation in Services?

It is sometimes claimed in the literature that slower productivity growth in services in Europe is related to a lack of innovation. However, there is little direct evidence to substantiate this claim. Although ICT investment – as was seen in the previous section – is an important enabler of innovation and productivity growth, and as the US has been more successful in obtaining productivity effects from ICT investment than EU, the productive use of ICT investment is strongly dependent on various dimensions of non-technological innovations.

There are different ways to go about measuring non-technological innovation and its impact on productivity growth. The 56 industries identified in Section 5.3 can be re-arranged to measure productivity growth on the basis of the type of innovation in the industry (van Ark, Broesma and den Hertog, 2003). A crucial consideration for such a service innovation typology is the way in which suppliers of inputs (machines, computers, human capital), the service company and its customers (consumers or intermediary users) interact. In the service patterns described below, the customer has an increasing influence on the innovation process in the first four patterns.

1. *Supplier-dominated innovation.* This usually involves technological innovations in the manufacturing sector that are implemented in the service sector through investment in new computers. Although there may be limited scope within a company for influencing the service itself, it may utilize the innovation by making non-technological changes to aspects such as staff training and the way in which the service is delivered.

2. *Innovation in services.* Actual innovation and implementation takes place within the service organization itself. These innovations may be technological or non-technological in nature or, as is usually the case, a combination of the two. Typical examples are the development of a new service concept, the combination of different service functions, or a new method of service delivery developed by the organization itself. These innovations are often implemented in co-operation with partners from the private and/or public sectors.

3. *Customer-led innovation.* This type of innovation is implemented by service providers in response to the specific and clear wishes of customers. In some cases, providers respond to the demand in specific market segments. In many other cases, the innovation is initiated by a single customer. This often happens in the market for business services. The client of an educational institute may request a customized IT course to teach specific IT skills to staff.

4. *Innovation through services.* According to this pattern of innovation, the service organization contributes to the customer's innovation process. In many cases, the supplier of the intermediate service provides the knowledge that is required by the customer for an innovation process. This pattern prevails in knowledge-intensive business services, such as engineering consultancies.[8]

Table 5.5 presents labour productivity growth rates in the EU and the US when industries are grouped according to their innovation patterns in services.

In supplier dominated services, the US acceleration in productivity growth is mainly due to the retail trade industry. The US also shows an improvement in productivity growth in communication, but the productivity growth in the EU communications sector is higher than in the US after 1995.

However, in specialised supplier services ('innovation through services'), the EU outperforms the US, which is mainly due to the strongly negative labour productivity growth rates in US computer services. Also knowledge intensive business services show a somewhat better performance in the EU. On the other hand, productivity growth rates in dedicated R&D firms in the US are higher than in the EU.

Organisational innovative services ('innovation in services') show a better performance in the US than in the EU during the period since 1995. Banking services have shown a strong productivity improvement in both regions, whereas insurance services have experienced a slowdown in both regions. But there is large heterogeneity across EU countries. The strong productivity advantage in EU air transport services over the US has been reversed after 1995.

Considering client led industries, a heterogeneous pattern can be seen in Table 5.5. The US experiences considerable growth in this sector, which includes industries such as wholesale, hotel and catering and business services, in the latter part of the 1990s. The EU lags behind the US, but when the country breakdown is taken into account, some countries are more similar to the US and experience less erratic labour productivity growth than other EU member countries.

It is difficult to draw any firm conclusions from the non-market services collection of industries since this is likely to consist of services where outputs and inputs are difficult to measure. On average the EU shows a better productivity performance in non-market services than in the US. But when the EU is broken down into individual countries, there is much heterogeneity within and between countries over the two time periods. One also should take into account the substantial measurement problems in non-market services.

Table 5.5   Labour productivity growth according to pattern of service innovation, 1979–1995 and 1995–2002 (%)

	1979–1995			1995–2002		
	EU	DEU	US	EU	DEU	US
Service industries						
Supplier dominated services	2.9	3.1	2.3	4.0	5.4	6.8
Specialised suppliers services	0.7	1.3	–0.4	0.8	0.3	–0.2
Organizational innovative services	2.6	3.2	1.4	2.1	3.0	3.3
Client led services	0.7	1.2	1.2	0.2	–0.2	4.2
Non-market services	0.8	0.9	–0.5	0.8	0.8	–0.5

Source: Groningen Growth and Development Centre, 60-Industry Database, February 2005, http://www.ggdc.net.

In summary, the most important observation on productivity growth in services related to innovation patterns, is the strong acceleration of US productivity growth in services that depend on innovation by their suppliers. This industry group is dominated by retail trade. The strong improvement in US retail trade has also gone together with strong productivity growth in wholesale trade, which explains the US advantage in client led services. These industries benefited from the supply of ICT, but have also undergone significant organizational innovations. Indeed in industries that are primarily characterized by organizational innovations, US performance has also strongly improved, in particular in banking. Within the EU, the experience in service productivity growth is mixed across industries and countries. Although services will be an important engine for future productivity improvements, the exploitation of the potential for productivity growth will be strongly dependent on national circumstances, including the nature of the innovation system and the working of product and labour markets.

5.4.3 A Lack of Reforms in Services?

There has been much discussion in the literature about the link between, on the one hand, the performance of product and labour markets and, on the other hand, innovation and productivity. The basic argument has been that regulation restricts competition to a much greater extent in Europe than in the United States. Quantifying these differences is difficult, but a wide variety of evidence suggests that regulation does indeed matter.[9]

However, explaining sluggish productivity growth in Europe by broadly casting it as overregulated and uncompetitive is not very useful analytically. There is much variety and subtlety in the way by which regulation affects service productivity and innovation. It is essential to understand if and how regulation constrains productivity. Instead of giving an overall view of the interaction, it may be preferable to focus on one specific industry. Given the major role of the retail sector in explaining the productivity growth differential in services, a more detailed discussion of regulation in this sector may help us to understand the issues better.[10]

One simple assessment of competition in retailing is to examine the absolute level of the margins retailers are able to make on sales. High margins are suggestive of a less competitive environment, because retailers are able to extract monopolistic rents. As competition increases, retailers will no longer be able to maintain very high margins – competitors will forcefully drive them down. Gross margins are generally lower in the United States than in any European country, with only Germany approaching US levels.[11] Nonetheless, margins are far from a perfect measure of competition and may indicate differences in capital and labour costs, as well as other factors.

There are three other categories of regulation that can be logically associated with stunted productivity growth in Europe – store opening hours, land usage restrictions (especially on large stores), and labour laws.[12]

Most European countries have some type of regulation on large stores operating on Sundays (the United Kingdom being a major exception). Germany has some of the tightest regulations in all of Europe, defined by the *Ladenschlussgesetz* (Shop Closing Hours Act), which currently only allows stores to open 6 a.m. to 8 p.m. The United Kingdom and France, on the other hand, generally have no limits on opening hours during the week. The trend has definitely been towards liberalisation, and both local and national regulations are moving in the direction of greater flexibility. But remaining restrictions still reduce shopping time and limit customer convenience. In the longer run short opening hours limit the potential for accelerated productivity growth.

Local planning rules also impact productivity in retailing, as restrictions on retail land usage cut back on both the creation of new stores and the elimination of old ones. The rules make it very costly to build new stores (fewer entrants) and artificially inflate the value of old stores based on the land they occupy. As land use regulations usually discriminate against large store sizes it affects the scale advantages that can contribute to productivity growth. The policies of European countries differ from those in the United States. The United States has taken a largely decentralised, disorganised, market-driven approach to retail development. While far from uniform, Europe is generally more restrictive of new retail establishments. By far the strictest regulation occurs in the United Kingdom where development sites are highly restricted, with the result that retail property costs are significantly higher than in continental Europe or the United States. Germany also has a complex zoning law, but the regulatory threshold is 1,200 square meters (as opposed to, for example, 300 square meters in France). Combined with the operating hour restrictions, this encouraged the development of relatively small, highly productive discounters like Aldi and Lidl.

The efficient and flexible use of labour is as critical for success as strategic management of space and land. European labour is generally more expensive than in the United States. France and Germany generally have much higher minimum wages than the United Kingdom or the United States, reducing the number of services provided in the retail environment of the former two countries. Leaving out from the labour force the low paid group may, paradoxically, increase measured productivity. French retail labour productivity has historically been very high, and up until 1995 was greater than in the United States. But this is not a real efficiency gain as work is simply transferred to the customer.

In summary, while the overall picture points in the direction of regulations hampering productivity growth in services in Europe, there are many subtleties in how it exactly impacts productivity growth. There are large differences between EU countries. In fact the lack of a harmonised regulation system in itself is often cited as a major difficulty in building cross-border operations within Europe. It should also be stressed that complete deregulation is not always the best way to raise productivity growth. Moreover, there is a substantial time lag in reforms impacting on productivity. In this respect, it remains an important question whether the European slowdown is just a reflection of a lagged reform process, or is due to rigid institutions and regulations hampering the adjustment process.

5.5 DOES THE EUROPEAN UNION NEED A PRODUCTIVITY AGENDA?

On balance, this chapter suggests that the European slowdown in productivity growth is a reflection of an adjustment process towards a new industrial structure, which has developed more slowly in the EU than in the US. But with some delay, rapid diffusion of new technology may ultimately facilitate the adjustment process towards a faster growth track in Europe. After all, the United States has also gone through a phase of slow productivity growth during the 1980s.[13] However, an institutional environment that slows down change may hold up the structural adjustment process in Europe and inhibit the reallocation of resources to their most productive uses.

In a market economy the main way for public policy makers to promote and support faster productivity growth is to try and encourage private enterprises to move in a productivity-enhancing direction. For this government can use a mix of four main policy mechanisms, which are only partly directly targeted towards productivity-enhancing measures.

The first mechanism concerns macro-economic management, which influences the relative prices of capital and labour inputs and hence determines the choice of technology. It may be argued that wage moderation policies and active labour market policies (which have been applied in a different mix and intensity in European countries) have lowered the price of labour relative to capital in Europe. Although conclusive evidence on the precise relationship is still lacking, the relative decline in the price of labour may have impacted the slowdown in the growth of the capital-labour ratio during the 1990s. For many European countries this slowdown can be clearly observed and is an important source for the slower growth in labour productivity.

However, the main explanation for the slowdown in Europe comes from slower growth in total factor productivity, that is, productivity growth corrected for the change in capital-labour ratios (Timmer et al., 2003). Total factor productivity growth is often related to technological change. The second policy mechanism, measures directed to support technological change and innovation, are, therefore, very popular with governments. However, direct support for particular industries or technology areas quickly raises questions as to whether governments are able to make the right choices. Nevertheless it is clear that governments have a responsibility for creating the 'rules of the game' concerning technology creation and diffusion. Technology creating measures are of particular importance for moving the productivity frontier and improving best practices, and include measures such as R&D subsidization and the creation of effective patent systems. Technology diffusing measures play a major role in reducing the productivity gap between average and best practice firms, including best practices abroad. They involve the facilitating of training programmes, support of innovation platforms and other means of co-operation between government and business.

The investment decisions concerning tangible and intangible capital, and the (re)allocations of these inputs to industries and firms, are taken in an environment governed by markets in which supply and demand for factor inputs (labour and capital markets) and product and services (product markets) are matched. Governments play an important role in setting the 'rules of the game' (or institutions) of these markets, which is the third main policy mechanism. In the past many existing institutional settings or regulatory arrangements have originally been set up with the motivation to smooth the functioning of the markets, by streamlining rules on competition, business conduct, labour markets, consumer protection, public safety, health and so on. However, regulations may have become a drag to the extent that they limit the efficiency of market functioning, reduce entry of new firms and delay exits. There has been an increasing awareness of the need for an innovation-specific focus on (de)regulation and its impact on growth and productivity performance in the knowledge economy. The opportunities to exploit new technologies are to a large extent determined by the regulatory environment. There is much evidence that higher entry and exit rates of firms within industries are supportive of faster productivity growth (OECD, 2003).

Finally, 'horizontal policies', which represent the fourth main policy mechanism, concern policies that are not directly related to innovation but are at least as important to improve service innovation activity. As human capital is a key input in the innovation process, there is a clear role for the government to provide an adequate formal education system. More specifically, governments should support a higher education system that has the flexibility to train excellent researchers, to support their mobility, and to allow business to tap into the knowledge of universities and other higher education institutions for commercial purposes.

The optimal mix of these four main policy mechanisms is difficult to determine. It depends on such factors as the distance relative to the world technology and/or productivity frontier which may differ between industries. It may also depend on the state of institutional reform in particular markets. Finally, the nature of the political reality implies that all public policy interventions are likely to involve costs as well as benefits.

The key to productivity improvements is with business itself. For business there is a choice between a strategy focused on cost reductions through scrapping and postponement of investments in new capital goods and intangibles, or by restructuring through upgrading the resources and overcoming the bottlenecks which account for the difference between average and best practice in a given (local) market. Of course, one may argue that rapid restructuring through cuts has also often been propagated as the recipe for the recovery of US and global firms in general. The fundamental difference is that when such a strategy is pursued in a market environment that is more flexible, it may help to reposition the firm, activate the resources and realize the potential. Another difference between the EU and the US is that when entry and exit of firms is speeded up, the reallocation of resources to the most productive uses is strengthened. Hence in a more flexible market environment the strategy towards restructuring can be more easily aligned with exploiting the potential for growth and reducing the gap between average and best practice through maximizing the returns on investments in high performing capital goods and intangibles.

NOTES

1. This chapter is largely based on earlier work, including van Ark, Inklaar and McGuckin (2003), van Ark, Broersma and den Hertog (2003), O'Mahony and van Ark (2003), McGuckin and van Ark (2004) and Timmer et al. (2003).
2. Business cycles in the US and the EU are not completely synchronised. However, the divergent trend growth rates are clear.
3. For comparisons of productivity in the European Union and the US at the aggregate level, see for example, van Ark et al. (2002) and Timmer et al. (2003)
4. See http://www.ggdc.net/index-dseries.html#top van Ark, Inklaar and McGuckin (2003) and O'Mahony and van Ark (2003). The main source is the new OECD STAN Database of national accounts, but greater industry detail is provided through the use of industry surveys and censuses.
5. See van Ark, Inklaar and McGuckin (2003) for an overview of all ICT producing, ICT using and non-ICT industries.
6. See, for example, Griliches (1992), Wölfl (2003) and Triplett and Bosworth (2004).
7. See, for example, Baumol (2004) and Triplett and Bosworth (2002).
8. A fifth category that may be considered is so-called paradigmatic innovation. Certain innovations are more radical than the incremental innovations that usually take place in service companies. They usually follow from breakthrough technologies, such as IT, and lead to far-reaching and complex changes. Paradigmatic innovations in the service sector primarily affect the value chain. They often require participation and a change of behaviour by all players in the innovation, including co-operating companies, the public sector and consumers. An example of paradigmatic innovation is the introduction of the chip-card or the construction of an underground transport system. This fifth pattern of service innovation has a somewhat different character than the previous four as it deals with how 'radical' an innovation is rather than where to place the source and sink of innovation in the value chain. This innovation pattern signals the possibility that some major service innovations may affect all players in a value chain and require major (interdependent) changes in behaviour by all players involved. However, our industry classification does not include any specific service industry that can be classified as 'paradigmatic' innovation.
9. See, for example, Nicoletti and Scarpetta (2003).
10. See McGuckin, Spiegelman and van Ark (2005).
11. Gross margin data are taken from Boylaud (2000).
12. Other regulations such as price controls and restrictions on promotional activities play some role, but they are not likely to be as significant.
13. See, for example, Dertouzos et al. (1989).

REFERENCES

Ark, B. van, J. Melka, N. Mulder, M.P. Timmer and G. Ypma (2002), 'ICT investments and growth accounts for the European Union 1980–2000', *Research Memorandum GD-56*, Groningen Growth and Development Centre, September (downloadable from http://www.eco.rug.nl/ggdc/pub/).

Ark, B. van, R. Inklaar and R.H. McGuckin (2003), 'Changing gear: productivity, ICT and service industries in Europe and the United States', in J.F. Christensen and P. Maskell (eds), *The Industrial Dynamics of the New Digital Economy*, Cheltenham, UK: Edward Elgar, pp. 56–99.

Ark, B. van, L. Broersma and P. den Hertog (2003b), 'Services innovation, performance and policy: a review', Research Series No. 6, The Hague: Strategy, Research & International Co-operation Department, Ministry of Economic Affairs.

Ark, B. van and R.H. McGuckin (1999), 'International labor productivity and per capita income,' *Monthly Labor Review*, July, pp. 33–41.

Baumol, W. J. (2004), 'Four sources of innovation and stimulation of growth in the Dutch economy', *De Economist*, **152**, pp. 321–51.

Blanchard, O. (2004), 'The economic future of Europe', *The Journal of Economic Perspectives*, 18, pp. 3–26.

Boylaud, O. (2000), 'Regulatory reform in road freight and retail distribution,' OECD Economics Department Working Papers, No. 255, Paris: OECD Economics Department.

Dertouzos, M.L., R.K. Lester and R.M. Solow (1989), *Made in America. Regaining the Productive Edge*, Cambridge, M.A.: MIT Press, 3rd edition.

European Commission (2004), 'Facing the challenge. The Lisbon strategy for growth and employment', report from the High Level Group chaired by Wim Kok, Brussels.

Gordon, R.J. (2004), 'Two centuries of economic growth: Europe chasing the American frontier', CEPR Discussion Paper No. 4415, London.

Griliches, Z. (ed.) (1992), *Output Measurement in the Service Sectors, Studies in Income and Wealth*, Volume 56, National Bureau of Economic Research, Chicago University Press.

Griliches, Z. (1994), 'Productivity, R&D, and the data constraint,' *American Economic Review*, **84** (1), pp. 1–23.

Hertog, P. den and R. Bilderbeek (1999), 'Conceptualising service innovation and service innovation patterns', mimeo, Utrecht: DIALOGIC.
    (http://www.eco.rug.nl/GGDC/dseries/SIID_frontpage.shtml).

Jorgenson, D.W. and K. Stiroh (2000), 'Raising the speed limit: U.S. economic growth in the information age', *Brookings Papers on Economic Activity*, **1**, pp. 125–211.

Jorgenson, D.W., M. Ho and K.J. Stiroh (2003), 'Growth of U.S. industries and investments in information technology and higher education,' forthcoming in C. Corrado, J. Haltiwanger, and D. Sichel (eds.) *Measuring Capital in a New Economy*, Chicago: University of Chicago Press.

McGuckin, R.H. and B. van Ark (2004), *Performance 2004: Productivity, Employment and Income in the World's Economies*, Research Report R-1351-04-RR, New York: The Conference Board.

McGuckin, R.H., M. Spiegelman and B. van Ark (2005), *The Retail Revolution. Can Europe Match U.S. Productivity Performance?*, Perspectives on a Global Economy, Research Report R-1358-05-RR, New York: The Conference Board.

Nicoletti, G. and S. Scarpetta (2003), 'Regulation, productivity and growth: OECD evidence', *Economic Policy*, Issue 36, pp. 9–72.

OECD (2002), *Measuring the Information Economy*, Paris: OECD.

OECD (2003), The Sources of Economic Growth in OECD Countries, Paris: OECD.

Oliner, S.D. and D.E. Sichel (2000), 'The resurgence of growth in the late 1990s: is information technology the story?', *Journal of Economic Perspectives*, **14**, pp. 3–22.

Oliner, S.D. and D.E. Sichel (2002), 'Information technology and productivity: where are we now and where are we going?', *Federal Reserve Bank of Atlanta Economic Review*, 3rd Quarter 2002, **87**(3), pp. 15–44.

O'Mahony, M. and B. van Ark (eds) (2003), *EU Productivity and Competitiveness: An Industry Perspective. Can Europe Resume the Catching-up Process?*, European Union, Luxembourg: DG Enterprise, (http://www.ggdc.net/pub/EU_productivity_and_competitiveness.pdf).

Timmer, M.P., G. Ypma and B. van Ark (2003), 'IT in the European Union: driving productivity divergence?', Research Memorandum GD-67, Groningen Growth and Development Centre, October (http://www.eco.rug.nl/ggdc/pub/).

Triplett, J. and B.W. Bosworth (2002), ' 'Baumol's Disease' has been cured: IT and multifactor productivity in U.S. services industries', mimeo, Washington D.C: Brookings Institution.

Triplett, J. and B. Bosworth (2004), *Productivity in the U.S. Services Sector. New Sources of Economic Growth*, Washington D.C: The Brookings Institution.

Wölfl, A. (2003), 'Productivity growth in service industries – an assessment of recent patterns and the role of measurement,' STI-Working Paper 2003-07, Paris: OECD.

PART III

RESEARCH LESSONS AND POLICY
IMPLICATIONS FOR THE LISBON STRATEGY

6. Is the American Model Miss World? Choosing Between the Anglo-Saxon Model and a European-Style Alternative

Henri L.F. de Groot, Richard Nahuis, and Paul J.G. Tang[1]

6.1 INTRODUCTION

'France had the seventeenth century, Britain the nineteenth, and America the twentieth. It will also have the twenty-first.' That was predicted in 1998 in Foreign Affairs. The author, Mortimer B. Zuckerman, was jubilant about the American economic performance and saw a happy marriage of the new economy and the older American culture. Indeed, in the second half of the 1990s the United States productivity growth accelerated and employment expanded. The contrast with Europe was sharp. Most European countries experienced sluggish productivity growth and struggled with high unemployment rates.

A cursory look at the data suggests that Europe has indeed a lot to learn from the US. Table 6.1 ranks the United States and European countries according to production per head of the population and shows the employment rate.[2] Clearly, the United States is much richer than any of the European countries. The second on the list, Ireland, has approximately 10% less income per capita (from production) than the United States. At the bottom of the list are countries in Southern Europe that entered the European Union relatively recently. They are still significantly behind the European average.

Not only is the United States richer, it is also better at providing jobs than most European countries. A few exceptions to this rule exist, though. Norway, Denmark, Sweden, the Netherlands and also Portugal can rival the United States in this respect. But, generally, the European welfare states lead to open and hidden unemployment and discourage labour market participation.

Table 6.1   Production per capita and employment in Europe and the United States, 2003

	Production per capita indices, US=100	Employment rate indices, US=100
US	100.0	100.0
Ireland	90.7	94.1
Norway	89.6	104.2
Denmark	83.7	104.2
The Netherlands	77.9	105.3
Austria	77.4	96.2
Sweden	76.0	101.8
Belgium	74.7	80.8
Germany	73.2	91.2
Finland	73.1	95.5
United Kingdom	73.1	97.2
Italy	72.4	87.4
France	71.4	85.6
EU15	71.0	91.2
Spain	60.2	86.6
Portugal	50.8	104.7
Greece	50.4	78.4

Source: own computations based on GGDC: Total Economy Database 2004 (University of Groningen and the Conference Board). We refer to the Appendix for an extensive description of the data sources.

The contrast between the two economic superpowers has led to a call for reform in Europe. Barriers to competition in goods, capital and labour markets – the result of too much and too diverse regulations across countries – are thought to stifle growth and to be one of the reasons behind the persistent problem of unemployment. The European Council has backed this call for reform. In Lisbon, it has drawn up an agenda for reform, which should make the European economy in 2010 the most competitive in the world. It has reaffirmed this agenda on later occasions. Nobel Prize winner Gary Becker (2002) sees a watershed in European economic policies: 'Until recent years, most continental European politicians and intellectuals dismissed what they derisively called the British and American "Anglo-Saxon" model of competition and price flexibility. Yet a quiet but enormous change may be taking place in European attitudes toward competition in labour and other markets.'

With the emphasis on reform towards an 'Anglo-Saxon' model comes the concern that Europe will not only become more competitive but also more unequal. The income differences within both the United States and the United Kingdom are generally larger than in continental Europe, and have significantly grown in the 1980s and 1990s. Introducing competition and flexibility, through deregulation and privatisation, could also introduce an 'Anglo-Saxon' society in which the winners are well off but the losers must work hard to get by. This is not in line with European traditions. The European Union acknowledges this concern and stresses social cohesion, which includes acceptable income differences.

This chapter puts reforms, aiming to turn Europe into the most competitive economy, in perspective. Two important points emerge from this. First, the United States is not a leading example for the European Union. The productivity difference between the United States and Europe is not nearly as large as the data on income per capita suggest. We show that the most important difference between the United States and (Western) Europe is not efficiency but the number of hours worked. The prediction that America will 'have' the 21st century thus seems somewhat haphazard, especially since Mortimer B. Zuckerman based it on ideas that 'accounting systems in the United States strive for clear corporate information' and that 'the United States is enjoying a [budget] surplus that looks likely to continue as far as the eye can see'. Moreover, the employment rate of the population in the United States is relatively high but so is (after-tax) income inequality. Europe has a relatively strong tradition in protecting the poor and the sick from the whims of the markets. For those who care about equity and income security,[3] interesting role models are countries that score well on all three aspects: productivity, employment and income inequality. Such countries are found in Europe.[4]

Second, we conclude that a trade-off exists between macroeconomic efficiency and social-economic equality. The reform of European labour markets meets fierce resistance. An important reason behind this resistance – apart from vested interests – is that the same institutions that are held responsible for unemployment – strong trade unions, employment protection, generous social security benefits, high and progressive taxes – yield equality in the income distribution. Indeed, the empirical analysis in this chapter reveals that a trade-off between efficiency and equality exists. This implies that the net social gains of reforming labour markets are not clear-cut. For example, unemployment benefits with a long duration have a negative effect on the incentives to work – some people draw on them for a long time – but contribute to a more equal distribution of income. The analysis also reveals that active labour market policies, that is, training of unemployed workers and assistance with job search, can escape this trade-off up to a point.

Much research on the macroeconomic equity-efficiency trade-off and the relation between labour market institutions and indicators of economic performance is already available. Characteristic for most of this literature, though, is that it tends to analyse the determinants of measures of economic performance more or less in isolation, focusing on unemployment, productivity or participation separately. The most prominent example of this literature – which also provides a good account of previous contributions – is Nickell and Layard (1999).[5] Their analysis is closely related to ours. We contribute to this literature by analysing more dimensions of economic performance – in particular, income inequality – in a unified framework. In doing so, our focus is on the impact of labour market institutions on economic performance, including inequality. A second strand of literature takes up the question as to what institutional setting serves best the goal of optimising economic performance. An interesting example of this literature is Boeri (2002).[6] He considers the economic performance of four different 'social policy models' that he associates with groups of countries, the Nordics, the Anglo-Saxon, Continental Europe and the Mediterranean. Economic performance is evaluated on the basis of income inequality, protection against labour market risk and rewards to labour market participation. Based on cross-country comparisons supplemented with micro-econometric evidence, Boeri concludes that both the Nordic and the Anglo-Saxon countries score well on all indicators and can compete with the USA. Characterising countries in terms of their institutional framework and resulting outcomes can thus provide useful information on the effectiveness of different policy instruments. Our analysis aims to elaborate on this literature by systematically focusing on the impact of a wide range of labour market institutions on macroeconomic outcomes. Our analysis expands on earlier approaches by considering a wide range of institutional characteristics and their effect on macroeconomic outcomes using systematic econometric analysis exploiting cross-sectional as well as time-series variation. Despite the attractiveness of cross-country analysis, the limitations of such approaches have to be acknowledged. These are concisely summarised in Freeman (1998).[7]

We proceed in the following manner. In section 6.2, we compare productivity across time and countries. This establishes that productivity differences between the United States and Europe are not very large. Differences are mainly driven by differences in hours worked per person, and to a lesser extent by the employment rate. Section 6.2 also reiterates the well-known fact that income inequality in the United States is larger than almost anywhere else. Section 6.3 discusses trade-offs among various indicators for economic performance. A central trade-off between participation and income inequality emerges in section 6.4. It shows how the usual, traditional policy instruments – the level of benefit income, employment protection and so on – affect the combination of the two, but do not improve on the fundamental dilemma. In contrast, active labour market policies have allowed some countries to achieve both higher participation and less income inequality.

6.2 THE INCOME GAP BETWEEN THE UNITED STATES AND EUROPE

The United States is by far the richest economy in the world. Its production and income per capita is unrivalled.[8] Various factors can explain this advantage. One of them is that the United States has a superior production technology, based on scope for entrepreneurship combined with investments in R&D and ICT, and a better skilled labour force than any other country. An altogether different explanation is that Americans work more (in terms of number of persons as well as in number of hours). In other words, the American economy is rather labour-intensive. To see which explanation holds ground, we decompose for various countries the production per capita difference with the US into three constituent factors:. the difference in production per hour, the difference in the number of hours worked per worker, and the difference in the number of workers relative to the total population.[9] Figure 6.1 shows for four relatively contrasting European countries – France, the Netherlands, Ireland and Finland – to what extent these three factors have contributed historically to the relative difference in production per capita with the United States.[10]

In 1950, the gap in production per capita was largely the result of a difference in productivity per hour. Hours worked and employment in the four countries did not deviate much from the United States. It was not the effective size of the labour force, but its average productivity, which made the United States much richer than the four countries. The most important historic reason was that Europe had only just started the process of reconstruction after the Second World War, requiring huge investments in private and public capital, whereas the United States had already made the change toward mass production of goods in the decades before the war.

From the 1960s onwards, Europe caught up rather quickly (De Groot and Van Schaik, 1997). It invested on a large scale and had the advantage that it could copy the new production technologies developed in the United States. The four countries outpaced the United States in growth of productivity per hour, although not to the same degree. In Ireland and Finland, somewhat at the periphery of Europe and starting with lower levels of productivity, the catching-up has continued up to now. In France and the Netherlands it continued until the early 1990s. In the second half of the 1990s they lost ground and experienced a decline in their productivity per hour relative to the United States.

Production per capita did not keep track with productivity per hour. At the same time that the growth in productivity per hour accelerated, the employment rate and the number of hours worked started to fall (relative to the United States). With the exception of France, the downward trend in the employment rate was reversed later on.

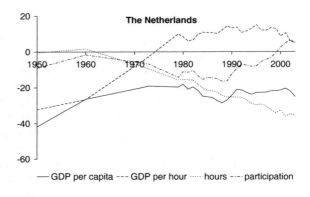

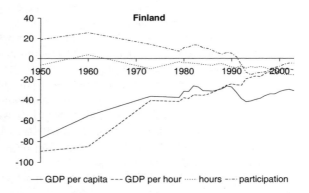

Figure 6.1 Decomposition of GDP per capita, 1950–2003 (US=0)

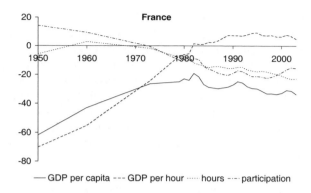

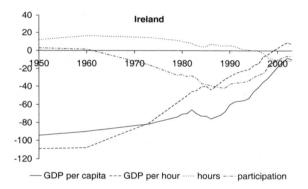

Figure 6.1 Decomposition of GDP per capita, 1950–2003 (US=0)(cont.)

In the 1990s the Netherlands, Ireland and Finland were among the fastest growing countries in the European Union. Measured by production per capita, they were able to keep up with the United States, but for different reasons. The Netherlands was able to improve the employment rate, Finland saw its productivity per hour increase further, and in Ireland both factors contributed to a fast growth in production per capita.

The previous description of trends in relative economic performance of European countries suggests that European workers are currently oftentimes as efficient per hour worked as their American colleagues. The fact that Americans are the richest in the world is by and large caused by the fact that they work more (both in persons as well as in hours per worker). The number of hours worked per employed person is an especially important difference between the two economic powers. Table 6.2 decomposes for a broader sample of (mainly European) countries the income gap with the United States in 2003. The countries are ranked from top to bottom according to their relative GDP per capita.[11] Ireland, Norway, Denmark, the Netherlands, Belgium, Germany, and France outperform the US in terms of production per hour worked. Nevertheless, their gap in GDP per capita exceeds almost 10%. This gap is largely caused by fewer hours worked. For most countries, low employment rates further add to the gap with the United States The Netherlands outperforms the US in terms of production per hour worked (by almost 5%) and employment (by about 5%) whereas the number of hours worked per worker is about 35% less than in the US, resulting in a GDP per capita gap of about 25%.

Table 6.2　The income gap with the US explained: a decomposition, 2003

Percentage difference in	GDP per capita	GDP per hour	Hours per worker	Employment rate
Ireland	−9.7	7.3	−10.9	−6.1
Norway	−11.0	18.0	−33.1	4.1
Denmark	−17.8	0.2	−22.2	4.1
The Netherlands	−25.0	5.0	−35.2	5.2
Austria	−25.6	−1.1	−20.6	−3.9
Sweden	−27.5	−12.8	−16.5	1.8
Belgium	−29.2	8.6	−16.5	−21.3
Germany	−31.2	3.8	−25.8	−9.2
Finland	−31.3	−11.1	−15.6	−4.6
United Kingdom	−31.3	−15.9	−12.6	−2.8
Italy	−32.4	−4.6	−14.2	−13.5
France	−33.8	4.7	−22.9	−15.6
EU15	−34.3	−8.0	−17.1	−9.2
Spain	−50.8	−33.2	−3.2	−14.4
Portugal	−67.8	−63.9	−8.4	4.5
Greece	−68.5	−47.5	3.4	−24.4

Substantially lagging in productivity per hour are the Southern European countries that have joined the European Union relatively late: Spain, Greece and Portugal. Low productivity per hour is the prime reason that the income per capita in these countries is below the European average and far below the American level. On top of that, Spain and Greece also perform particularly poorly in terms of the employment rate as compared to the USA.

To summarize, these results show that the United States is, in GDP per capita terms, richer than almost any country in the European Union. The difference with Northern and Western Europe is largely explained by differences in the number of hours worked, whereas the difference with Southern Europe largely results from a difference in productivity per hour.

The decomposition of income per capita (from production) into three factors – productivity per hour, hours per worker and workers per inhabitant – would not be straightforward to interpret if these three factors were interdependent. In particular, one might suspect that countries with a relatively low employment rate will have – ceteris paribus – a relatively high productivity (per worker as well as per hour). In such countries, workers with a below average level of productivity are most likely not participating in the labour market, but rather draw upon a social security benefit. This 'selection mechanism' would – ceteris paribus – have a positive effect on average productivity measured over employed workers. Reasssuringly, Cavelaars (2003) does not find statistical evidence for a relationship between participation and productivity per worker.

One might also expect hours worked and productivity per hour to be related. Working more hours by individual workers might run into decreasing returns giving rise to a negative relationship. On the other hand, part-time workers earn less per hour than full-time workers, suggesting a positive relationship. The latter also emerges from micro-econometric estimates; see for example Bell and Freeman (2001). Overall, the relationship between hours worked and productivity per hour is ambiguous.

6.2.1 How to Close the Income Gap?

The European Union has the ambition to be the most competitive economy in the world and to close the income gap with the United States. How can it achieve this ambition? The discussion thus far logically suggests three broad ways:

Increase the number of hours worked
For the richest members of the European Union, the main source for the income gap with the United States is the number of hours worked (per worker). However, increasing this number has serious drawbacks and does not unequivocally improve welfare. One drawback is that increases in hours worked might partly be paid for with decreases in productivity per hour (although the empirical evidence for such an effect is not strong; see before). A second, more important drawback is that more labour time means less leisure time. The value of leisure does not appear in income and production statistics, but this does not make its value any less real. Similarly, official statistics ignore the value of household-production.

One needs to argue that the individual choice between labour and leisure (or household production) is distorted to make the argument that an extra hour of work is socially more valuable than an additional hour of leisure.[12] Income taxes could be a reason for such a distortion, since they lower the financial revenue of extra work but not the benefits of extra leisure. However, this argument is not entirely clear-cut and convincing. Higher average income taxes not only induce substitution of labour for leisure, but also decrease (after-tax) income, which raises the incentive to work. Empirically the substitution and the income effect tend to cancel out; the estimated effects of average income taxes on hours worked are rather low.[13] On the other hand, marginal tax rates which are higher than average tax rates, that is, progression in the tax system, could lead to significant distortion in the choice between labour and leisure.[14]

Increase employment
In many European countries, the employment rate of the labour force is relatively low (and unemployment is relatively high.[15] In order to analyse how employment can be increased we first take a closer look at the causes. To this aim we decompose the differences in participation, analogously to the decomposition discussed earlier.[16] We decompose the employment rate (what we denote as participation) into employed as a fraction of the labour force, the labour force as a fraction of the working age population (15–65) and working age population as a fraction of the total population (Figure 6.2).[17] The gaps for a particular variable are again defined as the log–difference between the country that is considered and the United States.

For the Netherlands the development of employment is almost fully explained by an increase in participation in the labour force. Especially since the early 1980s, the labour force as a fraction of the working-age population has grown very rapidly. Differences in the age structure somewhat positively affect employment, although the trend has changed since the mid 1990s, and is expected to continue due to the relatively strong ageing of the baby-boom generation. France has experienced an almost continuous decline in the employment rate. As for the Netherlands, the development is largely attributable to the share of the labour force in the working-age population. Since the early 1980s, the remaining part of the difference is explained by a higher unemployment rate in France as compared to the United States. The development of Finland roughly mimics that of France, although the difference with the United States is less. Specific for Finland is that the contribution of the participation and unemployment rate have more or less moved in parallel. Decreases in participation were accompanied by increases in unemployment. This combined effect explains the steep decline in the employment rate in the early 1990s and the subsequent increase in the second half of the 1990s. Finally, in Ireland the employment rate started at an already relatively low rate in the 1970s (largely due to a relatively small share of the population in the working age). The employment rate further declined until the late 1980s driven by increases in unemployment and reductions in participation but has increased since the late 1980s. The increase is explained by a fairly unique combination of an increased share of the population in the working age, a reduction in unemployment and an increase in participation.

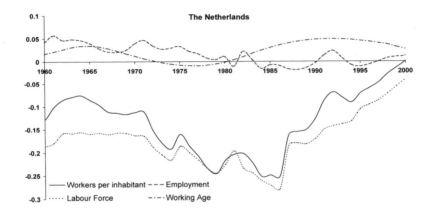

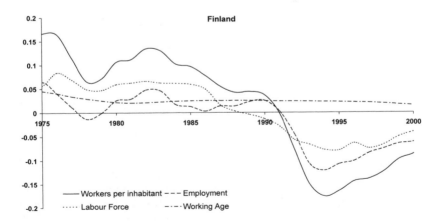

Figure 6.2 Decomposition of employment rate, 1950–2003 (US=0)

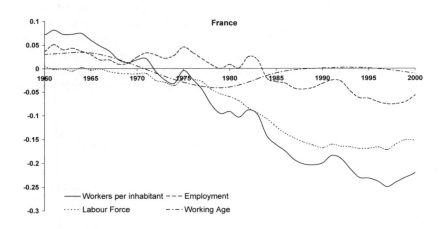

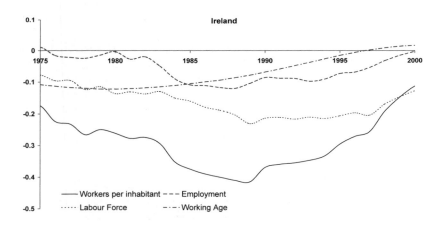

Figure 6.2 Decomposition of employment rate, 1950–2003 (US=0)(cont.)

So for most countries, participation and to a lesser extent unemployment are the driving factors behind changes in the employment rate. Labour market participation is low and unemployment is high among the less productive workers. Of course, when more less-productive workers participate in the labour market, this is expected to reduce the overall average productivity per hour due to a composition effect. But more easily than with the choice between labour and leisure, one can argue that open and hidden unemployment is an important distortion. Unemployment is often involuntary. And even if drawing an unemployment benefit or other type of social benefit is voluntary, the social security arrangements do distort the individual choice. An example may help to clarify this. The participation of workers older than 55 is strikingly low in many countries. The reason lies primarily in schemes for early retirement, which give little incentive to continue working. People who retire early hardly experience any income loss, while the close link between the last earned wage and old-age benefits makes elderly workers reluctant to accept lower wages when getting older – even though they are not as productive as they used to be. The social security system then provides firms and workers with a way to escape the conflict of interests.

Increase productivity (per hour)
A third way to raise income and production per capita is to increase the productivity per hour of each worker. Table 6.2 reveals that many European countries are not (far) behind the United States in terms of productivity per hour. This indicates that the gap in skills or technology between the two is small. Many European workers have invested heavily in training and schooling, and European firms often operate at the technological frontier. This does not apply to Southern European countries, like Greece and Portugal, and a fortiori for those Eastern European countries that have recently joined the European Union. These countries can still improve their productivity by learning to adapt existing technologies. The richer European countries, however, have no alternative but to invest in new and better production methods and products, although the return to shifting the technological frontier is uncertain.[18]

A general gap in technology and skills is not likely, but the European Union can still learn from the United States in at least one area, ICT. This does not immediately concern the production of ICT goods and services. The United States is strong in computer and communication hardware, but Europe is strong in telecommunication services. However, Europe seems to be lagging in the effective application of the new technologies, especially in domestic services (see Baily, 2001; de Mooij and Tang, 2003; Nahuis and van der Wiel, 2004).

Institutional reform
A fourth way to reduce the gap would be to engage in institutional reform. In this context, a much expressed concern is that – in order to transform the European Union into the most competitive economy in the world – a transformation towards an American-style society is required which might be

at the expense of the relatively equal distribution of income that characterises the European Union. The source of this concern is found in Figure 6.3, which reveals for various countries the before-tax and after-tax income inequality – measured by Gini coefficients – in the mid-1990s. At one end of the spectrum, we see Sweden; at the other are the United States and the United Kingdom. The relatively large inequality in the Anglo-Saxon countries does not fit well with continental European traditions. The European Union has therefore stressed in the Lisbon agreement that increased competitiveness should not harm social cohesion, which includes limited income differentials in society.[19] The twin goals of raising competitiveness (and thus income) and maintaining social cohesion may be noble. However, it neglects the fact that a fundamental trade-off between efficiency and equality may exist. For instance, to encourage participation of less-productive workers, one could trim the social security systems (restricting eligibility, limiting the duration or reducing the level of benefits), but this comes at the expense of larger income differentials. The next section investigates the trade-off between efficiency and equity or, more precisely, the trade-off between participation and income equality.

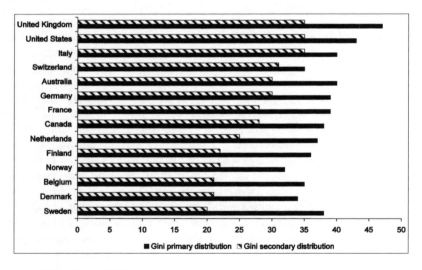

Source: Bradley et al. (2001).

*Figure 6.3 Country ranking according to after-tax income inequality in
         mid-1990s. Gini-coefficients for primary and secondary
         income distribution*

6.3 TRADING OFF EFFICIENCY AGAINST EQUALITY

6.3.1 A First Glance at the Data

The social models in continental Europe are better at delivering income equality but are worse at providing jobs than the Anglo-Saxon model. The run-of-the-mill explanation is that in Europe social security benefits and minimum wages provide a floor below which wage income cannot fall. This compresses the income distribution but at the same time raises unemployment and lowers the participation rate.[20] Figure 6.4 does not give clear support to this explanation. It plots for 12 countries in the period 1989–1994 the Gini-coefficient for the secondary income distribution against the participation rate. For both variables the percentage deviation from the sample mean is shown in the figure. In Belgium and the Netherlands a below average participation rate is combined with a below average degree of inequality, whereas countries like the United Kingdom and the United States match high participation with a large income inequality. This would point to a trade-off, were it not for countries in the upper-left quadrant and lower-right quadrant. The three largest economies in continental Europe – France, Germany and Italy – perform worse on both counts. They have a below average participation that is not compensated with a below average inequality, although inequality is not as high as in the United Kingdom and the United States. In contrast, the two countries in the lower-right quadrant, Denmark and Sweden, perform better on both counts. These are the interesting examples; they demonstrate that it is possible to have an important role for income redistribution, and at the same time a high participation rate.[21]

Figure 6.4 does not reveal a clear-cut trade-off between participation and income equality. It does, however, show that in order to improve economic performance, and in particular the participation rate, European countries do not necessarily have to embrace the Anglo-Saxon model. The do's and don'ts are found in Europe. A group of European countries performs about as well as the US in terms of productivity per hour and participation, but combines this with a far lower inequality. This group includes Denmark and Sweden, but probably also Finland and the Netherlands. On the other hand, a group of European countries performs poorly, not so much in terms of productivity per hour but in terms of labour market participation.

Observation: A first look at the data does not suggest a simple trade-off between participation and inequality. Instead, it leads to the conclusion that different European social models also provide useful lessons on how to reform, and how not to reform.

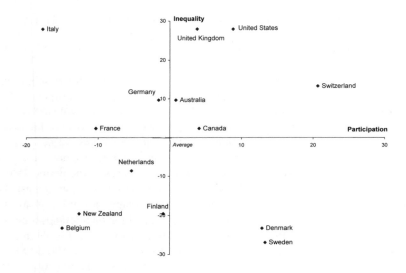

Source: Nickell and Nunziata (2001) for participation and Bradley et al. (2001) for the Gini-coefficients. The variables are constructed as percentage deviations from the (unweighted) average of all countries in the sample.

Figure 6.4 Participation versus income inequality in 14 OECD countries, 1989–1994

6.3.2 An Empirical Approach

The level of unemployment benefits defines a lower bound on the wage distribution. The higher this level is, the more even the wage distribution and the higher the rate of unemployment (or the lower the rate of employment). A first glance at the data (in the previous section) does not confirm this idea. However, the level of unemployment benefits in relation to the level of wages, that is, the replacement rate, is just one characteristic of national labour markets. Other institutional factors are important as well for the performance of labour markets. These factors include, for example, the duration of unemployment benefits and employment protection. They may provide an explanation as to why a trade-off does not seem to appear and thus why some (European) countries perform better than other (European) countries. The trade-off between equality and participation may well be conditional on other factors. We therefore resort to a multivariate analysis.

Central in this section are regressions in which the rate of participation and the degree of income inequality are related to various institutional characteristics of national labour markets. Our data-set covers 18 OECD countries[22] and averages for seven five-year periods from 1960 to 1995 which yields (at most) 126 observations.

Before turning to the regression results, we characterise our data-set. We do so by characterising the economic performance of clusters of countries. In defining the clusters, we follow Esping-Anderson (1999) who breaks down the group of rich countries into three categories according to the social models that the countries have adopted: corporatist, social-democratic and liberal. Broadly speaking, the first category includes countries in continental Europe, the second Scandinavian countries and the third Anglo-Saxon countries.[23]

Figure 6.5 shows for each of the categories three indicators for labour market performance: an estimated measure for inequality of disposable household income, the non-participation rate (defined as 100 minus the participation rate) and the unemployment rate. The latter two indicators are highly correlated, but not always interchangeable. On the axes is the measure of economic performance of the respective group of countries divided by the average measure of performance of all countries. A score of 100 thus means that the group of countries scores equal to the average of all countries. Figure 6.5 clearly reveals that the corporatist countries are more egalitarian but provide fewer jobs than liberal countries. Interestingly, a relatively low rate of participation does not necessarily translate into a high rate of unemployment. The social-democratic countries have the best score for equality and participation, but not for unemployment.

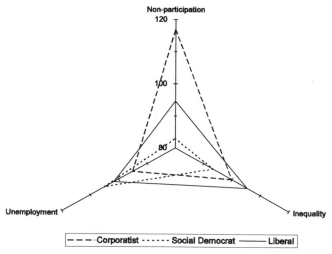

Figure 6.5 Performance in three Esping-Anderson groups
(average 1989–1994)

Figure 6.6 shows for the same three groups of countries several characteristics of labour market institutions. It is immediately clear that in the liberal countries the government intervenes less in the labour market than in the other (groups of) countries. For example, the level and duration of unemployment benefits are on average lower in the liberal countries than elsewhere. Figure 6.6 also illustrates an interesting difference among the European countries. The social-democratic countries have on average the highest benefit level (and the highest tax wedge). They have a higher benefit level than the corporatist countries and combine this with higher expenditures on active labour market policies, with a shorter benefit duration and less employment protection. This suggests that social security in the social-democratic countries is more geared towards reintegration in the labour market than in the corporatist countries, possibly explaining the difference in the participation rate between the two groups of countries. Let us now turn to the regression analysis to see whether it confirms these notions derived from a partial look at the data.

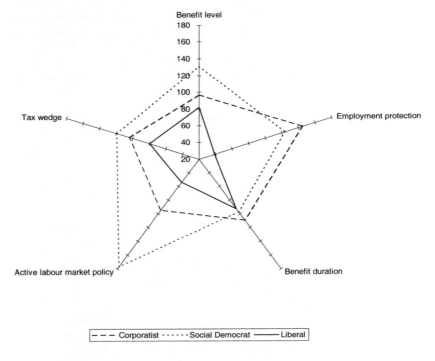

Figure 6.6 Labour market characteristics in three Esping-Anderson groups (average 1989–1994)

A complication for the regression analysis is that the labour market characteristics are mutually correlated. The effect of a single factor is hard to isolate, since it affects not only the performance of the labour market directly, but also the other institutional factors. For example, a country with trade unions in a strong position is likely to have a high replacement rate and a progressive tax system.

We proceed therefore in two steps. In the first step we include in the equation only variables for which the mutual correlation is relatively limited. In doing so, we avoid potential problems of multi-collinearity that might affect the results. Table 6.3 reports the correlation among the explanatory variables for the average of the period 1989–1994. The correlation coefficients are below 0.5 for four variables: benefit level or replacement rate, benefit duration, a measure for employment protection and a measure for active labour market policies. [24]

Table 6.3   Correlations between policy instruments

	Benefit level	Benefit duration	Employment protection	Active LM policies	Union coordination	Union coverage	Tax wedge
Benefit level	1.00	−0.25	0.32	0.41	0.15	0.25	0.36
Benefit duration		1.00	0.03	−0.26	0.27	0.42	−0.07
Employment protection			1.00	0.47	0.55	0.52	0.55
Active LM policies				1.00	0.33	0.36	0.51
Union coordination					1.00	0.36	0.06
Union coverage						1.00	0.06
Tax wedge							1.00

In the second step we separately include other variables of potential relevance in explaining differences in economic performance across countries and over time. Because of space constraints, we restrict attention to the results for addition of the tax wedge between the labour costs for employers and the net wage for employees. Results for addition of and the measures for the unions' role on the labour market, that is, the degree of centralisation in wage bargaining (called coordination) and the extent to which workers are covered by collective agreements (called coverage), can be found in De Groot et al. (2004). The inclusion of such variables exacerbates the potential problems with multi-collinearity and calls for a careful interpretation of the results. The fact that the qualitative results (the signs of the relationship) are not seriously affected by the inclusion of such variables gives confidence in the presented results. The sometimes substantial effects in terms of size of the estimated coefficient and its statistical significance is most likely to be caused by the problem of multi-collinearity and needs to be acknowledged in the interpretation of the results.

Table 6.4 reports the estimation results.[25, 26] We first discuss the results of the first step, in columns I, III and V. Later we shift attention to the other three columns. We discuss the results presented in Table 6.4 horizontally, that is, we discuss the effect of each policy instrument on the various indicators of economic performance separately.

Table 6.4   Labour market policy and economic performance, 1960–1995

| | Dependent variable, logarithm | | | | | |
| | Participation rate | | Unemployment rate | | Inequality | |
	I	II	III	IV	V	VI
Replacement	0.012	0.016	1.281*	0.722	−0.080***	−0.032
rate	(0.21)	(0.27)	(1.95)	(1.15)	(−3.66)	(−1.63)
Benefit	−0.060**	−0.032	0.456	0.818**	−0.051***	−0.109***
duration	(−2.08)	(−0.96)	(1.27)	(1.99)	(−3.1)	(−6.43)
Employment	−0.042**	−0.040**	−0.120	−0.303**	−0.006	0.018**
protection	(−2.59)	(−2.41)	(−0.65)	(−2.05)	(−0.65)	(2.17)
Active LM	0.0031***	0.0034***	−0.0120*	−0.0159***	−0.0030***	−0.0026***
policies	(4.81)	(4.71)	(−1.96)	(−2.66)	(−13.75)	(−10.61)
Tax wedge		−0.021		2.518		−0.287***
		(−0.19)		(2.66)		(−6.55)
Time trend	0.000	0.000	0.055***	0.045***	0.003***	0.004***
	(0.15)	(−0.17)	(7.18)	(5.40)	(5.46)	(7.19)
Constant	4.209***	4.207***	−4.715***	−5.447***	3.496***	3.599***
	(154.5)	(85.0)	(−9.9)	(−8.4)	(204.4)	(185.6)
R^2	0.20	0.20	0.37	0.38	0.51	0.68
# observations	126	118	126	118	95	89
F-statistic	6.11	4.75	14.07	11.37	18.61	28.39

Note: White heteroskedasticity consistent t-values are reported in brackets below the estimates. *** means statistically significant at 1%, ** at 5% and * at 10%.

A higher replacement rate corresponds to less inequality (column V) but to more unemployment (column III). For this policy instrument a trade-off between equity and efficiency seems to result. The effect on the participation rate is positive although small and far from statistically significant. Nickell

(1997) comes up with a similar result. One explanation is that the replacement rate has two opposing effects. A higher rate leads to less labour demand and, thus, to more unemployment. It also encourages labour supply. A better insurance against unemployment risk provides a higher incentive to enter the labour market. The net effect of the replacement rate on participation is hence ambiguous.

The duration of unemployment benefit has a similar impact on unemployment and inequality as the level. Specifically, duration is positively related to unemployment and negatively to inequality. In addition, it has a negative effect on participation. Thus for benefit duration, a clear trade-off arises.

Employment protection also has a negative effect on participation. Since it tends to reduce inequality, a trade-off seems to arise. However, the effect on inequality is small and statistically insignificant. Interestingly, employment protection does not have a clear impact on unemployment. The main effect of employment protection is to reduce flows on the labour market, from employment to unemployment and vice versa. This probably makes it more important for the duration of unemployment than for the rate of unemployment.[27]

The results for active labour market policies are remarkable. Whereas the other three policy instruments give rise to a trade-off, spending on active labour market policies (per unemployed) does not. This type of spending boosts the rate of participation (column I), lowers the rate of unemployment (column III) and reduces income inequality (column V). These results show that some forms of active labour market policies are effective, helping those with a relatively bad position on the labour market and a relatively low income. Of course, the results show only the benefits of these policies, but not their budgetary costs. Moreover, it remains unclear which forms of active labour market policies are effective.

The results of the second step in which the tax wedge is added seem to fit the rule that creating jobs comes at the expense of sharper inequality. The tax wedge reduces income differences and increases unemployment (the effect on participation is insignificant). Including additional variables in the second step does not alter the result that active labour market polices have allowed countries to achieve better combinations of equity and efficiency (see De Groot et al., 2004, for more details). The coefficient for spending on unemployed workers is hardly affected. Including the tax wedge reduces the effect of the replacement rate on unemployment and inequality. This may not seem surprising, given that a higher replacement rate implies more expenditure (on unemployment benefits) and a higher tax burden. However, including the tax wedge magnifies the effect of benefit duration on unemployment as well as on inequality. The effect of employment protection gets an unexpected sign.

For policy making, the results are interesting. Most European countries want to see the rate of overall participation rise. However, achieving that usually gives rise to a dilemma. As a rule, a trade-off between participation and inequality emerges. Reducing benefit duration, for example, has the effect of raising participation, but also brings about more income inequality. Not surprisingly, this and similar measures often meet fierce social and political resistance and fuel the fear of an American-style society in which everyone works – because they have to – but social-economic distinctions are sharp.

An exception to the rule are active labour market policies, which comprise among other things assistance with job search and schooling of (unemployed) workers. This type of instrument is effective in raising participation as well as reducing inequality. It seems to have allowed countries like Denmark and Sweden to combine relatively generous social security systems (when measured by the replacement rate) and limited inactivity among the labour force. The regression analysis is not conclusive evidence, but it at least suggests that European countries can improve participation while maintaining income equality by investing in active labour market policies. Not every form of active labour market policy is effective. The available evidence is scant but already makes that clear (see, for example, Koning and Vollaard, 2000, and Martin, 2000). Systematic evaluations are therefore needed. The OECD (2001) concludes from the few available evaluations that some inexpensive policies, like job-search assistance, are among the most cost-effective ones for a substantial number of unemployed.

Besides introducing additional controls as in columns II, IV and VI we performed some additional robustness checks (see De Groot et al., 2004). The result in general and especially the impact of active labour market policies are robust to differences in data sources, sample, time period that is considered, estimation technique, etc.

6.4 CONCLUSION

US citizens are on average far richer than Europeans. Production per capita is on average more than 30% higher in the United States than in the European Union. This does not result from a general gap in technology. In fact, in some European countries productivity per hour is higher than in the United States. Neither does it result from a general difference in participation on the labour market. In fact, some European economies are better at providing jobs than the American economy. Instead, the income difference arises from a difference in hours worked. Whereas the Americans work on average 1865 hours per year, Europeans only work around 1600 hours: there is difference in income per capita but not necessarily in welfare, since the income statistics ignore the value of leisure and household production.

Behind the averages are important differences in Europe. In Southern Europe productivity per hour is still significantly lower than in the United States (and in the rest of the European Union). Moreover, in continental Europe – Belgium, France, Italy and Germany – participation is far lower than on the other side of the Atlantic. The usual explanation is the extensive social security system in continental Europe. Making the systems less generous would help to make Europe more 'competitive' and would help to raise the rate of participation. The fear is that this comes at the expense of larger, American-style, income differences. Such a trade-off between participation and inequality does not appear at first sight. The worst combination (a below average participation and an above average inequality) is found in Europe, for example Italy. The best combination is found in Europe as well. Some small, mainly Scandinavian countries have found ways to combine relatively high participation with relatively modest income differences. This implies that the United States is not always the obvious role model.

A panel-data analysis for OECD countries shows why different countries achieve different combinations of economic performance. Income redistribution (through a social security system) does not necessarily lead to lower participation and higher unemployment as long as countries supplement it with active labour market policies. These results are robust in a statistical sense. Which types of active labour market policies are effective is something that the panel-data analysis cannot tell. A further analysis of this question would be an interesting extension of this chapter, but is left for future research. Finally, the results suggest that the provision of relatively high benefit levels with a relatively short duration may improve employment without widening the income distribution.

NOTES

1. The authors would like to thank Michèle Belot, Henk Don, Sjef Ederveen, Casper van Ewijk, Theo van de Klundert, Pierre Koning, Ruud de Mooij and participants to the workshop 'Competitiveness and Growth in Europe' (Bonn, September 2004) for discussions and comments. Henri de Groot and Paul Tang would like to dedicate this chapter to the memory of Richard Nahuis who so sadly and unexpectedly passed away during the proof-reading stage of this chapter.
2. We define the employment rate here as the share of employed in the total population. A more commonly used indicator for economic performance in this respect is the participation rate that is defined as the share of the labor force in the population aged between 15 and 65.

the unemployed in the numerator and neglects the people aged below 15 and above 65 in the denominator.

3. Equality can be valued for two principal reasons: the insurance motive in social security or egalitarian reasons per se. We do not discuss this any further.

4. Boeri (2002) comes to the related conclusion that the social-economic equality is a major advantage of the European social models over the Anglo-Saxon approach.

5. Other examples include Daveri and Tabellini (2000) and Scarpetta (1996).

6. See also Andersen (2004) for a more in-depth analysis of the Scandinavian welfare model.

7. Although Freeman acknowledges the usefulness of cross-sectional analyses as a complement to within-country studies that exploit changes in institutions over time and comparisons of groups of workers that are covered by different institutions, he points at two important drawbacks of cross-country analyses. Most importantly, he points at the possibility that countries differ in many institutional dimensions, implying that differences in outcomes can be explained in different ways. Furthermore, he points at the possibility that institutions that work in one country need not work in another country because of other differences in institutions that mutually interact. Acknowledging these drawbacks, we argue that macroeconomic cross-country studies extended with time series analysis are a useful complement to more microeconomic-oriented studies.

8. Actually there exist some small countries that – for fairly specific reasons – have higher per capita income than the United States, like Luxembourg. We do not include Luxembourg in the tables as this distracts attention from the main message.

9. More specifically, we use the definition $Y/P = (Y/H)* (H/L)*(L/P)$, where Y is real GDP, P is the population, H is the number of hours worked and L is employment. Taking logs and differences with the United States, we arrive at relative differences between a country and the United States.

10. Similar figures for all other countries are available in Annex 1 to this chapter, which is available at www.henridegroot.net/downloads.asp (under 'notes and appendices').

11. Note that the numbers in Table 6.1 and Table 6.2 are strongly related. In Table 6.1, we showed GDP per capita of a country relative to that of the US, whereas in Table 6.2 we decompose the difference between the log of GDP per capita of a country and that of the US into its components (see note 9 for the definition of GDP per capita resulting in our decomposition).

12. Of course, in many jobs hours worked is not a choice variable. Hours worked are often institutionally constrained. Workers whose constraint is binding might also face a different valuation at the margin.

13. Kimball and Shapiro (2003) write that

> One of the best-documented regularities in economics is that – when they affect all members of a household proportionately – large, permanent differences in the real wage induce at most modest differences in the quantity of labor supplied by a household. . . . The standard explanation is that the substitution and income effects of a permanently higher real wage are of approximately the same size; (. . .).

14. However, lowering tax progression is not without risks. It makes it more difficult to redistribute income but could also have important side effects on macroeconomic productivity, especially in Europe. For example, progressive taxes help to moderate wage demands (of trade unions) and in this way help to reduce unemployment.

15. For 14 OECD countries the simple coefficient of correlation between the average participation rate and the average standardised unemployment rate in the period 1989–1994 is –0.83.

16. For this aim, we define the employment rate (L/P) as $(1-U)LF/LF * LF / WA * WA / P$. The first term measures the share of the labour force that is employed (and thus not unemployed) where U measures the unemployment rate and LF is the labour force. The second term measures the fraction of the working age population (population between 15 and 65) that is in the labour force. Finally, the third term measures the share of the total population that is aged between 15 and 65.

17. The results of such an analysis for all countries can be found in Annex 2 to this chapter, which is available at www.henridegroot.net/downloads.asp (under 'notes and appendices').
18. Two important asides have to be mentioned here. The first is that, strictly speaking, technological leadership is to be established at a more disaggregated level (for example sectors). Second, the potential for catching up is strictly speaking not determined by the gap between the average productivity in one country and the average productivity of the leader country, but by the gap with the most productive firms in a leading country (see Bartelsman and De Groot, 2004, for an empirical elaboration of these issues).
19. A third component of the Lisbon Strategy concerns sustainable development, referring to the quality of the environment. We do not explore here the trade-off between a clean environment and economic growth (see, for example, Van den Bergh and De Mooij, 1999).
20. From this point onwards, in contrast to section 2, we use the participation rate instead of the employment rate as our measure for economic performance reflecting the provision of jobs in the economy. The former is taken from Nickell and Nunziata (2001) and defined as Total civilian employment normalised on the working age population (15–64).
21. The data apply to the period 1989–1994 and may not adequately characterize the current situation. However, since participation in Denmark and Sweden is still high in 2001 (see Table 6.1) and since there are no clear signs that these two countries have become much more unequal, they are likely still to outperform the United States. The Netherlands may have joined these two, since the Dutch participation rate has increased substantially in the 1990s (see Figure 6.1)
22. These countries are Australia, Austria, Belgium, Canada, Denmark, Finland, France, Germany, Ireland, Italy, Japan, the Netherlands, New Zealand, Norway, Sweden, Switzerland, United Kingdom and United States.
23. More specifically, the corporatist countries are Austria, Belgium, France, Germany, Italy, the Netherlands and Japan; the social-democratic countries are Denmark, Sweden, Finland and Norway; and the liberal countries are Ireland, United Kingdom, United States, Switzerland, Australia, Canada and New Zealand.
24. Even for these variables, the mutual correlation is not negligible, meaning that a careful interpretation of the regression results is called for.
25. Our data for active labour market policies are taken from Nickell (1997). Their availability is restricted to the periods 1984–1989 and 1989–1994. In order to optimally exploit the information in our dataset for the other variables and to avoid serious biases in the estimates for active labour market policies, we have filled the non-availables for active labour market policies in our dataset with expenditures on active labour market policies in the closest period for which data are available. We have analysed the robustness of our results by (i) performing the analysis without filling the series for active labour market policies (and accepting the loss of observations that results), (ii) using data on active labour market policies from the OECD that cover a longer time span, and (iii) using lags of active labour market policies to account for the possible problem of endogeneity. These sensitivity tests are reported in De Groot et al. (2004).
26. The data on benefit duration are taken from Nickell and Nunziata and contain several zeroes. We find these slightly suspicious. The results in Table 4 are based on information on benefit duration in which the zeroes have been replaced by the value for benefit duration in the closest year for which information is available. As with active labour market policies, we have made sensitivity analyses to establish the robustness of the results for this change to the original data supplied by Nickell and Nunziata.
27. Indeed, Nickell (1997) finds that employment protection has a positive effect on long-term unemployment and a negative effect on short-term unemployment.

REFERENCES

Andersen, T.M. (2004), 'Challenges to the Scandinavian welfare model', *European Journal of Political Economy*, **20**, pp. 743–54.

Baily, M.N. (2001), *Macroeconomic Implications of the New Economy*, Kansas City: The Federal Reserve Bank.

Bartelsman, E.J. and H.L.F. de Groot (2004), 'Integrating evidence on the determinants of productivity', in G. Gelauff, L. Klomp, S. Raes and T. Roelandt (eds), *Fostering Productivity*, Amsterdam: Elsevier, pp. 157–81.

Becker, G. S. (2002), 'The continent gets it', *Business Week*, April.

Bell, L.A. and R.B. Freeman (2001), 'The incentive for working hard: explaining hours worked differences in the US and Germany', *Labour Economics*, **8**, pp. 181–202.

Belot, M. (2003), 'Labor market institutions in OECD countries: origins and consequences', Ph.D. thesis, Tilburg: Center for Economic Research, Tilburg University.

Bergh, J.C., J M. van den and R.A. de Mooij (1999), 'An assessment of the growth debate', in J. C. J. M. van den Bergh (ed.), *Handbook of Environmental Resources*, Cheltenham: Edward Elgar, pp. 643–55.

Blanchard, O. and J. Wolfers (2000), 'The role of shocks and institutions in the rise of European unemployment: the aggregate evidence', *Economic Journal*, **110** (462), pp. C1–33.

Boeri, T. (2002), 'Let social policy models compete and Europe will win', conference paper, John F. Kennedy School of Government, April 11–12.

Bradley, D., E. Huber, S. Moller, F. Nielsen, and J. Stephens (2001), 'Distribution and redistribution in post-industrial democracies', Luxembourg Income Study Working Paper No. 265.

Cavelaars, P. (2003), 'Has the tradeoff between productivity gains and job growth disappeared?', *MEB Serie*, no. 2003–12, Amsterdam: DNB.

Daveri, F. and G. Tabellini (2000), 'Unemployment, growth and taxation in industrial countries', *Economic Policy: A European Forum*, April, pp. 47–88.

Esping-Andersen, G. (1999), *Social Foundations of Post-industrial Economics*, Oxford: Oxford University Press.

Freeman, R. (1998), 'War of the models: which labour market institutions for the 21st century?', *Labour Economics*, **5** (1), pp. 1–4.

Galbraith, J.K. and Hyunsub Kum (2003), 'Inequality and economic growth: data comparisons and econometric tests', mimeo, University of Texas.

Groot, H.L.F. de, R. Nahuis and P. Tang (2004), 'Is the American model Miss World? Choosing between the Anglo-Saxon model and a European style alternative', CPB Discussion Paper, The Hague: CPB Netherlands Bureau for Economic Policy Analysis (forthcoming).

Groot, H.L.F. de and A.B.T.M. van Schaik (1997), 'Unemployment and catching-up: Europe vis-a-vis the USA', *De Economist*, **145**, pp. 179–201.

Kimball, M.S., and M.D. Shapiro (2003), 'Labor supply: are income and substitution effects both large or both small?', mimeo, paper not yet published. It can be downloaded at: http://www-personal.umich.edu/~shapiro/labor-16may2003.pdf.

Koning, P. and B. Vollaard (2000), 'Arbeidsbemiddeling en -reïntegratie van werklozen Welke rol heeft de overheid te spelen?', *CPB Document*, no. 118, The Hague: CPB Netherlands Bureau for Economic Policy Analysis.

Martin, J. (2000), 'What works among active labour market policies: evidence from OECD countries' experiences', in OECD, *Policies Towards Full Employment*, Paris: OECD.

Mooij, R.A. de, and P.J.G. Tang (2003), *Four Futures of Europe*, The Hague: CPB Netherlands Bureau for Economic Policy Analysis.

Nahuis, R. and H.L.F. de Groot (2003), 'Rising skill premia: you ain't seen nothing yet?', *CPB Discussion Paper*, no. 20, The Hague: CPB Netherlands Bureau for Economic Policy Analysis.

Nahuis, R. and H. van der Wiel (2004), 'Europe's ambition and the role of ICT. Should there be a European ICT policy agenda?', *CPB Document*, forthcoming.

Nickell, S. (1997), 'Unemployment and labor market rigidities', *Journal of Economic Perspectives*, **11**, pp. 55–74.

Nickell, S. and R. Layard (1999), 'Labour market institutions and economic performance', in O. Aschenfelter and D. Card, *Handbook of Labor Economics, Volume 3*, Amsterdam, North Holland: Elsevier Science, pp. 3029–84.

Nickell, S. and L. Nunziata (2001), *Labour Market Institutions Database* (version 2.00; 1960–1995), http://cep.lse.ac.uk/pubs/download/data0502.zip.

OECD (2001), *Employment Outlook 2001*, Paris: OECD.

Scarpetta, S. (1996), 'Assessing the role of labour market policies and institutional settings on unemployment: a cross-country study', *OECD Economic Studies*, **26** (2), pp. 43–98.

Total Economy Database, 2004, Groningen Growth and Development Centre (GGDC), Groningen: University of Groningen and the Conference Board.

Zuckerman, M. B. (1998), 'Debate: a second American century', *Foreign Affairs*, **77** (3), pp. 18–31.

APPENDIX 6.A   DATA SOURCES

This Appendix describes the sources and content of the data used in this study.

Productivity per hour, participation, production per capita and hour per person

These data are taken from GGDC Total Economy Database 2003 (University of Groningen and the Conference Board, http://www.eco.rug.nl/ggdc). The database contains series for real GDP, population, employment, annual working hours, GDP per capita, GDP per person employed and GDP per hour. It covers 74 countries from 1950 onwards.

Inequality measures

There is a plethora of empirical measures proxying for income inequality, each with its own pros and cons. In this chapter, we have used the Gini measures for income inequality as gathered by the Luxemburg Income Survey (LIS) and by Deininger and Squire, percentile ratios gathered by LIS, and Estimated Household Income measures that were estimated by Galbraith and Kum (2003). Without going into detail on all these different measures, it is useful to characterize the essential differences between these measures as they have motivated our choice for the measures used in the main text. In order to provide some feeling for the differences (and similarities) among these measures of (or proxies for) income inequality, we have constructed a correlation matrix of all these measures for the year 1989. This matrix is contained in Table 6.5. The table reveals that almost all measures are highly correlated, with the exception of the Gini measure from Deininger and Squire that is poorly correlated with the Estimated Household Income measures. More details on income inequality measures can be found in Nahuis and De Groot (2003).

Table 6.5   Correlation matrix

	GINI	GINI_LIS	PERC90_10	PERC90_50	PERC80_20	EH112	EH114
GINI	1.00	0.60	0.61	0.51	0.59	0.11	0.17
GINI_LIS		1.00	0.94	0.97	0.97	0.62	0.58
PERC90_10			1.00	0.89	0.97	0.57	0.51
PERC90_50				1.00	0.93	0.68	0.66
PERC80_20					1.00	0.57	0.50
EH112						1.00	0.81
EH114							1.00

Sources for Table 6.4:

- Participation: taken from Nickell and Nunziata (2001). Defined as total civilian employment normalised on the working age population (15–64) (from CEP OECD data, updated by authors).
- Hours worked per worker: Own computations based on data taken from GGDC Total Economy Database 2003 and 2004 (University of Groningen and the Conference Board; data are available at www.eco.rug.nl/ggdc).
- Inequality: Estimated Household Income Inequality taken from Galbraith and Kum (2003). We refer to Nahuis and De Groot (2003) for a more extensive discussion on available inequality measures. An alternative though less attractive variable available for long time spans is the Theil inequality measure provided by the University of Texas Inequality Project (UTIP). This measure is based on pay inequality in the manufacturing sector. This variable is used for robustness analysis.
- Standardized unemployment rate: taken from Belot (2003).

- Replacement rate: taken from Nickell and Nunziata (2001). They use Benefit Replacement Rates data provided by OECD with one observation every two years for each country in the sample. The data refer to first year of unemployment benefits, averaged over family types of recipients, since in many countries benefits are distributed according to family composition. The benefits are a percentage of average earnings before tax.
- Employment protection: taken from Nickell and Nunziata (2001). They use information from Blanchard and Wolfers (2000) who constructed an employment protection time varying variable from 1960 to 1995, each observation taken every 5 years. Range is {0,2} increasing with strictness of employment protection.
- Benefit duration: An index. See Nickell and Nunziata (2001) for details.
- Active labour market policy: Nickell (1997).
- Coordination: Belot (2003).
- Union coverage: Belot (2003).
- Tax measures: Data on average and marginal taxes are taken from the OECD. Our measure for tax progression is derived from the average and marginal tax data.

COMMENT

John Fitz Gerald

This chapter draws together in an accessible form the results of a number of other useful pieces of research that contribute to our understanding of the choices facing policy makers in the EU. It highlights the very interesting contrast between Europe and the US in terms of the average number of hours worked by employees on both sides of the Atlantic. This raises the question of the appropriate measure of utility: is it GDP per head or should we be using some wider measure that takes into account the utility of 'leisure'?[1]

A paper by Freeman and Schettkat (2004) suggests that the consistent pattern of lower hours worked in the EU may represent legal constraints placed on employees in Europe and may also reflect the greater 'marketisation' of child-care in the US. Our understanding of the differences between the EU and the US would be enhanced if we could decompose the differences in hours worked into differences in holidays, differences in patterns of part-time working and differences in hours worked by full-time employees. The work of Bruyère and Chagny, 2002, throws some light on this issue. In the first case – higher holidays – it is hard to argue that the pattern of higher holidays in the EU than in the US is driven purely by legal constraints rather than representing a free choice made in terms of a greater preference for leisure.

As Freeman and Schettkat show, some of this increased 'leisure' is taken up with more time spent minding children. This could be a freely made choice, in which case the reduction in market earnings does not represent a loss of welfare. However, some of it may be due to higher child-care costs in much of the EU compared to the US. In turn the higher child-care costs may reflect a much lower dispersion in wage rates in the EU than in the US. It may not be profitable for many couples in the EU to employ someone to look after their children, given the high taxes and relatively lower dispersion in earnings. This issue as to what extent the difference in paid hours worked represents and actual difference in utility should be amenable to answer by further research.

The distribution of income can be affected by the welfare and tax system (including the replacement rate) in each country. However, it can also be affected by changes in the supply-demand balance for labour, especially the balance for unskilled labour. A reduction in the supply of unskilled labour through interventions in the educational or training systems could narrow the wage dispersion in a more sustainable manner than a rise in welfare rates. This could be part of the explanation for the superior performance of the Scandinavian EU members noted in the paper.

The suggestion that progressive taxes could help to moderate wage demands seems implausible. Economic theory and European experience would suggest that increases in the tax wedge (between what employers pay in labour costs and what employees receive in after tax income) will result in upward pressure on wage rates. Increased progressivity, if achieved by higher marginal tax rates, could be expected to add to pressures in the bargaining process for higher wage rates.

The duration of unemployment benefits will mean different things in different welfare systems. In many welfare systems, when an individual loses entitlement for unemployment benefit they may well be covered by other safety-net payments. As a result, the duration of unemployment benefits paints a starker picture of the choices facing the unemployed in many EU countries than is really the situation. In addition, in some countries, especially the Netherlands, the relative ease with which people can qualify for sickness payments will change the range of choices facing the individual unemployed person.

The chapter provides relatively good evidence that active labour market policies can be particularly beneficial for EU economies, achieving a more favourable distribution of income without a penalty in terms of higher unemployment. However, there is also a lot of evidence from around Europe that active labour market polices can often prove ineffective in achieving their goals (O'Connell, 2002). Policy makers will need to take this into account: there is no automatic guarantee that more spending on active labour market policies will achieve the goal of reducing unemployment at a low cost. Active labour market policies will need to be precisely targeted if they are to prove value for money.

NOTE

1. Also, 'leisure' includes other non-market kinds of work, including time spent child-minding.

REFERENCES

Bruyère, M. and O. Chagny (2002), 'Comparaisons internationales des durées du travail', *Revue de l'OFCE*, No. 82, July, pp.117–63.

Freeman, R. and R. Schettkat (2004), 'Your money or your time: marketization and work in advanced economies', mimeo.

O'Connell, Philip J. (2002), 'Are they working? Market orientation and the effectiveness of active labour market programmes in Ireland', *European Sociological Review*, **18**, pp. 65–83.

7. The Impact of Institutions on the Employment Threshold in European Labour Markets, 1979–2001

Christian Dreger

7.1 INTRODUCTION

Rigidities in national labour markets are widely seen as responsible for the weak employment performance in Europe. The average unemployment rate in the EU15 is around 8%, and is predicted to be stable at this level for the near future. According to OECD measures, a substantial part is due to long term unemployment: 45 (60)% of the unemployed are unemployed for longer than 12 (6) months. Despite a gradual decline since the mid 1990s the rates are highly persistent. Actually, long term unemployment rates exceed the US level by a factor of 4.

The high unemployment rates are accompanied by lower employment and participation rates.[1] After a rise in the 1990s, EU15 employment rates are 65%, which is not far below the Lisbon goal (70%). But, the gaps are wider for young people, older workers and women. Due to the weak economic recovery, the rise in the employment rate will not continue in the near future. At the same time, differences within the EU are larger than the difference between the EU average and the US. Long term unemployment rates exceed the average especially in Germany, Italy and Spain. Employment rates are relatively low in Belgium, Greece, Italy and Spain. The correlation between the long term unemployment and employment rate is –0.8 over the last decade. Hence, the unemployment problem is not caused by higher participation.

To some extent, labour market institutions may account for this outcome. Rigid institutions can reduce the chance of flexible adjustments in case of structural shocks. Examples of institutions include employment protection legislation, the system of wage bargaining and benefits in favour of the unemployed. Over recent years, several papers have investigated this issue, see for example Nickell (1997), Blanchard and Wolfers (2000) and IMF

(2003). The main topic analysed is the link between labour market institutions and unemployment. In contrast, the focus of this chapter is on the impact of institutions on the employment performance. Institutions should affect unemployment by enhancing employment. Looking at the unemployment rate might be misleading: if there is only a link from institutions to unemployment, workers who have lost their jobs would drop out of the labour force. This contradicts the Lisbon goal of high participation. To obtain robust results, different aspects of the employment record are examined. In addition to the participation rate, the threshold of employment is considered: due to productivity gains, output growth has to exceed a certain level to create new jobs. This threshold is inversely related to the marginal intensity of employment to output growth, that is, the elasticity of employment growth with respect to output growth. As both parameters are not observable they have to be estimated.

The chapter is organized as follows. In the next section (section 7.2) the threshold and marginal intensity for employment are derived. Then, the role of institutions is discussed and results of the literature are reviewed (section 7.3). The empirical section is divided into two parts. In the first step (section 7.4), estimates of the threshold and marginal intensity of employment are presented for a sample of EU countries. Second, in section 7.5 the impacts of institutions on the employment record are investigated. Finally, section 7.6 concludes.

7.2 DERIVATION OF THE EMPLOYMENT THRESHOLD

The law of Verdoorn (1949, 1993) states that faster output growth (y) will induce gains in labour productivity growth (p). Formally, the relationship

$$p_t = \theta_0 + \theta_1 y_t \, , \, \theta_1 > 0 \tag{7.1}$$

predicts increasing returns to scale if the Verdoorn coefficient θ_1 turns out to be greater than 0, see Fingleton (2001). A positive, but declining slope parameter is found in most empirical studies, see Harris and Lau (1998) and Léon-Ledesma (2000) for the UK and Spanish cases, respectively. Increasing returns may be explained by a variety of endogenous growth models, see Aghion and Howitt (1998) for a survey.

A serious issue with Verdoorn's law is the absence of the role of capital, which can be substituted for labour. Due to the omitted variable problem, estimation of the regression parameters from the relation (7.1) seems to be biased. Suppose output is produced by a Cobb-Douglas technology

$$y_t = \tau + \eta l_t + \gamma k_t \qquad (7.2)$$

where l, k and τ are the growth rates of labour, capital and technology, respectively. As employment growth is the difference between output and productivity growth, the relation

$$p_t = \tau / \eta + [(\eta - 1)/\eta]y_t + (\gamma/\eta)k_t \qquad (7.3)$$

is implied. Hence, the bias is proportional to the coefficient from a regression of capital growth on output growth, see Greene (2003). However, the link between productivity and output growth can be defended, if capital growth equals output growth. This is in line with the stylized fact of a roughly constant capital-output ratio, see Jones (1998). In that case, the relations $\beta_0 = \square / \square$ and $\beta_1 = (\square + \square - 1)/\square$ are supposed to hold, and unbiased estimates can be obtained from (7.1). But, the returns to scale parameter cannot be revealed from this expression without knowledge of the production elasticities of labour and capital. The intercept corresponds to the rate of technological progress, divided by the production elasticity of labour.

Because of the high correlation of output growth and productivity growth, spurious regressions may occur. If employment growth and technical progress were constant, a perfect correlation between productivity and output growth would appear, which is not informative at all. This problem can be avoided in a specification between employment and output growth,

$$l_t = \alpha_0 + \alpha_1 y_t, \quad \alpha_0 = -\beta_0, \alpha_1 = 1 - \beta_1 \qquad (7.4)$$

that has been already favoured by Kaldor (1975). A high correlation between output and productivity does not imply the same for employment and productivity growth: if the former are perfectly correlated, the latter variables are not related at all.

A Verdoorn coefficient of 0.5 in (7.1) implies a marginal employment intensity α_1 of the same size in (7.4). This means that a 1% acceleration in output growth would stimulate employment growth by half a % on the average. The less than proportional reaction is due to efficiency gains, which can be realized more easily in periods of higher growth. They may be traced, for example, to manpower reserves, increases in working hours, or higher labour intensities. The threshold of employment (y_E) indicates output growth for which employment is constant ($l_t = 0$). In terms of the model parameters the threshold level y_E reads:

$$y_E = -\alpha_o / \alpha_1 \qquad (7.5)$$

Due to the parameter $-\alpha_0$, it is positively related to the rate of technological progress (λ), and negatively related to the production elasticity of labour (β). In addition, a higher marginal employment intensity (α_1) is expected to reduce the threshold. Provided that output growth is above the threshold, employment will be stimulated. If growth falls beyond the bound, losses in employment are predicted on the average. In that case, output growth is not sufficient to compensate for the rise in productivity because of technological progress and employment will shrink. According to (7.4) and (7.5), the evolution of employment

$$l_t = \alpha_1 (y_t - y_E) \tag{7.6}$$

depends on the deviation of actual output growth from the threshold. Each percentage point of output growth above (below) the threshold comes with a positive (negative) employment reaction determined by the marginal employment intensity.

Most previous studies indicate a decline of the threshold over time, see Fingleton and McCombie (1998) and Walwei (2002), among others. Hence, the model parameters are subject to change. This finding may be caused by the decrease in total factor productivity (TFP) in most EU economies, see European Commission (2003). Furthermore, if deregulation in the labour markets had been successful in the past, the marginal intensity of employment should have risen over time.

7.3 THE ROLE OF LABOUR MARKET REGULATION

It is widely acknowledged that proper institutions are of key importance for a smooth working of the labour market, see Agell (1999), Blanchard (2004) and Bertola (2004). Information problems for both workers and firms generate imperfections in matching and monitoring processes. Different degrees of market power of wage contractors and the risk of becoming unemployed require an appropriate mix of the institutional framework. However, such regulations also cause rigidities which can impede the reallocation of labour in case of structural shocks. Overly restrictive elements may actually worsen the employment performance. To examine this issue, a set of variables has been developed in the literature, covering different aspects of the institutional setting. The set includes employment protection legislation, the structure of wage determination, measures in favour of the unemployed, like unemployment benefits and active labour market policies, and taxes on labour. In addition, product market institutions may be relevant for the employment record. However, they are highly correlated with labour market institutions, and are not considered separately.

Employment protection legislation may raise the effective costs to firms of employing workers and the costs of adjusting employment over the business cycle. Dismissals become more difficult and firms will be more cautious about filling vacancies. A higher degree of job security can be compensated by lower wage growth, although stronger employment protection may also raise the bargaining power of insiders. On the other hand, employment protection makes regular employment more stable. As personnel selections within firms are more effective, involuntary separations are reduced. In addition, a higher degree of employment protection can support investments in firm specific human capital, thereby inducing productivity and competitiveness gains, see Pissarides (2001) and Belot and van Ours (2002).

Trade unions are highly important for the wage setting process in Europe. Greater union power tends to raise wages above the competitive equilibrium. This effect may be boosted in countries with strict employment protection schemes and extensive measures in favour of the unemployed. Moreover, wages and other working conditions are determined by collective bargaining agreements either on the regional or on the sectoral level. The outcomes often bind not only the bargaining parties, but also employers and employees within a particular sector. Due to the centralisation of bargaining, flexibility is lost. But, if union power is accompanied by a high degree of coordination of firms and workers, employment can be supported, see Calmfors and Driffill (1988). For example, centralized bargaining may improve the responsiveness of wage to the overall macroeconomic conditions, and a greater internalisation of the consequences of high wage demands can be achieved.

Higher unemployment benefits and longer benefit duration periods reduce the gap between net wage earnings and public transfer payments, and thus the incentives of households to work. The unemployed will become choosier about filling vacancies, implying that the matching process appears to be less effective. As the fear of unemployment declines, an upward pressure on wages is generated. The positive impact of benefit levels and durations on the length of unemployment spells is well documented by numerous microeconometric studies. However, more generous unemployment benefits could also increase the incentives for human capital accumulation. As the search process can last longer, it becomes more likely to result in an appropriate job. Furthermore, participation in the labour force might become more attractive, as it is a prerequisite to be eligible for the benefits.

Active labour market policies aim to reduce the dependency of people on unemployment benefits by improving their chances to move into work. This is relevant in particular for low skilled workers, see OECD (2003). Strategies include public employment services, labour market training, subsidies on employment and measures for the young and disabled. Insofar as the employability of the participants is improved, labour market performance should improve. However, regular employment can be crowded out by public work. Policies are financed through taxes and contributions of employers and employees. Training programmes might not match with the qualifications really demanded by firms, see Martin and Grubb (2001).

Taxes on labour widen the wedge between the wages as employer's costs and wages as worker's income. The tax share that is borne by the employers will raise the effective costs of employment, thereby reducing labour demand. If higher labour taxes are fully compensated by lower wages, the product wage paid by firms will be unchanged, but the consumption wage received by households declines. Thus, the distance to transfer payments is narrowed, and the incentives of households to work are reduced. Overall, rising labour taxes should have a negative impact on the employment record, see Daveri and Tabellini (2000). Especially in the low income-low productivity range, high marginal tax rates can generate inactivity traps. A significant part of the relatively good employment performance in the Euro area between 1997 and 2001 can be traced to decreasing labour tax rates, see Mourre (2004).

According to Blanchard and Wolfers (2000), the interaction between macroeconomic shocks and institutions may be crucial for a proper understanding of the development in EU labour markets. In fact, a substantial part of the institutional framework was already in place in the 1960s and 1970s, when unemployment was quite low. The rise in unemployment since then may be explained by adverse supply shocks like the oil crises in the 1970s or financial crises of the social security systems because of unfavourable demographic trends. But, these shocks hit the EU countries in a symmetric way. Thus, they can account for a general increase in the unemployment rate, but the cross country variation is left unexplained. If institutions are not optimally designed, the persistence of unemployment in response to shocks might be prolonged. In recent years, several papers have examined this issue, see for example Nickell (1997), Elmeskov, Martin and Scarpetta (1998), Blanchard and Wolfers (2000), Fitoussi, Jestaz, Phelps, and Zoega (2000), and Nickell, Nunziata, Ochel and Quintini (2002). Most researchers have investigated the impacts of the institutions on unemployment for a sample of 20 OECD countries. More recent studies have controlled for interactions between institutions and macroeconomic shocks or within the set of institutions, stressing the relevance of the appropriate institutional mix, see Belot and van Ours (2001) and Bertola, Blau and Kahn (2002). For example, the effect of an increase in payroll taxes on the incentives to work will be larger in the country with the more generous unemployment benefit system.

Overall, the evidence taken from these studies is not straightforward, see Baker, Glyn, Howell and Schmitt (2002) for a survey. Most important, many of the institutional features are no more rigid among the group of high unemployment countries than among those with low unemployment. Results often appear to be counter-intuitive. In particular, employment protection legislation seems to have almost no impact on the course of unemployment. Stricter protection of jobs increases the long term unemployment rate, but the effect is no longer significant, when the overall rate is considered. Strength of trade unions and bargaining coverage tends to raise unemployment. However, this effect is usually compensated, if wage setting is highly coordinated on both the employers' side and that of the employees. Comparing the actual outcome with a model assuming fixed institutions over time, Nickell, Nunziata, Ochel and Quintini (2002) are able to explain half of the unemployment experience by institutional shifts in the 1960–1995 period, especially in the tax and transfer systems. But, the result is built upon substantial levels of endogenous persistence as reflected by a high coefficient of the lagged dependent variable in the regressions. This persistence should be caused by the institutional framework, but is left unexplained in the model. In the IMF (2003) study, institutions and interaction terms play a vital role for the evolution of unemployment in France and Italy, but not in Germany.

7.4 THRESHOLD AND MARGINAL INTENSITY OF EMPLOYMENT

Estimates for the threshold and the marginal intensity of employment are based on annual data of real gross value added and employment taken from the Groningen Growth and Development Centre (2004) database. The overall time span runs from 1979–2001. The parameters are determined via recursive OLS. Initially, the regression (7.4) is run country-by-country over the period 1979–1985, and the first set of parameters is computed (corresponding to 1985). Then, the observation period is prolonged by 1, and the process is repeated until the end of the sample is reached. Due to this procedure, country specific time series of the threshold and the marginal intensity of employment are obtained. Estimates are more reliable in later periods, because they are based on a broader information set. The results are presented for three subperiods: 1985–1990, 1985–1995, and 1985–2001, see Table 7.1. A few outliers occurred in the Italian threshold in 1991 and 1992.

They have been smoothed out, using 1990 and 1993 as the start and end point of the linear interpolation.

Table 7.1 Threshold of employment and marginal employment intensity

	1985–1990		1985–1995		1985–2001	
Austria	2.1 (0.7)	0.3 (0.2)	2.1 (0.4)	0.4 (0.1)	1.9 (0.4)	0.4 (0.1)
Belgium	2.1 (0.3)	0.6 (0.1)	2.1 (0.3)	0.5 (0.1)	1.6 (0.3)	0.5 (0.1)
Denmark	1.3 (0.4)	0.6 (0.1)	1.7 (0.4)	0.5 (0.1)	1.4 (0.3)	0.5 (0.1)
Finland	1.8 (1.0)	0.5 (0.2)	3.2 (0.7)	0.7 (0.1)	2.8 (0.5)	0.8 (0.1)
France	2.1 (0.3)	0.7 (0.1)	1.8 (0.3)	0.5 (0.1)	1.4 (0.3)	0.6 (0.1)
Germany	0.6 (0.8)	0.5 (0.2)	1.2 (0.5)	0.6 (0.1)	1.2 (0.3)	0.6 (0.1)
Ireland	4.4 (1.3)	0.2 (0.2)	2.7 (0.9)	0.5 (0.2)	2.8 (0.7)	0.6 (0.1)
Italy	0.5 (1.0)	0.3 (0.2)	1.3 (0.7)	0.4 (0.2)	1.0 (0.7)	0.4 (0.2)
Netherlands	1.1 (0.7)	0.9 (0.3)	0.8 (0.6)	0.8 (0.2)	0.8 (0.5)	0.8 (0.2)
Portugal	3.0 (1.5)	0.3 (0.2)	2.7 (1.2)	0.4 (0.2)	1.8 (0.9)	0.4 (0.1)
Spain	2.6 (0.3)	1.3 (0.2)	2.2 (0.3)	1.2 (0.2)	1.9 (0.3)	1.3 (0.1)
Sweden	0.2 (1.0)	0.3 (0.2)	2.1 (0.3)	1.0 (0.1)	2.2 (0.3)	0.9 (0.1)
United Kingdom	1.9 (1.3)	0.6 (0.2)	2.0 (0.7)	0.7 (0.2)	1.8 (0.5)	0.7 (0.1)

Notes:
Table shows averages over the respective period. Parameters are derived country-by-country using recursive OLS in (4). Standard errors in parentheses. The threshold is a ratio of two random variables; its variance has been calculated by a first order Taylor approximation. Output refers to gross value added, employment to persons employed. Data obtained from the Groningen Growth and Development Centre (2004) database.

Consider Austria as a numerical example. The threshold is 1.9 over the entire sample period. Hence, output growth has to be at least 1.9 on the average to generate jobs. As the marginal intensity of employment is 0.4, the constant in (7.4) is 1.9*0.4=0.76. Assuming a production elasticity of labour of 0.5, the implied rate of TFP growth is 1.5 percentage points on the annual base. For the majority of the EU countries, the threshold has declined over time, although the change is hardly significant. The threshold appears to be rather stable in Denmark and the UK, while an increase can be detected for Finland, Germany, Italy and Sweden. Moreover, the threshold has substantially converged across the EU. Its dispersion has fallen by 50% since the second half of the 1980s, as measured by the coefficient of variation.

The marginal intensity of employment is more or less constant. Although an upward trend in the parameter can be detected for most countries, the change is often insignificant. The threshold and the marginal intensity of employment are almost not connected over the entire sample, as their correlation is not significantly different from 0, see Figure 7.1. Over the last decade, only three countries (Austria, Ireland, Portugal) experienced a decrease in the threshold and an increase in the marginal intensity parameter. For the other countries, the evolution of the threshold parameter is largely due to fluctuations in the TFP growth rate.

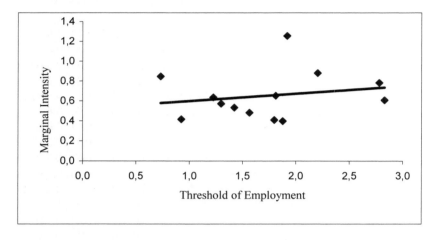

Figure 7.1 Relationship between changes of threshold and marginal intensity of employment

7.5   THE INSTITUTIONAL IMPACT ON THE EMPLOYMENT RECORD

Data on the participation and employment rate and the share of part time employment have been obtained from OECD labour force statistics. For institutions, Nickell and Nunziata (2001) have assembled an annual dataset for a sample of 20 OECD countries, covering the period from 1960–1995 (Labour Market Institutional Data Base, hereafter LMIDB). Measures include employment protection legislation, trade union density, that is, the share of unionised workers in total employment, bargaining coverage and the coordination of bargaining, benefit replacement rates and durations, and the tax wedge on labour income. See Nickell and Nunziata (2001) on how these variables are defined. As the series in the LMIDB usually show more variation than OECD indicators, they are preferred by most researchers. Data on active labour market policies start later (1985) and are taken from various issues of the OECD employment outlook.

As a main shortcoming, the LMIDB ends in 1995. Since then, employment rates have increased slowly in the EU, perhaps just because of some progress in the implementation of labour market reforms, see Mourre

(2004). Fortunately, Nickell (2003) has provided an update, extending the period to 1998. For both employment protection legislation and bargaining coverage, the length of the series can be further enhanced by the Fraser Institute database, see Gwartney, Lawson, and Emerick (2003). Correlations are about 0.8 in absolute value between the respective LMIDB and Fraser Institute measure (1995). Other variables, like benefit replacement rates and trade union densities, can be prolonged by OECD measures. Due to data merging, the time span can be extended to 2001. However, a few missing values remain, especially in 1999. They are replaced by the average of 1998 and 2000.

Results are based on the 1979–2001 period. Due to the derivation of the threshold and the marginal intensity of employment, the first six observations have been dropped, and the effective sample employed runs from 1985–2001. In contrast to previous studies, institutional information reaching back to the 1960s is not considered. Because of the shorter period, the results are supposed to be less affected by structural breaks. Macroeconomic shocks and their interactions with institutions are expected to play a less vital role, implying that the regressions are less complex and easier to interpret. Degrees of freedom are enhanced by estimating a panel model allowing for country individual fixed effects. The results refer to the average of EU15 economies. However, Luxembourg and Greece are excluded due to data limitations.

The models with the best empirical fit are reported for employment (Table 7.2) and for the threshold and marginal intensity of employment (Tables 7.3 and 7.4). As the results for participation rates are very similar to those obtained for employment rates, the former have been skipped. Initially, all institutions and reasonable interactions between them are included in the equations. The high correlation of the variables implies imprecise parameter estimates. Hence, the large models hide the relevant forces at work, and they need to be simplified successively. Simplification starts from different points to get a robust picture.

To control for the business cycle situation, the equations have been enhanced by macroeconomic variables, that is, output growth and inflation. Both variables behave procyclically. In addition, interactions with the institutional setting are taken into account. Note that for the derivation of the threshold and the marginal intensity of employment, output growth rate is already taken into account. In contrast to the dominant view, only a few channels of interactions with the institutional design turn out to be significant. This may be caused by the sample period, which is substantially shorter than in most other studies. In addition, the evidence may differ between the performance of employment and that of unemployment.

Table 7.2   Effects of labour market institutions on the overall employment rate in a panel of EU countries

	Coefficient	t-value (absolute)
UDS	−0.397	7.92
EPL	−0.045	2.88
TAX*BRR	−0.324	4.02
ALMP*BRR	−0.025	2.04
GP	0.525	5.04
COO*GY	0.177	4.49
Adjusted R^2	0.90	
F-Statistic	389.97	

Notes:
Panel estimation with country fixed effects. ALMP = Active labour market policy, BRR=benefit replacement rate, COO =bargaining coordination, EPL = employment protection legislation, TAX = tax wedge, UDS=trade union density, GY = growth rate gross value added, GP = CPI inflation. Employment rates obtained from OECD Labour Market Statistics, CPI from the OECD Main Economic Indicators.

Nevertheless, the results are more or less reasonable. For example, higher union power (union density) and stricter employment protection are expected to lower the employment rate (Table 7.2). This result might reflect labour demand behaviour. Provided that union power increases wages above the competitive equilibrium, employment prospects are worsened, leading to a decline in participation. Moreover, a rise in taxes or active labour market policies tends to reduce the employment rate. The negative impact is restricted to countries with a more generous unemployment benefit system. Both interaction terms emphasize the relevance of policies aiming at stronger incentives for households to work. Regarding active labour market policies, some ineffectiveness seems to be prevalent. This points to some ineffectiveness in the use of these policies. As the active labour market policies include several components, additional evidence can be provided. Here, the ineffectiveness is traced back mainly to a negative impact of public employment services on the employment rate, but not to labour market training measures. Significant crowding out effects of regular employment can be detected especially for the East German economy. Finally, an upturn of economic activity will contribute to an increase of employment rates. This effect seems to be more important, if wage bargaining is highly coordinated.

Union strength is relevant for the threshold of employment (Table 7.3). Higher union densities raise the threshold, especially in countries with more generous unemployment benefits. This is partly compensated by a high degree of coordination in wage bargaining. Furthermore, an increase in the tax wedge is expected to lower the threshold, which appears difficult to interpret. However, the reduction of the threshold might reflect a TFP slowdown, see equation (7.4). This view is supported by the analysis of the marginal intensity of employment, where the tax wedge is not significant at all. In an economic upturn, the threshold is reduced, thereby improving the employment outlook. However, this effect is compensated, if the countries have extensive employment protection legislation schemes.

Table 7.3   Effects of labour market institutions on the threshold and marginal intensity of employment in a panel of EU countries

	Coefficient	t-value (absolute)
UDS	0.041	3.49
UDS*BRR	0.117	8.42
COO	−0.005	2.59
TAX	−0.058	4.02
GP	−0.229	4.48
GP*EPL	0.179	6.14
Adjusted R^2	0.81	
F-Statistic	185.73	

Notes:
Panel estimation with country fixed effects. BRR = benefit replacement rate, COO = bargaining coordination, EPL = employment protection legislation, TAX = tax wedge, UDS = trade union density, GP = CPI inflation.

Employment protection legislation is the most important variable for the marginal intensity (Table 7.4). Stronger employment protection will reduce the job content of output growth. Empirically, the best fitting models point to some interaction of employment protection with other institutional and business cycle variables. In particular, a decline in the marginal intensity is expected, if union power is high, and the unemployment benefit system is more generous. Furthermore, higher levels of coordination tend to raise the marginal intensity of employment. A better consideration of the macroeconomic situation in wage negotiations can activate jobs to a larger extent, especially at the lower income range.

Table 7.4 Effects of labour market institutions on marginal intensity of employment in a panel of EU countries

	Coefficient	t-value (absolute)
COO	0.314	7.06
EPL*UDS	−0.358	3.18
EPL*BRR	−0.476	6.76
GP*EPL	−0.515	1.96
Adjusted R^2	0.80	
F-Statistic	291.36	

Notes:
Panel estimation with country fixed effects. COO = bargaining coordination, EPL = employment protection legislation, UDS = trade union density, GP = CPI inflation.

7.6 CONCLUSIONS

The analysis has shown that labour market institutions are important for the EU employment record. Most results have sensible interpretations. Policies should be directed to introduce more flexibility in the labour markets. Compared to the current setting, a less stringent employment protection legislation seems to be favourable, while both the need for flexibility and security have to be taken into account. The tax and transfer systems should be more aligned to support the incentives for households to work. In addition, fiscal consolidation is important, as it is a precondition for cutting taxes in the medium and long run.

Some progress has been made in recent years due to the liberalisation of temporary contracts with low separation costs and exceptions for small enterprises and business startups, see Young (2003). In the field of employment protection legislation, the use of temporary work arrangements has been eased, while the protection of regular employment remained mostly unaltered, see OECD (2004). Instead of partial reforms, the results point to a more comprehensive strategy, as interactions between institutions often turn out to be significant.

However, the institutions do not tell the whole story. Only a minor part of the employment record can be explained by the institutional setting. The bulk of the explanation is due to country individual fixed effects. On the other hand, institutions are partly embedded in these effects, as the institutional change is usually slow. Efforts should be undertaken to improve the institutional database to capture the complexity of the institutional framework, see Bertola, Boeri and Cazes (2000). In particular, the dataset should be enhanced to cover variables focusing on actual deregulation strategies. These include the use of temporary contracts, variable payment schemes, such as bonuses, and opening clauses in collectively bargained contracts.

NOTE

1. Employment rates are obtained as employment population ratios, where the number of employed persons aged 15 to 64 is divided by the total population of the same age group. Participation rates include the unemployed in the nominator.

REFERENCES

Agell, J. (1999), 'On the benefits from rigid labour markets: norms, market failures and social insurance', *Economic Journal*, **109**, pp. 143–64.

Aghion, P. and P. Howitt (1998), *Endogenous Growth Theory*, Cambridge: MIT Press.

Baker, D., A. Glyn, D. Howell and J. Schmitt (2002), 'Labour market institutions and unemployment: a critical assessment of cross-country evidence', Center for Economic Policy Analysis, Working Paper 2002-17.

Belot, M. and J. Van Ours (2001), 'Unemployment and labour market institutions: an empirical analysis', *Journal of Japanese and International Economics*, **15**, pp. 1–16.

Belot, M. and J. Van Ours (2002), 'Welfare effects of employment protection', CEPR discussion paper, 3396.

Bertola, G. (2004), 'A pure theory of job security and labour income risk', *Review of Economic Studies*, **71**, pp. 43–61.

Bertola, G., T. Boeri and S. Cazes (2000), 'Employment protection in industrialized countries: the case for new indicators', *International Labour Review*, **139**, pp. 57–72.

Bertola, G., F. D. Blau and L.M. Kahn (2002), 'Comparative analysis of labour market outcomes; Lessons for the US from the international long run evidence', in A. Krueger and R. Solow (eds), *The Roaring Nineties: Can Full Employment be Sustained?*, New York: Russell Sage and Century Foundations, pp. 159–218.

Blanchard, O. (2004), 'Designing labour market institutions', unpublished manuscript, http://econ-www.mit.edu/faculty/blanchar/papers.htm.

Blanchard, O. and J. Wolfers (2000), 'The role of shocks and institutions in the rise of European unemployment: the aggregate evidence', *Economic Journal*, **110**, Conference Papers, pp. C1–C33.

Calmfors, L. and J. Driffill (1988), 'Centralization of wage bargaining', *Economic Policy*, **2**, pp. 14–61.

Daveri, F. and G. Tabellini (2000), 'Unemployment, growth and taxation in industrial countries', *Economic Policy*, **15**, pp. 47–104.

Elmeskov, J., J. P. Martin and S. Scarpetta (1998), 'Key lessons for labour market reforms: evidence from OECD countries experiences', *Swedish Economic Policy Review*, **5**, pp. 205–52.

European Commission (2002), *Employment in Europe 2002*, Chapter 2: Structural changes in the European labour markets, pp. 47–78.

European Commission (2003), *The EU Economy: 2003 Review*, Chapter 2: Drivers of productivity growth, pp. 63–118.

Fingleton, B. (2001), 'Equilibrium and economic growth: spatial econometric models and simulations', *Journal of Regional Science*, **41**, pp. 117–47.

Fingleton, B. and J. S. McCombie (1998), 'Increasing returns and economic growth: some evidence from the European Union regions', *Oxford Economic Papers*, **50**, pp. 89–105.

Fitoussi, J.-P., D. Jestaz, E. Phelps and G. Zoega (2000), 'Roots of the recent recoveries: labour reforms of private sector forces?', Brookings Papers on Economic Activity, Brookings Institution, pp. 237–309.

Greene, W. H. (2003), *Econometric Analysis*, 5th edn, Upper Saddle River, NJ: Prentice Hall.

Groningen Growth and Development Centre and The Conference Board (2004), 60-Industry Database, http://www.ggdc.net.

Groningen Growth and Development Centre and The Conference Board (2004), Total Economy Database, http://www.ggdc.net.

Gwartney, J., R. Lawson and N. Emerick (2003), *Economic Freedom of the World: Annual Report of the Fraser Institute*, Vancouver, http://www.freetheworld.com.

Harris, R. and E. Lau (1998), 'Verdoorn's law and increasing returns to scale in the UK regions, 1968–91: some new estimates based on the cointegration approach', *Oxford Economic Papers*, **50**, pp. 201–19.

International Monetary Fund (2003), 'Unemployment and labour market institutions: why reforms pay off', April World Economic Outlook.

Jones, C.I. (1998), *Introduction to Economic Growth*, New York: Norton & Company.

Kaldor, N. (1975), 'Economic growth and the Verdoorn law – a comment on Mr. Rowthorn's article', *Economic Journal*, **85**, pp. 891–96.

León-Ledesma, M.A. (2000), 'Economic growth and Verdoorn's law in the Spanish regions, 1962–91', *International Review of Applied Economics*, **14**, pp. 55–69.

Martin, J.P. and D. Grubb (2001), 'What works and for whom: a review of OECD countries' experience with active labour market policies', *Swedish Economic Policy Review*, **8**, pp. 9–56.

Mourre, G. (2004), 'Did the pattern of aggregate employment growth change in the Euro area in the late 1990s', European Central Bank, Discussion paper 358.

Nickell, S. (1997), 'Unemployment and labor market rigidities: Europe versus North America', *Journal of Economic Perspectives*, **11**, pp. 55–74.

Nickell, S. (2003), 'Labour market institutions and unemployment in OECD Countries', CESifo DICE Report 2/2003, pp. 13–26.

Nickell, S. and L. Nunziata (2001), *Labour market institutions database*, vers. 2.00, LSE, Centre of Economic Performance,
http://cep.lse.ac.uk/pubs/download/data0502.zip.

Nickell, S., L. Nunziata, W. Ochel and G. Quintini (2002), 'The Beveridge curve, unemployment and wages in the OECD from the 1960s to the 1990s', in P. Aghion, R. Frydman, J. Stiglitz, and M. Woodford (eds), *Knowledge, Information and Expectations in Modern Macroeconomics*, Princeton: Princeton University Press.

OECD (2003), 'Benefits on employment, friend or foe? Interactions between passive and active social programmes', chapter 4, *Employment outlook*, Paris: OECD.

OECD (2004), 'Employment protection legislation and labour market performance', chapter 2, *Employment outlook*, Paris. OECD.

Pissarides, C. (2001), 'Employment protection', *Labour Economics*, **8**, pp. 131–59.

Verdoorn, P.J. (1993), 'On the factors determining the growth of labour productivity', *Italian Economic Papers*, **2**, pp. 59–68. Originally published: Verdoorn, P.J. (1949), 'Fattori che regolano lo sviluppo della produttivita del lavoro', *L'Industria*, **1**, pp. 3–10.

Walwei, U. (2002), 'Labour market effects of employment protection', *IAB Labour Market Research Topics*, **48**, Nürnberg: Institut für Arbeitsmarkt- und Berufsforschung der Bundesanstalt für Arbeit.

Young, D. (2003), 'Employment protection legislation: its economic impact and the case for reform', *EU Economic Papers*, **186**.

COMMENT

Jens Rubart

Motivation

What are the determinants of the (low) employment performance in European labour markets? This question is widely examined, for example, by Phelps (1994) and Sargent and Ljungqvist (2002). Nevertheless, particular questions concerning the importance of labour market institutions remain open.

It is generally accepted that the flexibility of labour market institutions is an important determinant of the performance of labour markets. However, they are almost always considered in order to explain the unemployment record within or across countries. In recent times the employment performance across countries has been analysed with growing interest.[1] Compared with the above mentioned theoretical work, the study by Christian Dreger is characterised by a detailed empirical analysis of the importance of labour market institutions for explaining the employment pattern across main European countries.

Christian Dreger's Approach

As already mentioned, complementing the theoretical work by, for example, Sargent and Ljungqvist (2002), the chapter by Dreger concentrates on a well founded empirical examination.

In particular, Verdoorn's law is applied in order to derive the employment threshold and the marginal employment intensity analytically. In a second step he applies OLS techniques to estimate the employment threshold and the marginal employment intensity. Furthermore, panel estimations with fixed country effects are applied in order to derive the specific impact of various labour market institutions on the employment rate, the employment threshold and the marginal employment intensity. Complementing Blanchard and Wolfers (2000) it is shown that labour market institutions are (almost always significantly) negatively correlated with the employment record across various European countries.

Comments

Beside the results, that the marginal employment intensity as well as the employment threshold are negatively correlated with various measures of labour market institutions, one particular kind of market imperfection is not considered by Christian Dreger: product market regulation. As pointed out by

Krueger and Pischke (1997) and Blanchard and Giavazzi (2003), the regulation of product markets is an important determinant of labour demand, vacancy creation and therefore the evolution of employment.[2]

Following a suggestion by Pissarides (2003) and assuming that the employment pattern of an economy depends on the rate of job creation, we relate an indicator of product market regulation with the vacancy rate, which can be seen as an indicator of the rate of job creation. Figure 7.1.C below shows that the rate of job creation is negatively correlated with product market regulation.[3]

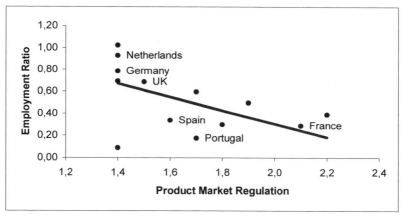

Source: Nickell and Nunziata (2001) and Nicoletti and Scarpetta (2003).

Figure 7.1.C Job creation and product market regulation

Using the employment rate and the employment threshold, as given by Christian Dreger's study, we obtain the result that the employment rate and the employment threshold are negatively correlated with product market regulation. Figures 7.2.C and 7.3.C below show the respective correlations.

In brief, (rigid) labour market institutions account significantly for the low employment performance of European labour markets. Nevertheless, product market regulation should be considered further in order to analyse this pattern, because product markets are important determinants of job creation, whereas labour market institutions notably determine the matching process of the labour market. However, if both product and labour market institutions are considered in regression experiments one has to avoid the problem of multicollinearity. This problem arises because of the fact that labour and product market legislation coincide positively (see, for example, Blanchard and Giavazzi (2003), figure IV).

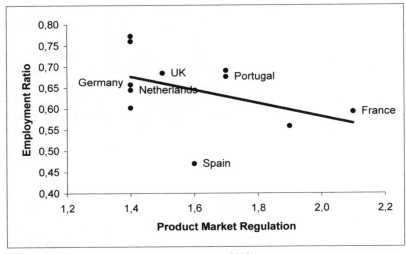

Source: Dreger (2004) and Nicoletti and Scarpetta (2003).

Figure 7.2.C Employment rate and product market regulation

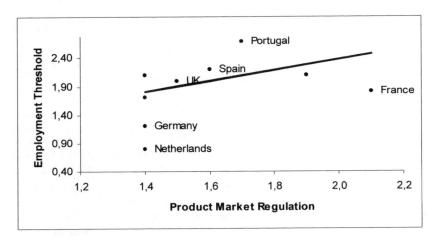

Source: Dreger (2004) and Nicoletti and Scarpetta (2003).

Figure 7.3.C Employment threshold and product market regulation

Furthermore, as also pointed out by Christian Dreger, many things are left for future research, particularly the development of reliable and comparable indicators of the regulation intensity for both product and labour markets, which can be used in order to derive detailed examinations of the specific impact of each kind of regulation on labour market performance.

NOTES

1. See also, for example, Krueger and Pischke (1997), Blanchard and Giavazzi (2003), Heckman (2003), and Pissarides (2003) for current research on this topic.
2. Detailed surveys on the pattern of regulation and its impact on the labour market performance can be found in Boeri et al. (2000), Nicoletti et al. (2000), Heckman (2003), and Nicoletti and Scarpetta (2003).
3. The data are selected analogue to Dreger (2004). The solid line in Figures 7.1.–7.3.C represents the respective OLS–estimator.

REFERENCES

Blanchard, O.J. (2004), 'The economic future of Europe', NBER Working Paper No. 10310, Cambridge, Massachusetts.

Blanchard, O.J. and F. Giavazzi (2003), 'Macroeconomic effects of regulation and deregulation in goods and labor markets', *Quarterly Journal of Economics*, **118** (3), pp. 879–908.

Blanchard, O.J. and J. Wolfers (2000), 'The role of shocks and institutions in the rise of European unemployment: the aggregate evidence', *The Economic Journal*, **110** (1), pp. C1–C33.

Boeri, T., G. Nicoletti and S. Scarpetta (2000), 'Regulation and labour market performance', CEPR Discussion Paper No. 2420, London.

Dreger, C. (2004), 'The impact of institutions on the employment threshold in European labour markets: 1979–2001', this volume.

Heckman, J.J. (2003), 'Flexibility and job creation: lessons for Germany', in P. Aghion, R. Frydman, J. Stiglitz and M. Woodford (eds), *Knowledge, Information, and Expectations in Modern Macroeconomics*, Princeton University Press, pp. 309–25.

Krueger, A.B. and J.S. Pischke (1997), 'Observations and conjectures on the U.S. employment miracle', NBER Working Paper No. 6146, Cambridge, Massachusetts.

Nickell, S. and L. Nunziata (2001), *Labour Market Institutions Database*, vers. 2.00, LSE, Centre of Economic Performance.

Nicoletti, G., S. Scarpetta and O. Boylaud (2000), 'Summary indicators of product market regulation with an extension to employment protection legislation', OECD Economics Department Working Paper No. 226, Paris.

Nicoletti, G. and S. Scarpetta (2003), 'Regulation, productivity and growth: OECD evidence', *Economic Policy*, **18**, pp. 9–72.

Phelps, E.S. (1994), *Structural Slumps*, Cambridge, Massachusetts: Harvard University Press.

Pissarides, C.A. (2003), 'Company start-up costs and employment', in P. Aghion, R. Frydman, J. Stiglitz and M. Woodford (eds), *Knowledge, Information, and Expectations in Modern Macroeconomics*, Princeton University Press, pp. 309–25.

Sargent, T. and L. Ljunqvist (2002), 'The European employment experience', mimeo, Stockholm School of Economics and Stanford University.

8. European Productivity Gaps: Is R&D the Solution?

Christoph Meister and Bart Verspagen*

8.1 INTRODUCTION

Industrialization, and the association between technological advance and economic growth, brought Europe world economic leadership in the 19th century. However, in the course of the 20th century, European leadership was lost to the United States, as well as a number of dynamic Asian economies, of which Japan was the first to emerge in the process of modern economic growth. This loss of European leadership is commonly associated with another major technological change: the rise of the mass production system in the United States (for example, David, 1975).

The process of European integration, started after the Second World War primarily as a way of achieving political stability and peace, became a major force towards the realization of economies of scale in the European economies, and hence as a way for Europe to benefit more than it had done before from the mass production system. This had its highpoint in the realization of the 'Europe 1992' programme, which created a single European market, without limitations for the free trade of goods and services or the free mobility of people (Tsoukalis, 1997).

As a result of this and other factors related to the diffusion of technology, Europe was able to catch-up to the United States over the long postwar period (for example, Abramovitz, 1979, Nelson and Wright, 1992, Pavitt and Soete, 1982), and close some of the productivity gap that had emerged in the first half of the 20th century (especially during the 1930s and 1940s). However, as we will document below, at the dawn of the 21st century Europe still faces a major productivity gap relative to the USA and other world economic leaders, such as Japan.

This fact of a European backlog relative to especially the USA and the dynamic Asian economies, led European political leaders to formulate an ambitious goal for the first ten years of the new millennium. At the Lisbon Summit in 2000 the governments of the European Union (EU) agreed on the goal of the EU becoming by 2010 'the most competitive and dynamic knowledge-based economy in the world, capable of sustainable economic growth with more and better jobs and greater social cohesion'.[1] This overall goal has been embedded in a set of policy guidelines that include the following elements:

- preparing the transition to a knowledge-based economy through better policies for the information society and R&D;
- stepping up the process of structural reform for competitiveness and innovation and completion of the single market;
- combatting social exclusion and modernizing the European social model by investing in people;
- sustaining the healthy economic outlook and favourable growth prospects by continuing with an appropriate macroeconomic policy mix and improving the quality of public finance.

To realize these goals, the review of the Lisbon process at the Barcelona Summit in 2002 has explicitly emphasized the importance of research and development (R&D).[2] One of its main recommendations calls for an increase in European R&D expenditure with the target to reach 3% of European GDP by 2010, two thirds of this to take the form of business R&D.[3] The main argument behind this target appears to be the concern that even if knowledge-intensive industries in the EU have been partially successful in creating employment over the last decade, productivity developments have been far less favourable (especially if measured against the US). This underperformance is seen as a threat for European competitiveness and economic growth in general and, more specifically, for the achievement of the Lisbon goals and for the growth of national incomes and living standards. A related concern is the fact that the EU has a relatively low performance in input (business R&D) and output indicators (such as patents) of innovative activity. Public policy, with the aim to promote investment in business R&D, is therefore seen as a key measure to prevent long-term economic decline (European Commission, 2002, Economic Policy Committee, 2002).[4]

As we argue below there is indeed major evidence that links R&D to productivity performance. Also, the adoption of the Barcelona target should contribute to closing the gap in R&D intensities between the EU and the US economies. However, the extent to which it can contribute to offset the productivity gap between the EU and the US remains to be seen. On the one hand, as pointed out in the official documents as well, regulatory and other institutional differences might play important roles. On the other hand, the EU's trading partners will also benefit from increased European R&D by a higher R&D content of exports. Thus, for relative productivity, achieving the Barcelona target is not a zero-sum game.

Based on a simulation exercise, which uses results from the literature and from a longitudinal dataset, the chapter tries to assess this issue. It starts with a short discussion on the link between R&D and productivity growth. Section 8.3 presents an overview of the existing productivity gap between the EU and the US and its development over time and sectors. Sections 8.4 and 8.5 provide and discuss the simulation results. A conclusion sums up the main findings and puts them into the perspective of the debate.

8.2 THE LINK BETWEEN R&D AND PRODUCTIVITY

Economic theorists have accepted the positive link between technological change, productivity and economic growth for a long time. Process innovation provides opportunities for cost reduction. Product innovation enhances either the range of available intermediate inputs for the production process, increasing real output, or increases the availability of consumer products with corresponding welfare gains. Indeed, in modern economies, the inputs of capital and labour alone cannot account for a large part of output growth (Solow, 1957). The concept of 'total factor productivity' (TFP) has been widely used as a measure to explain this residual (see Nadiri, 1970).

In a rich empirical tradition of work on productivity growth (for example, Griliches, 1979), the total factor productivity residual has been related to the accumulation of a 'knowledge stock', which is not accounted for in the measurement of the conventional capital stock but increases output via innovation and technological change. R&D expenditures have been suggested as a way of measuring this knowledge stock, and this has led to a range of works relating R&D expenditures to total factor productivity growth. This is consistent with the notion in 'new growth theory' of non-convexities of R&D and knowledge in output, which results in self-sustaining growth (as in Romer, 1986, 1990).

An important issue in this literature is the idea that R&D not only provides productivity benefits for the firms that undertake it, but also for other firms in similar or somehow related lines of business. This is the notion of R&D spillovers, indicating that the impact of innovation and technology is felt widely rather than being a private pay-off. In this context, Griliches (1979, 1992) pointed to the distinction between knowledge and rent spillovers. Pure 'knowledge spillovers' are externalities arising from the public goods characteristics of technology and research without the need to engage in economic transactions. These externalities can arise from learning, observation and copying such as 'reverse engineering' and 'patenting around'. Other transmission channels result from formal and informal contacts and networks of scientists, professionals, clients and customers, which go beyond market transactions (Mansfield, 1985). Rent spillovers, on the other hand, are defined by a shift of innovation rents from the producer to the user of a certain technology due to competitive market pressures. From the perspective of the whole economy, this constitutes an unwanted measurement error in attributing productivity increases to the wrong entity and can, in principle, be corrected by using adjusted output deflators (Triplett, 1996). Yet for an individual firm, industry or country, such effects result in real benefits with corresponding productivity increases.

Empirically, however, both notions are somewhat difficult to separate, as market interaction can facilitate the exchange of technological knowledge. To reflect the different mechanisms of spillover transmission and absorption the empirical literature uses basically three different weighting schemes to aggregate a stock of indirect, spillover-related R&D. Transaction-based weights emphasise to some extent the rent spillover component. Usually these are derived from interindustry sales (for example van Meijl, 1995), investment flows (for example Sveikauskas, 1981) or from a full input-output framework (for example Terleckyj, 1974, 1980, Wolff and Nadiri, 1993 or Sakurai et al., 1996). In contrast, weighting by technological distance measures accounts for the fact that the absorption of knowledge spillovers is mediated by the technological proximity between receiver and transmitter. Such distance may be measured by the type of performed R&D (Goto and Suzuki, 1989), the qualifications of researchers (Adams, 1990), the distribution of patents between patent classes (Jaffe, 1986) or patent classifications and citations (Verspagen, 1997a,b). Technology flow matrices in a sense combine the two concepts of technological and 'market' proximity by identifying originators and (potential) users of a technology or an innovation. Scherer's user-producer matrix as well as the Yale matrix have been derived from patent statistics (Scherer, 1982, Putnam and Evenson, 1994).[5] Many empirical studies have found indeed a relatively high influence of R&D and related spillovers on productivity growth but the results depend in some measure on the construction of the spillover variable.[6]

The findings that market transactions and technological closeness matter for productivity imply an extension of any meaningful empirical analysis to the global level, at least to the major trading partners. There is no *a priori* reason why international spillovers should be modelled differently than domestic spillovers. The total technology content of a product or a sector that matters for productivity contains the R&D performed by itself as well as the technology acquired by inputs from both domestic and foreign sources. For that reason, besides the more static advantages of getting an expanded set of inputs at lower cost (including frontier-technology), international trade is an important source for long-term development and catching-up (Fagerberg, 1987, Abramovitz, 1986). Especially small open economies can benefit disproportionately from international spillovers, not only in a development context (Coe et al., 2002) but also amongst developed countries as shown by Coe and Helpman (1995).[7] In fact it may be argued that the potential of the global R&D stock for catching-up should be *relatively* high for developed economies that already have a high level of absorptive capacities and would yield *comparatively* marginal benefits from investment in education and other social capabilities (Archibughi and Mitchie, 1998).

8.3 EUROPEAN PERFORMANCE RELATIVE TO THE US

The eagerness of European policy makers to bring Europe to the economic frontier of the world is obviously rooted in the feeling that Europe is behind relative to the USA and other leading countries in the world in terms of technology and productivity. The aim of this section is to document the European gap in this respect. We focus on the manufacturing industry, which we subdivide into 20 sectors, documented in Table 8.1. The sources of the data are the OECD STAN database, and various parts of the Groningen Growth and Development database. The newest version of the STAN database, using the ISIC rev. 3 classification, covers the period 1980–1998, while the older version of it, using the ISIC rev. 2 classification covers the period 1970–1994. Merging these editions and accounting for the different classification schemes we obtain a dataset that covers the period of 1973–1997. We derive the growth rates of total factor productivity from this database, in the way that is described in more detail below.

We use additional data on hours worked per person, unit value ratios (for value added) and value added deflators from the GGDC database to set up a benchmark of total factor productivity levels relative to the USA for 1997 (on the general nature of the data, see, for example, Van Ark, 1996).[8] The TFP growth rates derived from STAN are used to retrapolate this benchmark on a yearly basis to the early 1970s. Because the STAN database has serious holes in terms of the coverage for some countries, we focus on only four European countries, and compare these to the USA. The four European countries are Germany, France, Italy and the United Kingdom.

We use employment (in number of jobs) as our indicator of labour input in the total factor productivity growth rate calculations. In this part of the calculations, no correction for hours worked is made, because the data on hours in the GGDC database is not available for a large part of the period we are interested in. Value added is our output indicator, and a constructed capital stock is taken as the only other production factor. The capital stock is constructed on the basis of the investment time series, using a perpetual inventory method (with a depreciation rate equal to 0.15). We have to resort to using aggregate purchasing power parities for the capital stocks supplied by the Penn World Tables, because the GGDC database does not supply sectoral data on capital stocks (or investment flows). In summary, the 1997 benchmark for total factor productivity levels is based on state-of-the art methods that take into account differences between sectors in terms of unit value ratios and hours worked, but the growth rates that are used to retrapolate this benchmark are based on more rough measures.

Table 8.1 Sectors in the analysis

ISIC rev.2	ISIC rev.3	Short description
31	15-16	Food, beverages & tobacco
32	17-19	Textiles, apparel & leather
33	20	Wood products & furniture
34	21-22	Paper, paper products & printing
351+352	24	Industrial chemicals, drugs & medicines
353+354	23	Petroleum & coal products
355+356	25	Rubber & plastic products
36	26	Non-metallic mineral products
37	27	Iron & steel, non-ferrous metals
381	28	Metal products
3825	30	Office & computing machinery
382-3825	29	Non-electrical machinery
3832	32	Radio, TV & communication equipment
383-3832	31	Electrical apparatus, nec
3841	351	Shipbuilding & repairing
3843	34	Motor vehicles
3845	353	Aircraft
3842+3844+3849	352, 359	Other transport
385	33	Professional goods
39	36-37	Other manufacturing

Figure 8.1 describes the evolution of total factor productivity gaps (ratios) in manufacturing sectors between the European countries and the USA. A value larger than one indicates a European lead. The vertical axis of these figures gives the frequency of sectors with the specific value of the gap displayed on the horizontal axis. Thus, a peak in the plotted surface points to a cluster of sectors at the specific value of the productivity gap. The

distribution displayed in the figure is smoothed using a so-called kernel density estimation method (see Härdle, 1990).[9] The raw data consist of the value of the productivity gap for each of the 21 sectors in the four countries (hence there are 84 observations for each year) for the period specified in the graphs. The kernel density estimates can be seen as smoothed histograms (one for every year) of these values. Peaks in the figure indicate that relatively many sectors cluster at the value of the productivity gap displayed on the horizontal axis below. The value 1 on the horizontal axis demarcates the difference between European productivity leadership (>1) and a European productivity deficit (<1).

In Figure 8.1, it is obvious that on average, the European countries indeed face a productivity gap relative to the USA, although it is a relatively small one.[10] The peak (modal value) of the density plot in 1997 lies at a value of 90% (0.9), that is, the point where European countries trail 10% behind US productivity. 53% of the total density (sectors) has a 10% or higher productivity deficit, that is, is found to the left of the peak for 1997. 36% of the density is found in the right tail that represents European sectors leading over the USA in terms of total factor productivity (values larger than 1).

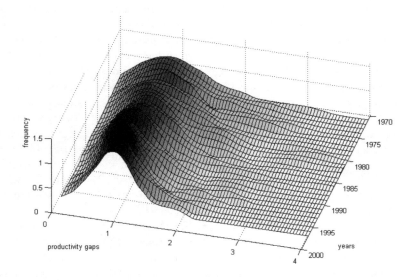

Figure 8.1 Kernel density estimates of the distribution of total factor productivity gaps of four European countries vs. the United States

Over time, the evolution is one in which the distribution becomes more narrow and peaked, but the overall centre of the distribution does not shift very much. In the early 1970s, the peak lies at 85%, that is, a somewhat larger European backlog, but at the same time, a larger fraction (48%) of the total density is found at values larger than one (a European lead). The early periods also show a relatively long trail of sectors on the right hand side, which corresponds to a limited number of European sectors that operate at the 'leading edge' of productivity. This 'leading edge' largely disappears over the 30-year period in the graph, until we have the relatively narrow and peaked distribution of the late 1990s.

8.4 R&D IN EUROPE AND THE GLOBAL ECONOMY: REALITY AND THE BARCELONA TARGET

The large majority of R&D in the world is carried out by firms, universities and public or semi-public research organizations.

Figure 8.2 shows the total R&D intensity in Europe, on the one hand, and USA on the other hand. R&D intensity is defined as total R&D as a % of GDP. Over the period 1980–2000, this value fluctuates between 2.5% and 3% in the USA, while it is almost a full %-point lower in the European Union[11] (all averages across countries are calculated as weighted averages). For the four European countries identified in the previous section, the value is slightly higher than the EU-average: it fluctuates around 2%.

Figure 8.2 thus supports the impression of a European backlog in R&D that led to the Barcelona target of a 3% R&D intensity. In order to achieve this target, and given the value of GDP in the year 2000, Europe's R&D effort in that year would need to be expanded by (roughly) one third. Obviously, this is a large increase, and one may question the possibility of achieving this, especially so in times of a downturn in the world business cycle. Also more than two years have passed since the Barcelona meeting, without clear policy measures aimed at stimulating extra R&D expenditure having been undertaken in many European countries.

While we believe that the Barcelona R&D targets will be rather hard to achieve, we undertake the analysis in the remainder of this chapter under the assumption that it will indeed be possible to achieve these targets. The aim of this analysis is to assess the impact that increased R&D intensity may have on the productivity gaps facing the European economy.

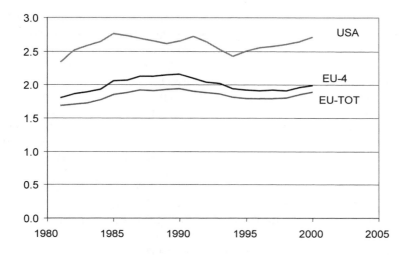

Figure 8.2 R&D intensity (total R&D as % of GDP)

8.5 ASSESSING THE IMPACT OF 'BARCELONA' ON EUROPEAN PRODUCTIVITY GAPS

The empirical and theoretical literature on R&D and productivity provides a practical framework to assess the impact of increased R&D efforts in Europe on technology gaps between Europe and the USA. In this assessment, account will have to be taken of the fact that R&D does not only have an impact in the firm/sector where it is undertaken, but also partly spills over to other sectors in the domestic and foreign economy. Viewed in this way, much of the increased R&D efforts as a result of 'Barcelona' will be absorbed within the EU itself due to the nature of the integration of European economies. However, it will also add to the technology content of exports to the main non-European competitors with the potential to generate productivity increases there. The aim of this section is to employ a simulation exercise to assess the net effect of the mechanisms on the productivity gaps identified in Section 8.3 above.

For the calculation of productivity effects we use the concept of 'direct and indirect' R&D from the spillovers literature (as in, for example Griliches, 1979).[12] We take the same sectors as above, and focus on business R&D only. The method we employ will be to add one-third to the R&D stocks of European sectors. The 3% Barcelona R&D intensity target actually implies a somewhat larger multiplication factor, but in light of the above discussion, we feel that this is a too ambitious target.[13] This implies that current R&D levels in Europe increase by (roughly) 33% (taking GDP as given, something we will do for all analysis in this section). We assume that the distribution of R&D over private and non-private sources does not change,that is, that the one-third increase applies to both types of R&D.

We take 1997 as the reference year (this is the most recent year for which disaggregated R&D stocks can be calculated for the countries in our sample). Because our R&D stocks are simply summations over time (taking into account also knowledge depreciation), a once-and-for-all multiplication of R&D investment by 1.33 also implies a multiplication of the R&D stocks by 1.33. We therefore perform a simulation in which all European R&D stocks are multiplied by 1.33 and compare the total factor productivity levels implied by this to the levels implied by the actual 1997 R&D stocks.

From the 'direct' R&D stocks, we calculate domestically and internationally acquired 'indirect' R&D stocks (see appendix for mathematical details). For the construction of these we rely on a weighting scheme developed by Verspagen (1997a). This scheme uses patent statistics, and is based on co-classification of patents in terms of their technological class. When a patent is classified in more than a single technology class, and these classes 'belong to' different industries, this is taken as a spillover from one sector (where the main technology class of the patent is) to another sector (where the supplementary technology class of the patent is). In this way, a matrix can be set up that gives the share of all patents generated in a sector that spillover to all other sectors. In Verspagen (1997b) these weights were used to construct domestic and foreign indirect R&D stocks, and the results were applied to an estimation of the impact of R&D and R&D spillovers on total factor productivity. We use the elasticities obtained in Verspagen (1997b), and documented in Table 8.2, in the simulation exercises in this section. In addition to these 'technology weights', domestic indirect R&D is weighted by the share of domestic producers on the market; 'imported' R&D is weighted by the share of foreign producers (broken down at the country level). TFP growth is simply given as the sum of the three components (own sector R&D, domestic indirect R&D from other sectors, foreign indirect R&D), weighted by their output elasticities.

Table 8.2   Empirical coefficients (output elasticities) used in the simulations

	OwnR&D	Domestic indirect R&D	Foreign indirect R&D
High-tech (Radio, TV & communication equipment; Office & computing machinery; Professional goods; Aircraft)	0.177	0.025	0.061
Medium-tech (Industrial chemicals, drugs & medicines; Non-electrical machinery; Electrical apparatus)	0.078	0.022	0.032
Low-tech (Food, beverages & tobacco; Textiles, apparel & leather; Wood products & furniture; Paper, paper products & printing; Petroleum & coal products; Rubber & plastic products; Non-metallic mineral products; Iron & steel, non-ferrous metals; Metal products; Shipbuilding & repairing; Motor vehicles; Other transport; Other manufacturing)	0.084	0.040	0.045

Source: Verspagen (1997b).

Table 8.3 documents the productivity effects in the four European countries and the USA for the various simulation experiments. Our first experiment, described above, is to multiply all European R&D stocks by 1.33, the value associated with the Barcelona target. This corresponds to an 'untargeted' or uniform R&D impulse, that is, one in which all sectors increase R&D expenditures by the same proportional rate. The effect of this is to raise total factor productivity levels in Europe across the 20 sectors of our analysis by an average of 4.4%, with a relatively narrow variation (standard deviation equal to 1.0%-points) over the sectors. The USA also benefits from this European R&D policy, and realizes a projected 0.6% increase in total factor productivity levels (with a standard deviation equal to half this value). Thus, both European and USA levels of productivity may be expected to rise across the board of manufacturing sectors as a result of the Barcelona targets, if and when successfully achieved.

Table 8.3   Average growth rates over sectors of total factor productivity in simulation experiments

Description of simulation experiment	Growth of productivity relative to base case (1997 real data)		
	EU-4	USA	Ratio increase EU to USA
Uniform R&D impulse in EU	4.4 % (1.0%)	0.6% (0.3%)	7.3
Targeted high-tech R&D impulse in EU	8.0% (12.5%)	1.5% (1.9%)	5.3
Targeted medium-tech R&D impulse in EU	8.9% (4.1%)	2.5% (1.1%)	3.6
Targeted low-tech R&D impulse in EU	13.3% (11.6%)	0.4% (0.6%)	33.3

The result is, obviously, a reduction in European technology gaps. This is documented in Figure 8.3, which gives the kernel density estimations for the first simulation experiment and the real data for 1997. The latter is taken from Figure 8.1 (last year), but is now reproduced in a 2-dimensional format. The evenness of the impact of increased R&D across sectors is evident from the almost parallel shift of the density curve. The peak (modal value) of the distribution shifts to the right, and is now found at a value of 0.95, that is, where European productivity lags behind US productivity 5%-points. 41% of the total density is now found in the domain where European productivity leads over US productivity (to the right of 1 on the horizontal axis). Although this is clearly an improvement, it does not represent Europe overtaking the US. In other words, although the increased R&D levels as a result of the Barcelona targets are beneficial for European industry, they do not seem to lead to the targeted European productivity leadership.

In order to compare the impact of the different sectoral R&D stocks on the distribution of European productivity gaps, we also document the results of some other thought-experiments, in which only a number of sectoral R&D stocks are varied at the same time. In these experiments, we employ the commonly used distinction between high-tech, medium-tech and low-tech sectors. This classification is based on average R&D intensity across the OECD countries, and is documented in Table 8.2 in the specific way in which it was used here. Note that because our level of disaggregation of sectors does not completely correspond to the usual scheme, we had to change some of the usual definitions. The most notable of these changes is that we merge pharmaceuticals (normally considered as a high-tech sector) with chemicals (normally considered as a medium-tech sector), and treat the resulting sector as a medium-tech sector.

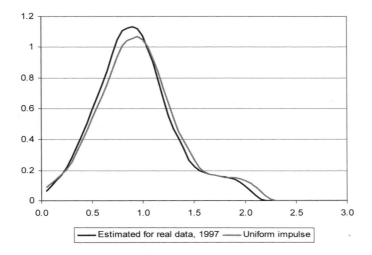

Figure 8.3 Kernel density estimates for real productivity gaps (1997) and simulated gaps (a European R&D impulse uniformly distributed over sectors)

In the sectoral experiments, we employ a broad reasoning that corresponds to 'putting all the eggs in one basket'. This means that we still start from a one-third increase in total R&D efforts (stocks), but now put these additional expenditures into only one of the three broad sectoral classifications (low-, medium or high-tech). In order to find the multiplication factor of R&D stocks that corresponds to this, we use the following formula:

$$\frac{R_{L,t+1} + R_{M,t+1} + R_{H,t+1}}{R_{L,t} + R_{M,t} + R_{H,t}} = \frac{R_{L,t+1}}{R_{L,t}} \sigma_{L,t} + \frac{R_{M,t+1}}{R_{M,t}} \sigma_{M,t} + \frac{R_{H,t+1}}{R_{H,t}} \sigma_{H,t} = 1.33,$$

where R represents R&D stocks, the subscripts H, M and L indicate high-tech, medium-tech and low-tech, respectively, the subscripts t and $t+1$ indicate before and after experiment periods, and σ indicates a share in total R&D. A 'focused' R&D impulse is calculated using this formula, by setting the ratio $R_{i,t+1}/R_{i,t}$ to 1 (that is, no change) for the two sectoral classes on which the R&D impulse is focused, and then solving for the same ratio for the sectoral class on which the R&D is focused. For example, in the case of an R&D impulse focused on low-tech, this yields

$$\frac{R_{L,t+1}}{R_{L,t}} = \frac{0.33}{\sigma_{L,t}} + 1.$$

This shows that we can calculate the ratio at which R&D stocks in the focused sectoral class must be increased as a function of the targeted overall increase (one third, or 0.33) and the share of the sectoral class in total R&D stocks. For sectoral classes that represent a small (large) share in total stocks, a large (small) proportionate increase is necessary to accommodate the increase of total R&D by one third.

Figures 8.4 and 8.5 document the sectoral distribution of total R&D stocks for the broad aggregates used in the experiments. Obviously, the low-tech R&D stocks make up the smallest part of total R&D stocks in both the EU-4 and the USA, accounting for approximately 10% at the end of the period. In the USA, the medium-tech sectors are somewhat smaller than in Europe, and the reverse holds (by implication) for the high-tech sectors. We use the EU-4 shares in 1997 to calculate the implied multiplication factors for the high-, medium and low-tech sectors according to the above formula. This yields a factor of 5.0, 3.5 and 11.4, respectively. It must be noted that these factors are quite high, especially so for low-tech sectors, and hence it is not very realistic to assume that such a focused R&D strategy could ever be actually implemented. The calculations using these multiplication factors are, however, intended to illustrate the differences in sectoral impact, rather than to make actual predictions of what could happen.

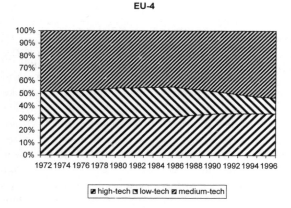

Figure 8.4 Percentage distribution of R&D stocks in high-, medium- and low-tech sectors, EU4

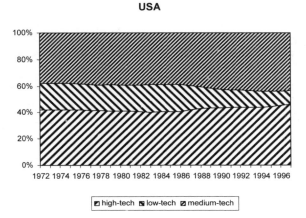

USA

high-tech low-tech medium-tech

Figure 8.5 Percentage distribution of R&D stocks in high-, medium- and low-tech sectors, US

Table 8.3 shows that the largest productivity effects of increased R&D are to be expected from the medium-tech sectors. For the focused low-tech R&D impulse, an average 13.3% total factor productivity increase in Europe is found, while this value is almost 0.4% in the USA (as a result of increased European R&D). Moreover, the effects of increasing high-tech R&D are highly variable over sectors, as indicated by the fact that standard deviation is larger than the mean (this is less so the case for medium- and low-tech sectors). The ratio of the increase of productivity in Europe and the USA is highest for the focused low-tech impulse, indicating that in this sectoral class, increased European R&D efforts are 'appropriated' to the largest extent.

Figure 8.6 shows the effects in terms of the distribution of total factor productivity gaps over sectors for the focused high-tech impulse. The latter is compared against two different baseline cases, that is, the kernel density estimate of the productivity gaps resulting in the first experiment (uniform R&D impulse), and the empirical observation for 1997. While the uniform R&D impulse shifts the kernel estimate almost in a parallel fashion, this is much less the case for the focused high-tech R&D impulse. For the focused high-tech R&D impulse, the peak of the distribution actually shifts slightly to the left, to a value of 0.85 (15% European productivity backlog). 42% of the total density lies to the right of the value 1 in case of the focused high-tech R&D impulse, indicating that, overall, there is a rightward shift of the distribution (the value is 36% for the empirically observed distribution). But what is most striking in the case of the focused high-tech impulse is that a small number of sectors on the right hand side of the distribution benefits most. This 'leading edge' of European sectors gains relatively more as a result of a targeted high-tech impulse.

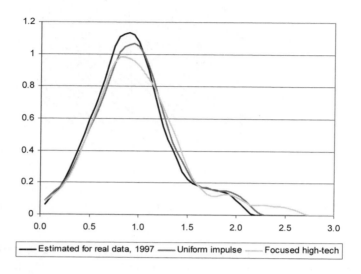

Figure 8.6 Kernel density estimates for simulated productivity gaps (a European R&D impulse focused on high-tech sectors)

The focused medium-tech impulse is displayed in Figure 8.7. Here we note a shift of the kernel density that is almost equal to the case of a uniform R&D impulse, and almost exactly parallel to the empirically observed density. The peak of the distribution stays, however, at a value of 0.9 (10% productivity lag for Europe), which is also the empirically observed peak. In this case, 44% of the total density lies to the right of 1 (European productivity lead).

Finally, Figure 8.8 displays the result of a focused low-tech R&D impulse. In comparison to the two earlier focused R&D impulses (high-tech and medium-tech), the effects are more dramatic for low-tech. We observe a relatively strong shift of the part of the distribution that is immediately to the right of the peak, while the peak itself (by implication, because the total density is constant) shifts markedly downwards. Also the 'leading edge' European sectors (to the far right) shift relatively more as a result of the focused low-tech R&D impulse. The fraction of the density that lies to the right of the value 1 is 51% in case of the focused low-tech impulse, and the peak of the distribution occurs at 0.95 (5% European productivity lag).

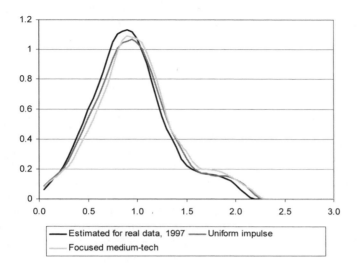

Figure 8.7 Kernel density estimates for simulated productivity gaps (a European R&D impulse focused on medium-tech sectors)

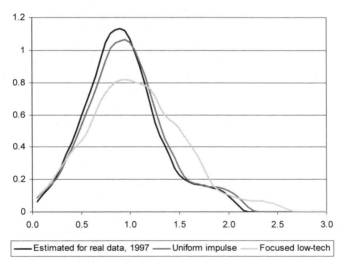

Figure 8.8 Kernel density estimates for simulated productivity gaps (a European R&D impulse focused on low-tech sectors)

Summarizing, it seems indeed to be the case that R&D policies aimed at different sectors may have different effects in terms of the distribution of productivity effects over sectors. Perhaps surprisingly, the most dramatic effects are associated with R&D in low-tech, while medium-tech sectors have the most evenly distributed impact.

8.6 DISCUSSION AND CONCLUSIONS

In this chapter we have documented European total factor productivity gaps relative to the USA. Although our method of calculating productivity levels in these countries is imperfect, it was shown that Europe indeed lags behind the USA somewhat in terms of total factor productivity in many manufacturing industries. We discussed the European ambition, expressed at the Lisbon Summit, to become 'the most competitive and dynamic economy in the world'. Because of the relationship between R&D and productivity we were especially interested in the targets set in Barcelona for European R&D intensity. In an analysis of current R&D trends, it was concluded that these targets are indeed ambitious, implying an increase of European R&D intensity by one third.

We then proceeded to apply a simple simulation method, based on the empirical literature on R&D and productivity, to estimate the impact of the Barcelona targets, assuming they can successfully be implemented, on the productivity gaps in manufacturing industry between Europe and the USA. Our model makes many simplifying assumptions, but its main virtue is that it does take into account the indirect impact of R&D, in terms of spillovers, in other sectors and countries than where the R&D effort is originally made. Thus, it was shown that the USA may also expect to benefit from increased European R&D, although at relatively low rates. The net effect on European productivity gaps is expected to be positive from the European perspective, that is, it will lead to a catching-up of total factor productivity levels relative to the USA.

However, the results also indicate that the expected effects are relatively small compared to the size of existing productivity gaps facing European industries. According to our estimates, which are to be seen as a rough indication of orders of magnitude, achievement of the Barcelona targets in a purely quantitative sense (that is, *ceteris paribus* raising R&D intensity to 3% of GDP) will not put the European economy clearly in the lead in terms of productivity relative to the USA. According to our simulations, a focused R&D impulse in low-tech industries can be expected to have the strongest effect, but it is unrealistic to assume that these sectors alone can achieve the Barcelona R&D target.

These results imply that, according to the estimations of our model, a policy solely aimed at increasing R&D expenditures, without paying any attention to the broad institutional context in which innovation and technological development take place, is not likely to succeed. Raising R&D expenditures may be one part of the story behind the European productivity lag but factors such as absorptive capacity, interaction between researchers in public and private organizations, finding the right level of intellectual property rights protection, and so on, may be just as important in achieving the Lisbon ambition. Our model does not have much to say on these factors (which, it can be argued, represent changes in the R&D elasticities that our models takes as given), but it does point out that more research on these issues may be useful, and that the task of regaining European technological and economic leadership may be a more complicated one than the Lisbon and Barcelona summits suggested.

NOTES

* We thank Colin Webb, Agnès Cimper (OECD, Directorate for Science, Technology and Industry, Economic Analysis and Statistics Division) and Marcel Timmer (GGDC) for provision of and advice on the data, Eddy Szirmai for advice on data issues, Alessandro Nuvolari, Bart van Ark and participants at the workshops on 'The Many Guises of Innovation: What we have learnt and where we are heading', Statistics Canada, 23–24 October 2003, on 'Current Issues in Economic Growth', Österreichische Nationalbank, 5 March 2004, and on 'Competitiveness and Growth in Europe: Lessons and policy implications for the Lisbon Strategy', ZEI/INFER, 3–4 September 2004, for comments and suggestions.

1. Presidency Conclusions, Lisbon European Council, 23 and 24 March 2002, para. 5.
2. For a broader description and a general assessment of the other goals of the Lisbon process see the chapter by Dierx and Ilzkovitz in this volume.
3. Presidency Conclusions, Barcelona European Council, 15 and 16 March 2002 para. 47. For a review of the progress of the Lisbon process up to then see 'The Lisbon Strategy. Making Change Happen', Communication from the Commission to the Spring European Council in Barcelona, COM(2002) 14 final, 15.1.2002.
4. See also 'Productivity. The Key to Competitiveness of European Economies and Enterprises', Communication from the Commission to the Council and the European Parliament COM(2002) 262 final, 21.05.2002.
5. The intermediate position of technology flow matrices is confirmed by van Pottelsberghe (1997), who applies the different weights to the same dataset. Moreover, these results vindicate the approach of most empirical studies to use one and the same matrix across different countries.
6. See Cincera and van Pottelsberghe, 2001, Mohnen, 2001 and Los and Verspagen, forthcoming, for recent in-depth reviews of the empirical spillover literature.
7. Also the simulation results of Verspagen (1997b) exhibit to some degree a relatively high contribution to productivity growth for the smaller economies in the sample.
8. The specific way in which this is done involves retrapolating the 1997 unit value ratios in the GGDC database to 1990 by means of the value added deflators.
9. We use Stata's kdensity function, with the default Epanechnikov kernel.
10. Our four European countries display above-EU average productivity, so that the results in this section must be seen as a lower boundary to the gap of the total EU.
11. The European Union is defined as EU-15 over the complete period.
12. Although the so-called Jones-critique of strong scale effects has led to a debate in which the possibility of some form of scale economies related to knowledge and R&D has not been

ruled out (Jones, 1995), we implement a model in which the level of total factor productivity depends on the level of the knowledge stock, and the rate of growth of total factor productivity thus depends on the growth of a knowledge (or R&D capital) stock. The reason for adopting this relatively conservative approach is that this model can still be considered as the main theoretical workhorse for the empirical work in this area. Moreover, since an important part of our calculations will take the form of extrapolating on the basis of increased R&D stocks in Europe, a model incorporating scale effects that have not been empirically verified over a large range of the relevant variables may be too optimistic in assessing the increased productivity effects.

13. The calculated effects are linear in the growth rates.

REFERENCES

Abramovitz, M.A. (1979), 'Rapid growth potential and its realisation: the experience of capitalist economies in the postwar period', in E. Malinvaud (ed.) *Economic Growth and Resources, vol. 1 The Major Issues, Proceedings of the fifth World Congress of the International Economic Association*, London: Macmillan.

Abramovitz, M.A. (1986), 'Catching up, forging ahead and falling behind', *Journal of Economic History*, **46**, pp. 385–406.

Adams, J.D. (1990), 'Fundamental stocks of knowledge and productivity growth', *Journal of Political Economy*, **98**, pp. 673–702.

Archibughi, D. and J. Mitchie (1998), 'Trade, growth, and technical change: what are the issues?', in D. Archibugi and J. Mitchie (eds), *Trade, Growth and Technical Change*, Cambridge: Cambridge University Press, pp. 1–15.

Cincera, M. and B. van Pottelsberghe de la Potterie (2001), 'International R&D spillovers: a survey', *Cahiers Economiques de Bruxelles*, no. 169, pp. pp. 3–32.

Coe, D.T. and E. Helpman (1995), 'International R&D spillovers', *European Economic Review*, **39**, pp. 859–87.

Coe, D.T., E. Helpman and A. Hoffmaister (2002), 'North-South R&D spillovers', *The Economic Journal*, **107**, pp. 134–49.

David, P. (1975), *Technical Choice, Innovation and Economic Growth*, Cambridge: Cambridge University Press.

Economic Policy Committee (2002), *Report on Research and Development*, EPC/ECFIN/01/777-EN Final. Brussels, 22 January.

European Commission (2002), 'European Competitiveness Report 2002', Commission Staff Working Paper, SEC(2002) 528. Luxembourg: Office for Official Publications of the European Communities.

Fagerberg, J. (1987), 'A technology gap approach to why growth rates differ', *Research Policy*, **16**, pp. 87–99.

Goto, A. and K. Suzuki (1989), 'R&D capital, rate of return on R&D investment and spillover of R&D in Japanese manufacturing industries', *Review of Economics and Statistics*, 71, pp. 555–64.

Griliches, Z. (1979), 'Issues in assessing the contribution of research and development to productivity growth', *The Bell Journal of Economics*, **10**, pp. 92–116.

Griliches, Z. (1992), 'The search for R&D spillovers', *Scandinavian Journal of Economics*, **94**, pp. S29–S47.

Groningen Growth and Development Centre, *60-Industry Database*, http://www.ggdc.net.

Groningen Growth and Development Centre, *ICOP Industry Database*, http://www.ggdc.net.

Härdle, W. (1990), *Applied Nonparametric Regression. Econometric Society Monographs*, **19**, Cambridge: Cambridge University Press.

Jaffe, A.B. (1986), 'Technological opportunity and spillovers of R&D: evidence from firms' patents, profits and market value', *American Economic Review*, **76**, pp. 984–1001.

Jones, C. (1995), 'R&D based models of economic growth', *Journal of Political Economy*, **103**, pp. 759–84.

Los, B. and B. Verspagen (forthcoming), 'Technology spillovers and their impact on productivity', forthcoming in H. Hanusch and H. Pyka (eds), *The Edward Elgar Companion on Neo-Schumpeterian Economics*, Cheltenham, UK: Edward Elgar.

Mansfield, E. (1985), 'How rapidly does new industrial technology leak out?', *Journal of Industrial Economics*, **34**, pp. 217–23.

Mohnen, P. (2001), 'International R&D spillovers and economic growth', in M. Pohjola (ed.), *Information Technology, Productivity, and Economic Growth: International Evidence and Implications for Economic Development*, Oxford: Oxford University Press, pp. 50–71.

Nadiri, M.I. (1970), 'Some approaches to the theory and measurement of total factor productivity: a survey', *Journal of Economic Literature*, **9**, pp. 1137–77.

Nelson, R.R. and G. Wright (1992), 'The rise and fall of American technological leadership: the postwar era in a historical perspective', *Journal of Economic Literature*, **30**, pp. 1931–64.

Pavitt, K. and L. Soete (1982), 'International differences in economic growth and the international location of innovation', in H. Giersch (ed.), *Emerging Technologies: The Consequences for Economic Growth, Structural Change and Employment*, Tübingen: Mohr, pp. 105–33.

Putnam, J. and R.E. Evenson (1994), 'Inter-sectoral technology flows: estimates from a patent concordance with an application to Italy', Yale University, mimeo.

Romer, P. (1986), 'Increasing returns and long run growth', *Journal of Political Economy*, **94**, pp. 1002–37.

Romer, P.M. (1990), 'Endogenous technological change', *Journal of Political Economy*, **98**, pp. S71–S102.

Sakurai, N., E. Ioannidis and G. Papaconstantinou (1996), 'The impact of R&D and technology diffusion on productivity growth: evidence for 10 OECD countries in 1970s and 1980s', STI working paper 1996/2, Paris: OECD.

Scherer, F.M. (1982), 'Interindustry technology flows and productivity growth', *Review of Economics and Statistics*, **64**, pp. 627–34.

Solow, R.M. (1957), 'Technical progress and the aggregate production function', *Review of Economics and Statistics*, **39**, pp. 312–20.

Sveikauskas, L. (1981), 'Technology inputs and multifactor productivity growth', *The Review of Economics and Statistics*, **63**, pp. 275–82.

Terleckyj, N.E. (1974), *Effects of R&D on the Productivity Growth of Industries: An Exploratory Study*, Washington/DC: The National Planning Association.

Terleckyj, N.E. (1980), 'Direct and indirect effects of industrial research and development of productivity growth of industries', in J. Kendrick and B. Vaccara (eds), *New Developments in Productivity Measurement and Analysis*, Chicago: The University of Chicago Press, pp. 339–86.

Triplett, J.E. (1996), *High Tech Industry productivity and Hedonic Price Indexes*, Washington, D.C: Bureau of Economic Analysis.

Tsoukalis, L. (1997), *The New European Economy Revisited*, 3rd edn., Oxford: Oxford University Press.

Van Ark, B. (1996), 'Sectoral growth accounting and structural change in post-war Europe', in B. van Ark and N. Crafts (eds), *Quantitative Aspects of Post-War European Economic Growth*, Cambridge: Cambridge University Press, pp. 84–164.

Van Meijl, H. (1995), 'Endogenous technological change: the case of information technology', Ph.D. dissertation, University of Limburg, Maastricht: Universitaire Press.

van Pottelsberghe de la Potterie, B. (1997), 'Issues in assessing the impact of interindustry R&D spillovers', *Economic Systems Research*, **9**, pp. 331–56.

Verspagen, B. (1997a), 'Measuring intersectoral technology spillovers: estimates from the European and US patent office databases', *Economic Systems Research*, **9**, pp. 47–65.

Verspagen, B. (1997b), 'Estimating international technology spillovers using technology flow matrices', *Weltwirtschaftliches Archiv*, **133**, pp. 226–48.

Wolff, E.N. and M.I. Nadiri (1993), 'Spillover effects, linkage structure, and research and development', *Structural Change and Economic Dynamics*, **4**, pp. 315–31.

APPENDIX – DATA, METHODS AND VARIABLES

The analysis draws on the OECD STAN, ANBERD and BITRA databases, merging their ISIC-Rev.2 and ISIC-Rev.3 versions for a longitudinal dataset, covering 21 industries in 7 countries for the period of 1973–1997 (Table 8.1). These sectoral data are used to calculate both domestic and 'international' (imported) R&D stocks. To derive constant price series in US dollars, implicit deflators from STAN and PPPs from the Penn World Tables were employed. The countries covered include the EU member states of France, Germany, Italy and the United Kingdom, as well as the United States. Japan is included as a country from/to which spillovers flow, but this country is not included in the productivity comparisons.

Following Verspagen (1997b) we start from an augmented Cobb-Douglas production function

$$Y_{ijt} = A_{ijt} K_{ijt}^{\alpha} L_{ijt}^{\beta} RD_{ijt}^{\rho} IRD_{ijt}^{\delta} IRF_{ijt}^{\phi} \qquad (8.1)$$

where Y represents production, A the usual scale variable, and K and L capital and labour inputs respectively. RD is 'own', that is, direct R&D, IRD is domestic indirect R&D, IRF is 'foreign', that is, indirectly imported R&D. α, β, ρ, δ, ϕ are the relevant output elasticities. The indices i, j and t refer to country, sector and time.

Neglecting indices, total factor productivity can be measured as a function of total R&D:

$$TFP \equiv Y / (K^{\alpha} L^{\beta}) \qquad (8.2)$$

or, combining (8.1) and (8.2), in the form of growth rates:

$$\frac{\dot{TFP}}{TFP} = \rho\frac{\dot{RD}}{RD} + \delta\frac{\dot{IRD}}{IRD} + \phi\frac{\dot{IRF}}{IRF} \tag{8.3}$$

Capital stocks are constructed by applying the perpetual inventory method, that is,

$$K_t = (1-\psi)K_{t-1} + I_t \tag{8.4}$$

with I being investment in fixed capital, the depreciation rate ψ set to 0.15 and an initial capital stock of 5 times I_{t+1} (assuming an initial growth rate of 5 per cent). The 'own' R&D stocks are constructed similarly using R&D expenditures.

For indirect domestic R&D, the sectoral R&D stocks are weighted by coefficients from a patent citation matrix based on EPO statistics (Verspagen, 1997a). For domestically acquired R&D we set their diagonal elements to zero to avoid double-counting. Finally, we weight with the share of domestic inputs; that is,

$$IRD_{ik} = \sum_j \omega_{jk}(1-m_{ij})RD_{ij}, \quad j \neq k \tag{8.5}$$

where ω_{jk} designates the share of sector j in sector k's citations and m_j stands for the import penetration of the domestic market. For imported R&D we keep the diagonal elements and aggregate as

$$IRF_{ik} = \sum_h \sum_j \omega_{jk}m_{ij}RD_{hj}s_{ihj} \tag{8.6}$$

using import penetration-weighted input coefficients, and RD_{hj}, the R&D stock of the export country h, being weighted by its import share in country i, s_{ihj}. We take this variable as a proxy for the degree of interaction between two countries (Verspagen, 1997b).

The simulation uses hypothetical R&D stocks as explained in the main text and calculates corresponding indirect R&D as in (8.5) and (8.6). To calculate hypothetical TFP growth the elasticity estimates (as in Table 8.3) by Verspagen (1997b), who uses a comparable set of OECD countries and sectors, were employed and fed into (8.3).

COMMENT

Guntram B. Wolff*

When the editors asked me to discuss the chapter by Christoph Meister and Bart Verspagen, I happily agreed, since the chapter addresses a very important topic in a very innovative way: Can R&D close the existing productivity gaps between European manufacturing sectors and US manufacturing? It is an important topic for economic policy since one tool of the Lisbon Agenda is to increase research expenditure in Europe from 2 to 3% of GDP, the level of the US. The chapter is innovative in the way that it addresses the potential of structural change taking into account sectoral R&D spillovers. In the following I will briefly summarize the approach and results of the chapter and then give some comments on possible future research in this area.

The literature on economic growth has emphasized the importance of technological change for economic growth, for example, Arrow (1962), Romer (1990), Aghion and Howitt (1992). Most of these papers are one sector models of the economy, in which the rate of endogenous technological progress directly increases total factor productivity. Empirical evidence suggests that TFP indeed is influenced by R&D intensity (for example Griliches 1979). Little evidence exists, however, on the effects of R&D on a sectoral level, which potentially can explain a large proportion of growth differences between economies.

The present chapter compares productivity on a sectoral level in Europe relative to the US levels. While not all European sectors have lower productivity levels than the US, the mean and median sector is less productive in Europe than in the US. The distribution has shifted in the last thirty years such that now even more European sectors have lower productivity levels than their corresponding US sectors.

The policy experiment of this chapter is the following: Suppose that the R&D stocks in Europe were increased by 33%, what would the distribution of relative productivity levels look like? [1] In this simulation, R&D spillovers across sectors and to the US are taken into account (Verspagen 1997a), and the elasticities of output to R&D stocks are taken from Verspagen (1997b). A uniform increase of R&D stocks in all considered sectors is found to shift the distribution of relative productivity to the right, reducing the gap to the US, but also increasing absolute productivity in the US due to spillover effects. The shape of the sectoral distribution does not change much. For a second simulation, the sectors are classified in low, medium and high technology sectors. If the increase in R&D stock could be targeted to one of these three sectors, where would the increase be most beneficial in terms of (relative) productivity growth? The somewhat surprising result: the efforts should be concentrated on the low technology sectors.

I have three main comments to make: the first relates to the measurement of the productivity gap, the second to the surprising last result. Finally I want to identify a research idea of sectoral productivity and R&D, which I believe deserves further attention.

The chapter measures the productivity gap between Europe and the US by looking at an unweighted distribution of sectoral productivity gaps. As policy makers, we are interested in the aggregate productivity gap, which is an employment weighted sum of sectoral productivity gaps. Suppose that the largest part of employment were in those sectors, in which the European productivity is larger than the US. In this case, aggregate productivity per worker would be larger in Europe than in the US, that the distribution of the sectoral productivity gaps still indicates a lower European productivity.

My second remark concerns the use of a distribution for measuring the impact of the policy experiment. While a distribution gives detailed information on the shape of sector productivity, I would like to learn more about the performance of individual sectors. As we have seen, increasing the R&D stock in all sectors has little effect on distribution. This can be interpreted in two ways: If the sector ordering of productivity stays constant, all sectors will shift to the right and spillovers across sectors seem to be uniform. If, however, the ordering of sectors has changed, spillovers will become really important. Only in this case, it might be useful to target the increase of R&D stocks to the low technology sector, as we might hope that this sector generates the highest spillovers to other sectors. Otherwise, I interpret the last finding as mainly reflecting the fact that the number of low technology sectors is largest. Obviously, this will imply that targeting R&D changes to this group will most strongly affect the distribution.

This discussion takes me to my last point, the importance of changes in sector employment. Burhop and Wolff (2005) show with German historical data, that while TFP growth of the economy is large, for individual sectors this increase is smaller. Large parts of aggregate productivity increase can be explained by labour reallocation to more productive sectors. Suppose that a single sector experiences a path breaking innovation, which increases productivity in this sector strongly. This will have few consequences for total economy productivity, if this sector is small (for example, IT in the 1980s). Much of the subsequent aggregate productivity increase will then be driven by the speed at which the economy can free workers in less productive sectors to move to this more productive sector. The unique data set employed in the discussed chapter provides a great opportunity to quantify the importance of labour reallocation for aggregate productivity growth. The management of this structural change of the economy represents one of the major policy challenges in today's world.

NOTES

* The opinions expressed in this discussion do not necessarily reflect the opinions of the Deutsche Bundesbank or its staff.
1. The authors do not address the question, how policy makers can increase enterprise research. Reinthaler and Wolff (2004) show that subsidies have a positive impact on R&D employment but also result in significant wage increases for researchers. This implies that increased subsidies only partly result in higher R&D output and should be complemented by efforts to increase the supply of well-qualified researchers.

REFERENCES

Aghion, P. and P. Howitt (1992), 'A model of growth through creative destruction', *Econometrica*, **60** (2), pp. 323–51.
Arrow, K. (1962), 'The economic implications of learning by doing', *Review of Economic Studies*, **29** (2) pp. 155–73.
Burhop, C. and G.B. Wolff (2005), 'A compromise estimate of German net national product 1851–1913 and its implications for growth and business cycles', *Journal of Economic History.*, **65, pp.** 613-657.
Griliches, Z. (1979), 'Issues in assessing the contribution of research and development to productivity growth', *The Bell Journal of Economics*, **10**, pp. 92–116.
Reinthaler, V. and G.B. Wolff (2004), 'The effectiveness of subsidies revisited: accounting for wage and employment effects in business R&D', ZEI Working Paper B04-21.
Romer, P. M. (1990) 'Endogenous technological change', *Journal of Political Economy*, **98** (5), pp. 71–102.
Verspagen, B. (1997a), 'Measuring intersectoral technology spillovers: estimates from the European and US patent office databases', *Economic Systems Research*, **9**, pp. 47–65.
Verspagen, B. (1997b), 'Estimating international technology spillovers using technology flow matrices', *Weltwirtschaftliches Archiv*, **133**, pp. 226–48.

9. Measuring Inventive Performance of the OECD Countries Using Triadic Patent Families: Reinventing the Lisbon Challenge

Marc Baudry and Béatrice Dumont

9.1 INTRODUCTION

The European Union set itself ambitious goals in March 2000. Indeed, at the Lisbon European Council, European Member States set the Union the goal of becoming by 2010 'the most competitive and dynamic knowledge-based economy in the world, capable of sustainable economic growth with more and better jobs and greater social cohesion'. Two years later at the Barcelona European Council, which reviewed progress towards the Lisbon goals, they agreed that research and technological development (R&D) investment in the EU must be increased with the aim of approaching 3% of GDP by 2010, up from 1.9% in 2000.[1] They also called for an increase of the level of business funding, which should rise from its current level of 56% to two-thirds of total R&D investment, a proportion already achieved in the US and in some European countries.

The lack of performance of European countries in terms of innovation is regularly pointed out. As shown by Figure 9.1, since the mid-1990s, the gap between the European Union as a whole[2] and the US both in terms of the inputs involved in the innovation process, that is, public and private R&D investments (at constant 1995 prices and purchasing power standard), and the output as measured by the number of triadic patent applications, has been widening steadily, with consequences for the long-term potential for innovation, growth and employment creation in Europe.[3] This poor performance is supposedly due to the low growth of R&D activities in the business sector for EU countries during the second half of the 1990s. In Europe, the private sector's share of research funding stood at only 56% compared with 68% in the US and 72% in Japan in 2002. Of course, this global observation masks important differences among Member States. For example, the Nordic countries are in the lead, with investment levels and growth distinctly higher than in the US. A second group, made up of Greece, Portugal and Ireland, has built up strong momentum which could see them catch up at a very rapid pace. By contrast, most European countries are around the European average, lagging behind the US, while certain big countries like Italy or Spain need to make an extra effort. Starting from these observations, one of the arguments underlying the Lisbon Strategy is that the gap between the US and Europe could simply be due to a different level of investment in R&D on both sides of the Atlantic. Accordingly, the R&D investment objectives set at Barcelona arise from the recognition that attaining the 3% goal would help to close the gap with the US and have a major impact on long-term growth and employment in the EU, in the order of 0.5% of supplementary output and 400,000 additional jobs every year after 2010.[4]

Interestingly, Figure 9.1 stresses, however, that the gap in terms of patent applications is growing at a slower rate than the gap in terms of R&D investments in the business sector. This suggests that maintaining the growth rate of public effort in R&D at the same level as in the United States could allow some European countries to partly compensate the weakness of their R&D effort in the business sector and/or that there exist some non observed factors (institutional or cultural factors) that may positively influence the innovation process of Member States compared with the United States. Indeed, the role of R&D as a driving force for a competitive and dynamic knowledge-based economy is linked to the economy's capacity to turn new knowledge into technological innovation. As a result, if greater R&D investment in the business sector is necessary, it is not enough on its own. This means that the Lisbon strategy as such could be ill conceived: it is therefore vital for Member States to identify whether they have a competitive advantage with regards to non observed factors influencing the innovation process, and thus whether they should focus on qualitative rather than quantitative objectives.

In order to analyse these issues of perennial policy relevance, the remaining presentation will be organised as follows: section 9.2 will present the state of play and will try to give some statistical arguments with regard to the fact that European countries may benefit from some qualitative advantages compared to the United States. Section 9.3 is devoted to a more technical but more complete approach based on the econometric estimation of some innovation production functions of Poisson type, at a macroeconomic level, by using panel data for OECD countries from 1994 to 2000. The emphasis is put on the development of a macroeconomic production function for innovations which is consistent with the aggregation of essentially individual innovation processes. In section 9.4, estimation results are presented and then used to measure both the efficiency of the allocation of R&D investments between the public and the private sector for each country and the fixed effects that reflect the influence of non observed factors. Finally, in section 9.5, we conclude by comparing the results of our estimations with the objectives set in the Barcelona Agenda.

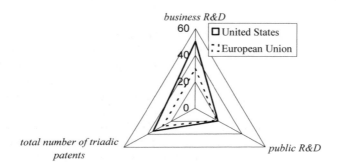

Figure 9.1   *Percentage of variation for several indicators of innovation, 1994–2000*

9.2   DATA AND METHODOLOGY

9.2.1 Sample Description and Selection

The first step in constructing our sample involved collecting data on technology performance across countries. Knowledge creation and innovation are difficult to measure but traditionally counts of patents applications to a single patent office (PTO) have been considered as the best indicator on this matter. Nevertheless this choice is not exempt from criticism. While the richness of traditional patent indicators is broadly recognised, they are affected by home advantage bias where, proportionate to their inventive activity, domestic applicants tend to file more patents in their home country compared to foreign applicants. Moreover, the value distribution of patents is skewed as many patents have no industrial applications (hence, are of no value), whereas others are of substantial value.

The restriction of our analysis to the OECD triadic patent families[5] answers some of the previous criticisms and improves the quality and international comparability of our data. 'A patent family is defined as a set of patents (originating from the priority filing) taken in various countries that protect the same invention.'[6] The triadic patent families refer to a sub-set of patents all applied for at the European Patent Office (EPO), the Japanese Patent Office (JPO), and granted by the US Patent and Trademark Office (USPTO) that share one or more priority applications.[7]

The choice to use 'triadic' patent families was justified by the fact that by applying the same filter, patent families indicators, after consolidation, provide an improved measure of the innovative performance and technological change at an international level. In particular, the home advantage bias and the impact of a country's specific rules and regulations are reduced or eliminated, double counts of a specific invention are avoided, as well as biases resulting from the fact that some countries have a high level of patenting activity at a foreign PTO (like Japan in Germany or Canada in the US). But most importantly, these OECD patent families generally represent patents of high value due to the self-selection process. Indeed, to create a patent family, a patent must be filed in several countries. This means that a patentee takes on additional costs to extend protection to other countries only if it seems worthwhile to do so. Thus, as shown by Harhoff and Reitzig (2001) but also Lanjouw and Schankerman (2001), patents that are members of families will generally be of higher value that those filed in a single country, and will more likely correspond to radical innovations.

The second step in constructing our sample has led us to collect data on R&D expenditures both for the private and the public sector. These variables were collected by using R&D investment spending as a percentage of GDP. They have been modified by using the GDP purchasing power standard of each country. The GDP used here are in 1995 constant prices and expressed in dollars. As a result, these data are expressed in constant terms.

Finally, we took as a reference 29 OECD countries. Because of a lack of data, Luxemburg is not on our list. However, some countries that do not belong to the triadic area belong to our sample because their inventions are protected in Europe, the United States and in Japan. We collected data for the years 1991 till 2000. More recent data could not be collected. Indeed, one of the main drawbacks with counting patent families according to the earliest priority date is the increase in lag between priority date and the availability of information. The time lag between priority and publication dates is 18 months, while the time lag between priority and grant dates stands on average between 3 to 4 years. As a consequence, triadic patent families are subject to the problem of timeliness. Therefore, from all the publicly available information in 2004, a data set of complete triadic patent families can only be computed up to 2000. Nevertheless these seven years have allowed us to increase the number of degrees of freedom in our model. This has also allowed us to better examine the evolution of the innovation indicators across the OECD countries.

9.2.2 Descriptive Analysis

One of the arguments underlying the Lisbon Strategy is that the gap between the US and Europe could simply be due to a different level of investment in R&D on both sides of the Atlantic. A preliminary analysis of the data at our disposal confirms the existence of a gap among OECD countries. Of the 40,334 triadic patents granted in 1998, 34,262 patents (85% of the total of triadic patent families applications) were applied for by 5 countries (US, Japan, Germany, UK and France).

As illustrated by our data, in terms of patent production, the United States are the model of reference for the other countries. Indeed, in 1998 the United States accounted for around 36% of the OECD total, followed by the European Union (33%) and Japan (25%). However, it is worth examining the level of investments necessary for the United States to reach these levels of performance. In other words, in terms of productivity, are the United States as efficient as is traditionally agreed? Figure 9.2 shows that the alleged leadership of the United States is far from being confirmed when comparing the average productivity of total R&D expenditures (defined as the number of patents in triadic patent families per million of dollars invested in R&D). Indeed, most northern European countries as well as Japan are characterised by a higher average productivity. Moreover, the average productivity of the European Union as a whole amounts to 9.30 triadic patents per million of dollars invested and thus exceeds that of the United States (6.84 triadic patents per million of dollars invested).[8] Of course, one may argue that the ranking of countries on the basis of their average R&D productivity is biased due to the existence of decreasing returns to scale in the innovation process at the firm level: the relatively low average productivity for the United States would then be explained by the high level of R&D investments of American firms. Hence, in Figure 9.2 the ranking of OECD countries according to their average productivity of R&D is compared with the ranking of the same countries according to an index of their relative effort in R&D (the Gross Domestic Expenditures in R&D as a percentage of Gross Domestic Product). Accordingly, countries characterised by the lowest values of R&D as a percentage of GDP, that is, countries where firms have low investment levels in R&D, should have a higher average R&D productivity than the other countries. Figure 9.2 clearly shows that this is not the case. Similarly, one may reasonably consider that in countries characterised by a similar value of R&D as a percentage of GDP, firms are also characterised by similar individual levels of R&D so that decreasing returns to scale in the innovation process should not affect the value of the average productivity of national R&D expenditures. Figure 9.2 also shows that it is not the case. Indeed, Germany, Switzerland, Finland, Japan and Sweden have an index of R&D effort which is quite similar to, or sometimes even higher than, that of the United States, whereas these countries exhibit a higher average productivity of R&D. Therefore, it seems that decreasing returns to scale are not, as such, a determinant factor when one tries to explain the differences that exist across OECD countries in terms of average R&D productivity.

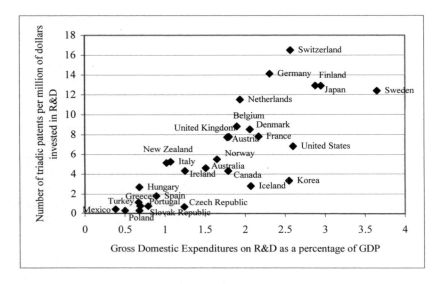

Figure 9.2 Ranking of OECD countries according to their average productivity of R&D and their relative effort of R&D, 1998

Assuming that the results regarding the comparison of the average R&D productivity expenditures are sufficiently robust, the question then arises whether the difference may be explained by a different allocation of total R&D expenditures between business R&D and public R&D or by some non observed factors. Some indications are given by Figure 9.3 which shows the number of patents in triadic patent families according to the division of R&D expenditures between the private and the public sector. Our data show that there is a semi-strong correlation between the number of patent families and business enterprise expenditure on R&D (BERD). Sweden, the United States, Japan, Switzerland, Finland and Germany have both a high level of BERD and a high number of patent families. Turkey, Portugal, Greece and Spain have both a low level of BERD and a low number of patent families. It is also worth noticing that for similar levels of business and public R&D expenditures per capita, the number of patents obtained by the OECD countries differs significantly. The United States for instance are close to Sweden and Switzerland in terms of public and business R&D efforts per capita but obtain a lower number of triadic patents per capita than these countries, suggesting that there are non observed factors playing a key role in the innovation process.

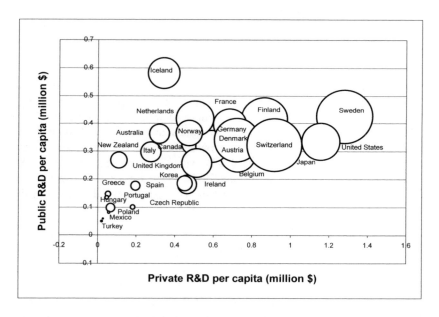

Figure 9.3 Number of patents per million population as a function of business R&D expenditures and public R&D expenditures per million inhabitants, 1998

9.3 ECONOMETRIC APPROACH OF THE INNOVATION PRODUCTION FUNCTION

9.3.1 Specification of the Count Data Model

In order to confirm or invalidate the idea that a simple catching up of R&D expenditures would be sufficient for European countries to reach the same level of competitiveness as the US, we used panel count data models applied to patent applications. More precisely, we first considered that, at the firm level, innovations are the outcome of a production process where individual R&D expenditures are the main input. However, the three following features distinguish the innovation process from usual production functions:

1. The output is not directly observed. Thus, the number of triadic patents applications is used as a proxy variable for innovations ;
2. The output is an integer;
3. The functional link between the inputs and the output is not purely deterministic. For instance, a different number of patents may result from the same level of R&D expenditures.

These main features of the innovation process are dealt with by following the methodology initially developed by Hausman, Hall and Griliches (1984). Accordingly, it is assumed that the number of innovations for a firm or a public research organisation (research institutes, universities and so on) is the outcome of a Poisson process whose parameter depends on the individual level of the main input, the level of R&D expenditures. More precisely, if Y_{it} denotes the random number of patents filed by firm i (or public organisation i) in the year t, the probability that a number y_{it} is observed is given by the following Poisson distribution of probabilities:

$$\Pr[Y_{it} = y_{it}] = \frac{e^{-\lambda_{it}} \lambda_{it}^{y_{it}}}{y_{it}!} \qquad (9.1)$$

where $\lambda_{it} > 0$ stands for the parameter of the Poisson distribution and may depend on the firm and on the year taken into consideration. λ_{it} also yields the mathematical expectation of Y_{it}:

$$E[Y_{it}] = \lambda_{it} \qquad (9.2)$$

From the properties of the Poisson probability distribution, it follows that the number Y_{jt} of patents filed by the N_j firms and public research organisations of country j in year t is also a Poisson random integer, the distribution of which is given by:

$$\Pr[Y_{jt} = y_{jt}] = \frac{e^{-\lambda_{jt}} \lambda_{jt}^{y_{jt}}}{y_{jt}!} \qquad (9.3)$$

with $Y_{jt} = \sum_{i=1}^{N_j} Y_{it}$ and $\lambda_{jt} = \sum_{i=1}^{N_j} \lambda_{it}$. Therefore, it turns out that the following linear specification for λ_{it} is particularly suitable:

$$\lambda_{it} = A_{jt}\, e^{\beta t}\, r_{it} \tag{9.4}$$

where β is a parameter and A_{jt} is a country specific term. t stands for a time index and r_{it} denotes firm's i or public organisation's i R&D expenditures at time t. From (9.4), it follows that

$$\lambda_{jt} = A_{jt}\, e^{\beta t}\, r_{jt} \tag{9.5}$$

with $r_{jt} = \sum_{i=1}^{N_j} r_{it}$ the total (business and public) R&D expenditures in country j at time t. The count data model defined by (9.3) and (9.5) is based on aggregate data but is consistent with the microeconomic nature of the innovation process. Consistency highly relies on the assumption of constant returns to scale. However, due to the fact that public R&D is rather oriented towards basic research and serves as a basis for a more applied business R&D within the private sector, one may expect that the performance of the innovation process for a given country depends on the allocation of total R&D expenditures between the business sector and the public sector. In order to take account of the different nature of public and business R&D, we hereafter assume that the country specific term A_{jt} in (9.5) varies with the fractions v_{jt} and $1-v_{jt}$ of total R&D expenditures due respectively to the business sector and to the public sector. It turns out that the following CES (Constant Elasticity of Substitution) specification is particularly suitable:

$$A_{jt} = \alpha_j \left(v_{jt}^{-\rho} + \theta \left(1 - v_{jt} \right)^{-\rho} \right)^{-1/\rho} \tag{9.6}$$

Indeed, as $v_{jt} = x_{jt}/r_{jt}$ and $1-v_{jt} = z_{jt}/r_{jt}$ where x_{jt} and z_{jt} respectively stand for R&D expenditures of the business sector and R&D expenditures of the public sector in country j at time t, (9.6) and (9.5) imply that:

$$\begin{aligned} \lambda_{jt} &= \alpha_j\, e^{\beta t}\, r_{jt} \left(v_{jt}^{-\rho} + \theta \left(1 - v_{jt} \right)^{-\rho} \right)^{-1/\rho} \\ &= \alpha_j\, e^{\beta t} \left(x_{jt}^{-\rho} + \theta\, z_{jt}^{-\rho} \right)^{-1/\rho} \end{aligned} \tag{9.7}$$

where α_j is a country fixed effect reflecting the influence of non observed national factors on the innovation in country j such as institutional (for example, the relationships between business and public R&D activities) or cultural factors (for example, a national preference for secrecy rather than patenting). Accordingly, the expected number of triadic patents for country j at time t is given by a CES type production function with constant returns to scale, the arguments of which are the R&D expenditures in the business sector and the R&D expenditures in the public sector. The assumption of constant returns to scale makes it possible to rewrite (9.7) in terms of per capita variables so that results from the estimation of the Poisson model characterised by (9.3) and (9.7) essentially capture the same ideas as those illustrated by Figure 9.2 above.

According to (9.7), a difference in the value of the fixed effect α_j across countries implies that, even for the same level of public and business R&D expenditures, countries will not achieve the same level of innovation. Therefore, we are able to define an index of efficiency for the innovation process in country j compared with an arbitrarily given country j' as follows:

$$\frac{\mathrm{E}\left[Y_{jt}/x \text{ and } z\right]}{\mathrm{E}\left[Y_{j't}/x \text{ and } z\right]} = \frac{\alpha_j}{\alpha_{j'}} \tag{9.8}$$

This index serves as a basis in what follows for international comparison of the efficiency in the innovation process at a macro level. Note that the elasticities of the expected number of triadic patents in country j at time t with respect to public R&D expenditures and aggregate business R&D efforts depend neither on the fixed effects α_j nor on the time index t. The Poisson count data model with random effects defined by (9.3) and (9.7) is typically estimated by maximum likelihood (see Cameron and Trivedi, 1998).

9.3.2 Measurement of Allocative Efficiency

Although the output of the innovation production function is intrinsically stochastic, usual methods to measure allocative efficiency in production decisions may be used. We successively examine the case of R&D expenditures minimisation for a given expected number of inputs and the case of output maximisation for a given level of total R&D expenditures.

The first case, the case of R&D expenditures minimisation for a given expected number of inputs, relies on the following optimisation programme:

$$e^*\left(z_{jt}^0, x_{jt}^0, t\right) = \underset{\{z,x\}}{Min}\left\{z + x\,;\,\lambda_{jt}(z, x, t) \geq \lambda_{jt}\left(z_{jt}^0, x_{jt}^0, t\right)\right\} \tag{9.9}$$

where z_{jt}^0 and x_{jt}^0 respectively denote the observed public R&D expenditures and the business R&D expenditures in country j at time t while $\lambda_{jt}(z, x, t)$ stands for the expected number of triadic patents in country j at time t given levels z and x of public and business R&D expenditures as defined in (9.7). The value function e^* yields the minimum total expenditures in R&D compatible with a level of innovation characterised by the expected number of patents $\lambda_{jt}(z_{jt}^0, x_{jt}^0, t)$. The ratio between e^* and the observed total expenditures in R&D $z_{jt}^0 + x_{jt}^0$ is used as an input oriented index of allocative efficiency for the different kinds of R&D expenditures:

$$Ef_{input} = \frac{e^*(z_{jt}^0, x_{jt}^0, t)}{z_{jt}^0 + x_{jt}^0} \qquad (9.10)$$

This index takes values between zero and one. The more efficient is the allocation, the closer to one is the index and conversely. Let z_{jt}^* and x_{jt}^* denote the solution to programme (9.9). Figure 9.4 illustrates this first approach.

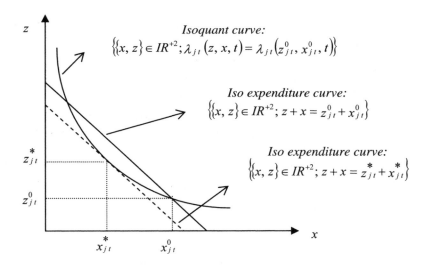

Figure 9.4 Total R&D expenditures minimisation for a given expected number of triadic patents

The second case, the case of output maximisation for a given total amount of R&D expenditures, relies on the alternative optimisation programme:

$$y^*\left(z_{jt}^0, x_{jt}^0, t\right) = \underset{\{z, x\}}{Max}\left\{\lambda_{jt}(z, x, t); z + x \le z_{jt}^0 + x_{jt}^0\right\} \qquad (9.11)$$

where notations are similar to those used in (9.9). Programme (9.11) is the twin of the previous programme (9.9). The value function y^* yields the maximum expected number of patents reachable given that the total expenditures in R&D do not exceed the observed level $z_{jt}^0 + x_{jt}^0$. In this case, it is the ratio between the expected number of triadic patents for the observed amounts of public and business R&D expenditures, $\lambda_{jt}\left(z_{jt}^0, x_{jt}^0, t\right)$, and y^* that is used as an output oriented index of allocative efficiency for the different kinds of R&D expenditures:

$$Ef_{output} = \frac{\lambda_{jt}\left(z_{jt}^0, x_{jt}^0, t\right)}{y^*\left(z_{jt}^0, x_{jt}^0, t\right)} \qquad (9.12)$$

Again, this index takes values between zero and one and, the more efficient is the allocation the closer to one it is. Let z_{jt}^{**} and x_{jt}^{**} denote the solution to programme (9.11). Figure 9.5 illustrates this second approach.

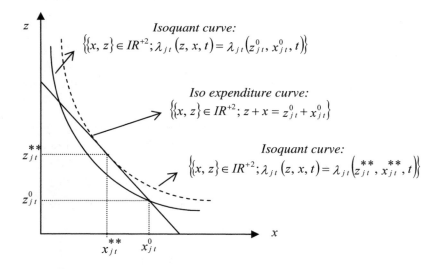

Figure 9.5 Maximisation of the expected number of triadic patents for given total R&D expenditures

One can easily check that, due to the homogeneity of the CES production function used, these two indices take the same value in the present case. This single efficiency index has been computed in order to evaluate how efficient is the trade off between public and business R&D expenditures in OECD countries. The results are examined in the following section.

9.4 RESULTS

9.4.1 Countries' Fixed Effects

As already outlined in the previous section, fixed effects capture the influence of non observed factors on innovation in a given country. Values of the relative index of efficiency defined in (9.8) and computed on the basis of the estimated fixed effects in the CES Poisson count data model with random effects characterised by (9.3) and (9.7) for OECD countries and years 1994 to 2000 are reported in Table 9.1 with the United States as the reference country.

Table 9.1   *Relative index of efficiency for the innovation process (reference country: United States)*

Country	Efficiency Index	Country	Efficiency Index
Australia	0.884* (0.027)	Japan	1.810* (0.016)
Austria	1.237* (0.040)	Korea	0.350* (0.006)
Belgium	1.243* (0.024)	Mexico	0.171* (0.020)
Canada	0.634* (0.017)	The Netherlands	2.074* (0.052)
Czech Republic	0.088* (0.011)	New Zealand	1.561* (0.110)
Denmark	1.377* (0.045)	Norway	0.870* (0.038)
Finland	1.998* (0.0.51)	Poland	0.089* (0.012)
France	1.184* (0.026)	Portugal	0.219* (0.038)
Germany	1.924* (0.033)	Slovak Republic	0.102* (0.024)
Greece	0.291* (0.0.43)	Spain	0.359* (0.015)
Hungary	0.876 (0.067)	Sweden	1.734* (0.023)
Iceland	0.878 (0.155)	Switzerland	2.306* (0.030)
Ireland	0.566* (0.034)	Turkey	0.064* (0.012)
Italy	1.078* (0.027)	United Kingdom	1.090* (0.024)

Notes: *: coefficient significantly different from 1 at 5%

A striking result outlined by Table 9.1 is that European countries are highly heterogeneous.[9] Some of them, mostly in North Europe, are far more efficient (Finland, Germany, The Netherlands, Sweden, Switzerland) or significantly more efficient (Austria, Belgium, Denmark) than the United

States, while other countries from East and Central Europe (Czech Republic, Poland, Slovak Republic) or South Europe (Greece, Portugal, Spain) plus Ireland are less efficient than the United States. Only two countries, Hungary and Iceland, are not found significantly less or more efficient than the United States. Although they exhibit a coefficient significantly different from one, one may also consider that France, Italy and the United Kingdom are just as efficient as the United States. From a policy point of view, these results point out the need for tailored solutions, namely a differentiation of the measures aimed at promoting innovation and growth according to groups of countries, focusing either on an increase of the effort in terms of R&D expenditures for those countries which are at least as efficient as the United States and/or on other institutional or cultural factors influencing the efficiency of the innovation process for those countries which are less efficient. Although our focus is on European countries, one may note that among non European countries Japan and New Zealand are more efficient than the United States. However, it is worth noting that the fixed effect in favour of innovation for some European countries compared with the United States may be offset by allocation inefficiencies between public and business R&D efforts. This is examined in the following subsection.

9.4.2 Optimal Trade-off between Public and Business R&D Efforts

Prior to an examination of the allocative efficiency index for public and business R&D expenditures, it is worth presenting the estimation results for the parameters other than the fixed effects in the CES Poisson count data model. These results are given in Table 9.2. The R_p^2 and R_d^2 indices for the quality of the regression are those presented in Greene (1997) for count data models. They show that our model fits the data well. The elasticity of technical substitution between business and public R&D effort, σ, indicates that there is a high degree of complementarity between these two kinds of R&D. Moreover, the optimal ratio between business R&D and public R&D that ensures a maximum expected number of triadic patents for a given total R&D expenditures θ^σ amounts to 2.51, which means that an optimal allocation of total R&D expenditures implies that business R&D represents 71.51% of the total amount.

Because of the high degree of complementarity between business and public R&D efforts, there is no gain to be expected from departing from the value of 2.51 for the ratio between these types of R&D expenditures by increasing one without adjusting the other. As a result, countries characterised by a ratio between business and public R&D expenditures that exceeds the critical value of 2.51 may not expect an important effect from an increase in their business R&D expenditures, ceteris paribus, where the elasticity of the expected number of patents with respect to this type of R&D expenditure is close to zero. However, they may expect a significant effect from increasing their public R&D expenditures, the elasticity of which is close to one. Conversely, countries characterised by a ratio between business and public R&D expenditures that is below the critical value of 2.51 may not expect a great impact from an increase of their public R&D expenditures, ceteris paribus, where the elasticity of the expected number of patents with respect to this second type of R&D expenditure is close to zero, whereas they may expect a significant impact from an increase of their business R&D expenditures with an elasticity close to one. This is confirmed by the estimated elasticities reported in Table 9.3.

Table 9.2   Estimated coefficients for the Poisson CES model with fixed effects

Coefficients	Estimations (t-stats)
β	0.0051 (3.336)
θ	0.000001 (1.376)
ρ	14.00 (7.007)
$\sigma = -1/(1+\rho)$	-0.066
θ^{σ}	2.51
Log likelihood	-1371.23
R_p^2	0.999096
R_d^2	0.998279

The study of efficiency in the allocation of the total amount of R&D expenditures focuses on the measure of the index of allocative efficiency defined in (9.10) (or equivalently in (9.12)). Table 9.4 gives an overview of the results. Interestingly, our results show that some countries like Austria, the Netherlands or Sweden have a high fixed effect but a relatively low value of their index of allocative efficiency while other countries like Ireland, Korea or the Slovak Republic are characterised by a low fixed effect but a relatively high index of allocative efficiency. This means that the positive influence of non observed factors on the innovation process may be partly offset by a misallocation of resource between the business and the public sector or, conversely, that an appropriate allocation of resource may compensate a weak influence of non observed factors positively influencing the innovation process. Nonetheless, some European countries (Belgium, Denmark, Finland and Germany) exhibit both a higher fixed effect and a higher index of allocative efficiency than the United States. Another important feature of the results reported in Table 9.4 is that the gap between Member States from Southern and Eastern Europe on the one hand and

Northern European countries on the other hand is less obvious when examining the allocative efficiency than when examining fixed effects.

Table 9.3   Elasticities of the expected number of triadic patents

Country	with respect to business R&D expenditures	with respect to public R&D expenditures	Ratio between business and public R&D expenditures
Australia	*1.00*	*0.00*	0.90
Austria	*0.99*	*0.01*	1.75
Belgium	*0.52*	*0.48*	2.66
Canada	*0.99*	*0.01*	1.49
Czech Republic	0.99	0.01	1.50
Denmark	0.98	0.02	2.01
Finland	0.79	0.21	2.44
France	0.99	0.01	1.67
Germany	0.85	0.15	2.37
Greece	1.00	0.00	0.44
Hungary	1.00	0.00	0.80
Iceland	0.99	0.01	1.29
Ireland	0.67	0.33	2.55
Italy	0.99	0.01	1.00
Japan	*0.78*	*0.22*	2.45
Korea	*0.30*	*0.70*	2.85
Mexico	*1.00*	*0.00*	0.42
The Netherlands	*0.99*	*0.01*	1.39
New Zealand	*1.00*	0.00	0.49
Norway	0.99	0.01	1.37
Poland	1.00	0.00	0.56
Portugal	1.00	0.00	0.39
Slovak Republic	0.99	0.01	1.92
Spain	0.99	0.01	1.16
Sweden	0.06	0.94	3.23
Switzerland	0.31	0.69	2.83
Turkey	1.00	0.00	0.50
United Kingdom	0.99	0.01	1.91
United States	0.15	0.85	3.03

*Table 9.4   Measure of efficiency in the trade-off between public and
business R&D expenditures, 2000*

Country	Index of allocative efficiency
Australia	0.680189
Austria	0.910577
Belgium	0.994322
Canada	0.856307
Czech Republic	0.859169
Denmark	0.955355
Finland	0.998664
France	0.894904
Germany	0.995254
Greece	0.438185
Hungary	0.634366
Iceland	0.807633
Ireland	0.999714
Italy	0.717421
Japan	0.999045
Korea	0.973276
Mexico	0.426729
The Netherlands	0.833405
New Zealand	0.473985
Norway	0.828394
Poland	0.516944
Portugal	0.39809
Slovak Republic	0.941604
Spain	0.768972
Sweden	0.903856
Switzerland	0.975440
Turkey	0.478281
United Kingdom	0.938815
United States	0.941510

9.5   SUMMARY AND CONCLUSION

The lack of performance of European countries in terms of innovation is
regularly pointed out. Starting from this observation, one of the arguments
underlying the Lisbon Strategy is that the gap between the US and Europe
could simply be due to a different level of investment in R&D on both sides
of the Atlantic. In 2002 attention has therefore been centred on targets in
terms of an increase of the R&D effort, the so-called Barcelona goals, rather

than towards a better allocation of this R&D effort or a better comprehension and consideration of the non observed factors influencing the innovation process.

But several years after these targets have been set, the picture is a mixed one. Some progress has been made. However, the pace of reforms at Member States level needs to be significantly stepped up across all areas if the credibility of the process and hence the 2010 targets are to be achieved. Indeed, it is important to bear in mind that in order to reach the 3% target by 2010, research investment in Europe should grow at an average rate of 8% every year, shared between a 6% growth rate for public expenditure and a 9% yearly growth rate for business investment. But as underlined in the 2003 European Innovation Scoreboard 'at the current rates of change, none of the current EU/US gaps would be closed before 2010' (EC 2003).

Such a quantitative conception and thus the Lisbon strategy as such, appears ill-conceived because if greater investment is necessary, it is not enough on its own. Indeed, our results show that for some European countries, mostly Southern and Eastern European countries, the 'deficit' of innovation cannot only be attributed to a weakness of their total R&D effort or to an inefficient allocation of their R&D effort between the public and the private sector, but is rather due to some non observed effects (institutional or cultural factors). Moreover, the question arises whether the United States should be used as a reference for innovation policy or not. Indeed, we find that ceteris paribus, and more particularly for identical R&D total expenditures, some European countries like Finland or Germany are able to attain a higher level of innovation than the United States thanks to a better allocation between the business and the public sector and to a better consideration of non observed institutional or cultural factors. This means that if Member States want to bridge the gap with the United States and become more competitive, they will have to define policy objectives in the field of innovation, reflecting specificities of their respective innovation systems and to set their own quantitative and/or qualitative targets on a voluntary basis.

NOTES

1. Throughout the chapter, R&D will always refers to the Frescati definition. See OECD (1993).
2. More precisely: Austria, Belgium, Czech Republic, Denmark, Finland, France, Germany, Greece, Hungary, Ireland, Italy, Netherlands, Poland, Portugal, Slovak Republic, Spain, Sweden and United Kingdom.
3. For example, Sheehan and Wyckoff (2003) for a detailed analysis.
4. See European Commission, 'Innovation and technological transfers', 5/03, p.4 and COM 2003 EC, DG Research (Luxembourg), Third European report on science and technology indicators. Declaration of Barcelona (2002), wwww.cordis.lu/indicators

5. We gratefully acknowledge the OECD, and notably Dominique Guellec and Hélène Dernis (Economic Analysis and Statistics Division, Directorate for Science, Technology and Industry) for access to the triadic patent families database (OECD, 2003).
6. Dernis and Khan (2004), p.7.
7. In the OECD database, patent families are presented according to the earliest priority date associated with each set of patents in the family (several priorities can be associated with elements of the family).
8. Results for the European Union are based on member states for which data are available, including new member states. The European Union thus includes the following countries: Austria, Belgium, Czech Republic, Denmark, Finland, France, Germany, Greece, Hungary, Ireland, Italy, the Netherlands, Poland, Portugal, Slovak Republic, Spain, Sweden and the United Kingdom.
9. Members of the European Union and associated countries like Norway, Iceland and Switzerland are designated as European countries.

REFERENCES:

Cameron, A. and P. Trivedi (1998), 'Regression analysis of count data', *Econometric Society Monograph*, No.30, Cambridge: Cambridge University Press.

Dernis, H. and M. Khan (2004), 'Triadic patent families methodology', *STI Working Paper 2004/2*, http://www.oecd.org/sti/working-papers

European Commission (2003), *European Innovation Scoreboard 2003*, COM (2003).

Greene, W.H. (1997), *Econometric analysis*, 3rd ed., Upper Saddle River, NJ: Prentice-Hall International, Inc.

Harhoff, D. and M. Reitzig (2001), 'Strategien zur Gewinnmaximierung bei der Anmeldung von Patenten', *Zeitschrift für Betriebswirtschaft*, 5, pp. 509–29.

Hausman, J., B.H. Hall and Z. Griliches (1984), 'Economic models for count data with an application to the patents R&D relationship', *Econometrica*, 52 (4), pp. 909–38.

Lanjouw, J.O. and M. Schankerman (2001), 'Characteristics of patent litigation: a window on competition', *The Rand Journal of Economics*, 32 (1), pp. 129–51.

OECD (1993), 'Proposed Standard Practices for Survey of Research and Experimental Development', *Frescati Manual*, Paris: OECD.

OECD (2003), *Database on Triadic Patent Families*, Paris: OECD.

Sheehan, J. and A. Wyckoff (2003), 'Targeting R&D: economic and policy implications of increasing R&D spending', OECD STI Working Paper (DSTI/DOC 2003/8), 24 July, http://www.oecd.org/sti/working-papers.

COMMENT

Adriaan Dierx[*]

This chapter makes a valuable contribution to the literature by assessing the efficiency of public and private spending on R&D in improving the innovative performance of OECD countries.

The chapter includes two main novelties. First, triadic patent families are used as a measure of innovative performance. In standard analyses patent applications at a single patent office are frequently used as an indicator of innovation, making it difficult to compare the innovative performance of EU Member States with that of the US or Japan, as inventors tend to file more applications in their home country. The use of triadic patents, that is, the subset of patents for which applications were filed at the European Patent Office and the Japanese Patent Office, and granted by the US Patent and Trademark Office, therefore improves the cross-country comparability of patents as an indicator of innovative performance. Moreover, by limiting the sample to high-value patents only, it partially resolves the problem of the large heterogeneity of patents. However, it does not resolve the problem of 'patent inflation', that is, the observation that inventors file more and more patents not because of an increased rapidity of innovation but rather to claim territory before competitors do. Within the chapter, this problem does not appear as such, as the analysis seems to be based on the yearly average number of triadic patents recorded during the sample period (1994–2000).

The second contribution of the chapter lies in the distinction made between productive and allocative efficiency of R&D spending. In this context, the allocative efficiency of R&D spending refers to the relative importance of public and business spending on R&D. The basic underlying assumption is that public and business R&D expenditures are complementary and that based on this complementarity an 'optimal' share of business in total R&D spending may be determined. Interestingly, Baudry and Dumont find that under an optimal allocation of total R&D expenditures, business R&D represents 71.5% of the total, a share that is not that far removed from the EU target of two thirds agreed at the Barcelona Spring European Council of March 2002. The productive efficiency of R&D spending can only be defined in relative terms, that is, in comparison with the best performer. From this perspective as well, the analysis fits very well with that of the Lisbon strategy, which uses benchmarking and peer pressure as major tools to push forward the process of structural reforms in the EU Member States. According to the chapter, the Northern European countries appear to be more efficient in producing patents in comparison with the US, while the countries from East and Central and from Southern Europe are generally less efficient.

However, one needs to be very careful in drawing policy conclusions from this. It might very well be that the countries in East, Central and Southern Europe, which are generally further removed from the research frontier, use their R&D expenditures as a tool to facilitate the diffusion of technologies developed elsewhere rather than as a way to encourage the domestic development of innovative technologies meriting new patents. Such a policy may well be optimal, given the situation within which a country finds itself.

Another issue that could be developed further in the analysis is the distinction between the optimisation problem faced by the government and that by a representative private firm. While presumably the government would want to maximise the total number of triadic patents being registered by domestically active business enterprises subject to a budget constraint limiting its own R&D expenditures, a private company would only be interested in maximising the number of patents registered under its own name. In such a theoretical model one would have to take account not only of the positive spill-overs of public R&D spending on innovations developed within private firms but also of the positive spill-over effects between research activities in different private firms (possibly even being located in different countries). One would expect that in such a situation, the private firm would spend less than optimal on R&D because it would ignore these positive spill-over effects. This would be an argument for the government to introduce a tax regime in support of private R&D activities. Given its overall budget constraint, the government would thus face a trade-off between financing public R&D and supporting private R&D through tax relief.

In making the empirical link between a country's R&D expenditures and the number of triadic patents recorded, proper account should be taken of the substantial time lags involved. This is a particularly problematic issue as there does not appear to exist a time series on triadic patents of sufficient length to apply the correct econometric tools. Moreover, as already mentioned above, even if such a time series existed the problem of patent inflation would need to be dealt with. In this respect, the option to relate triadic patents in a single year to past expenditures on public and business R&D may not be the worst.

Finally, it is important to place the chapter in the correct political context. The focus of the chapter on the effectiveness of R&D spending in improving the innovative performance of a country is particularly relevant in connection with the target agreed at the Barcelona Spring European Council that 'overall spending on R&D and innovation in the Union should be increased with the aim of approaching 3% of GDP by 2010. Two-thirds of this new investment should come from the private sector'. The Barcelona target is only an element of the Lisbon strategy, which is much wider in scope including targets for creating a more competitive and dynamic economy (implying amongst other things increased innovation) as well as employment targets and objectives related to social cohesion and sustainable development. Moreover, the tool kit for achieving the Lisbon objectives is by no means limited to increased spending on R&D. It includes measures aimed at encouraging market integration, deregulation and entrepreneurship as well as a series of labour market reforms. It also foresees an improvement of the framework conditions for R&D more generally.

NOTE

* The opinions expressed by the author are his own and do not reflect in any way the position of the European Commission on the issues discussed.

10. Education, Research, and Economic Growth – Some Tests for the US and Germany

Volker Caspari, Jens Rubart and Günther Rehme

10.1 INTRODUCTION

The importance of knowledge and human capital for long run economic growth has been known for a long time. For example, Young (1928) has pointed out that the productivity differences between US and UK industries at that time might by explained by different levels of inventive activities and better organizational structures of American industry. The statement of Young (1928) can be regarded as an early description of the importance of human capital and technological change for economic growth. The importance of higher education which fosters the diffusion of new technologies and therefore drives economic growth was pointed out by Nelson and Phelps (1966). In recent times, at least since Lucas (1988) or Romer (1990), the importance of knowledge and human capital has become a subject of political and politico-economical discussion.

Taking the role of human capital and innovations as given and comparing the economic development of Germany with that of the US economy during the last two decades, we find a strong decline in the growth trend (1980–90: 2.31%, 1991–2002: 1.4%), whereas the US growth trend remained constant at 3.2%.[1] Of course, one has to point out that the German economy had to overcome the burden of the reunification in 1991, but other reasons, which are pointed out by economists and also various political parties, are deficiencies of the German educational system and the system of inventive activities, particularly research and development activities. At least, since the so-called 'PISA shock'[2] a possible lack of human capital has become obvious. Since then, 'elite universities' or an increase in competition between universities in order to generate higher rates of innovation, and so on, have been called for in public discussion. Concerning the role of human capital one has to point out that the structure of human capital becomes more and more important in explaining the differences in economic growth between the US and Europe and particularly Germany. In recent studies Krueger and Kumar (2004a, b) point out that too intensive training in specific skills rather than general skills, leads to a lower degree of adoption of new technologies which results in a decrease in growth rates.

If we recapitulate the existing literature on economic growth due to human capital (for example, Aghion and Howitt, 1998, Ch. 10) one finds that one has to differentiate between different levels of education because each level has different effects on economic growth. There, particular importance is attached to tertiary education, because this type determines technological change due to inventive activities.

The present study examines the efforts and outcomes of the German and US educational and research systems on a macro level. Although it is difficult to compare these countries we derive some insights as to where the German system might fail and where it is able to compete with the US system. In particular, we show that, while there is not a general lack of human capital in Germany, it seems that the structure of Germany's human capital is not 'growth-enhancing'.

In our analysis we use time series data rather than cross sectional data which enables us to determine 'turning points' where one or the other system turns out to be more efficient. Furthermore, this approach is, from our point of view, in line with the perspective of the new growth theories. This means that we attempt to analyse long term economic development by applying time series data.[3] In order to examine indicators of efficiency or productivity of both systems we follow an approach where we combine efforts and outcomes of each system.

The remainder of this chapter is structured as follows. Section 10.2 outlines stylised facts of the US and German educational and R&D systems. In section 10.3 we conduct various tests on a set of indicators which describe aspects of the productivity of educational and research systems. Section 10.4 concludes.

10.2   SOME STYLIZED FACTS

In this section we outline some basic facts of US and German educational and research and development (R&D) efforts. Particularly, we consider relative expenditures per GDP as an input measure which show the country's efforts in education and research. Furthermore, we outline the structure of skills relative to employees as an output measure. The latter indicator enables us to derive indicators of the supply of skills (in terms of 'manpower') which determine the 'production' and adoption of new knowledge. Figures 10.1 and

10.2 below show educational and R&D expenditures relative to GDP for the US and Germany.

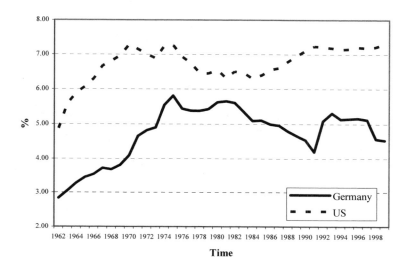

Source: *National Statistics.*

Figure 10.1   Educational expenditures (as % of GDP), Germany and US, 1962–1999

Figure 10.1 shows total, public and private, educational expenditures relative to GDP for the US and public expenditures for Germany. For recent years it is not possible to differentiate between private and public educational expenditures in Germany because of the lack of proper data. However, referring to the Federal Statistical Office Germany, one can derive that in 1998 private educational expenditures account for 25% of total expenditures compared to 19% in the US.[4] It is obvious from Figure 10.1 that over time the US educational efforts are about 50% higher than in Germany. In particular, since the beginning of the 1980s we observe a steady decrease for Germany whereas for the US, after a decline during the 1970s, the series remained constant since the end of the 1980s.

Concerning the total research and development expenditures relative to GDP (Figure 10.2) we observe that the US effort fluctuates around 2.5% if defence related R&D expenditures are included. Differentiating between defence and non-defence related R&D expenditures we observe a steady increase in the latter from 1.4% in 1962 to 2.3% in 2002. For Germany

Figure 10.2 shows an increase in relative R&D expenditures until the middle of the 1980s. During that time Germany's relative R&D efforts were higher than the US. Since then we observe a significant decline of this number.

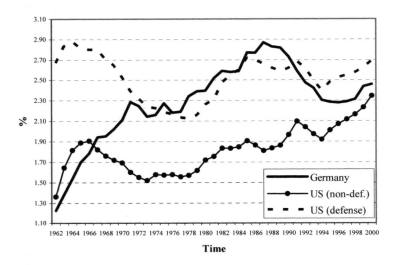

Source: National Statistics.

Figure 10.2   Total R&D expenditures (as % of GDP), Germany and US, 1962–2000

The indicators of educational and research efforts presented in Figures 10.1 and 10.2 show only the input side of educational and research systems. Therefore, we consider further indicators which show relative participants in each system. Figure 10.3 below presents the number of students at colleges and universities relative to employment.

As shown by Figure 10.3 it seems obvious that the relative participation in higher education is much higher in the US than in Germany. However, one has to point out that we compare very different educational systems. In particular, the German post-school education is characterized by apprenticeships, and people participating in the latter system are not covered by the data shown in Figure 10.3. That the attainment in the apprenticeship system is very important is shown by the following numbers. For example, in 2000 about 53.5% of the age cohort 20 to 29 years served an apprenticeship. In comparison, only 6.1% of this cohort earned a university degree.[5] However, Figure 10.3 shows that the relative number of students has increased significantly between 1960 and 1980 in the US and until 1990 in

Germany, respectively. Since 1990, the ratio remains relatively constant. These findings hold also, if one considers the educational attainment by various age groups. Considering the cohort of 22–25 years old, one finds that the enrolment in post-secondary education has increased slightly from 17.3% to 18.5% in the US and from 15.9% in 1990 to 18.7% in 1999 in Germany.[6] Considering the enrolment in tertiary education only, Table 10.1 below gives the results for some main OECD countries.

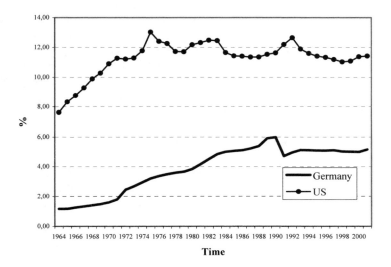

Source: National Center for Education Statistics (US), Federal Statistical Office (Germany).

Figure 10.3   *Students at colleges and universities relative to employment, Germany and US, 1964–2001*

Table 10.1   *%-Enrolment in tertiary education (age: 25–34 years), 1991–2002*

	1991	1996	2001	2002
France	20	26	34	36
Germany	21	20	22	21
UK	19	24	29	27
US	30	35	39	38

Source: OECD (2003a, 2004).

As can be seen from Table 10.1, the attainment in tertiary education has increased largely for France, UK and the US. However, for Germany a constant educational attainment, which is (in 2001) also below the OECD mean (28%), is reported by OECD (2003a).

In order to obtain comparable indicators of the outcomes of educational systems we focus on tertiary education only. Referring to Krueger and Kumar (2004b) this approach seems reasonable in that education by apprenticeships can be conceived as the acquisition of specific skills, whereas general skills, which drive technological change, are acquired through university education. In particular, we consider the distribution of college or university degrees in science and engineering as a share of total degrees. Although a wide range of fields exist (law, health, and so on), the field of science and engineering is, from our point of view, one of the most important from a growth perspective. One can easily imagine that most innovations that drive technological progress are related to the latter field. Tables 10.2 and 10.3 below report the distribution of degrees in science and engineering.[7]

Table 10.2 Degrees in science and engineering, US, 1966–2000

Year	Bachelor[a]	Master	Doctorate	Ph.D. / Master all	Ph.D. / Master S&E[b]
1966	35.2	29.2	64.5	12.8	28.2
1980	32.4	21.4	57.3	10.4	27.7
1990	30.5	23.9	63.4	11.1	29.4
2000	31.8	21.0	62.8	9.1	27.2

Notes:
[a] Degrees in S&E as percentage of all degrees.
[b] Doctorate Degrees in S&E as percentage of all Master's Degrees in the field of Science and Engineering

Source: National Center for Educational Statistics, US 2002.

As shown by Table 10.2, in the US about 32% of bachelor's and about 24% of master's degrees are earned in the field of science and engineering. However, about two thirds of doctoral degrees are earned in this field. That the attainment in science and engineering turns out to be very important at the highest educational level is also indicated by the last column of Table 10.2. Only 10% of all master's degrees earn a doctorate degree, whereas this ratio increases to 28% for the doctoral relative to master's degrees in science and engineering.

For Germany, Table 10.3 shows there is a large fraction of degrees awarded in science and engineering at the 'lower' level of tertiary education (comparable to a Bachelor's degree).

Table 10.3   Degrees in science and engineering, Germany, 1980–2000

Year	Univ.of App.Sc.[a]	University	Doctorate	Ph.D. / Master all	Ph.D. / Master S&E[b]
1980	89.3	59.0	40.1	26.3	17.9
1990	91.2	62.8	45.9	22.7	16.6
2000	91.4	61.0	51.6	27.0	22.8

Notes:
[a] Degrees in Science and Engineering in % of all degrees awarded at Universities of Applied Sciences (Fachhochschulen).
[b] Doctorate Degrees in S&E as percentage of all university degrees in Science and Engineering

Source 'Grund- und Strukturdaten', Ministry of Science and Education 2000.

As shown by Table 10.3 we have to take into account the structure of the German system of tertiary education which is characterized by three kinds of degrees: Degrees awarded at Universities of Applied Sciences (comparable to B.A. studies), university degrees (comparable to M.Sc. degrees) and doctoral degrees.

According to Table 10.3, 60% of total university degrees (diplomas) are awarded in S&E. However, the ratio of doctoral degrees in science and engineering has increased from 40.1% to 51.6% between 1980 and 2000 in Germany, whereas the US ratio remained constant around 60%. Furthermore, it is obvious that a higher fraction of university graduates earn a doctoral degree in Germany than in the US (> 20% to 10%). However, in Germany only 19% of all graduates in science and engineering earn a Ph.D. in comparison to 28% in the US (average values calculated from the last columns of Tables 10.2 and 10.3).

Last but not least, we consider an indicator which shows the employment of scientists and engineers in research and development relative to total employment.[8]

In comparison, the US employs more scientists in research and development than Germany. But, the gap between both countries is decreasing over time. This might be due to the fact which is reported in Table 10.3 that about 60% of German university degrees (without doctorates) are earned in the field of science and engineering.

Drawing a preliminary conclusion from the results reported in this section one has to state that the efforts in R&D and education are lower in Germany than in the US. On the other hand the educational participation in science and engineering is significantly higher (up to master's degrees) in Germany than in the US. This changes if one considers postgraduate education.

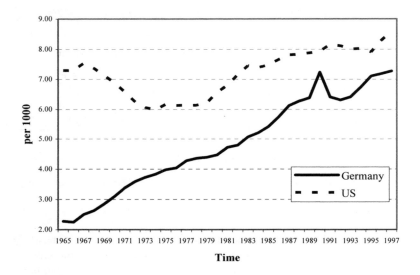

Source: OECD Main Technological Indicators (1998).

Figure 10.4   Scientists and engineers per 1000 employees, Germany and US, 1965–1997

The number of scientists and engineers engaged in R&D in Germany increases over time compared to a slight increase in the US. However, considering graduate education the situation is rather different.

10.3   EMPIRICAL EXAMINATION

In this section we try to obtain further insights into the relationship between education and educational efforts, and research and development activities which determine technological change.

Concerning the workers who studied at college or graduate schools, one possible indicator of the value of a higher degree of productivity due to higher education is the so called college or wage premium which a college graduate earns relative to a high school graduate. According to Temple (2000) this is a general approach in labour economics in order to estimate the productivity of different skill levels. Furthermore, it is generally shown, for example by Ingram and Neuman (2000), that the returns to education increase with the educational level.[9] Therefore, the application of the college premium as a possible measure of the outcome of tertiary education seems reasonable. Figures 10.5 and 10.6 below show the evolution of the wage spread over time for the US and Germany.

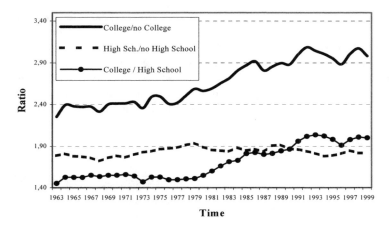

Source: US Bureau of the Census 2000, and own calculations.

Figure 10.5   Wage spread, US, 1963–1999

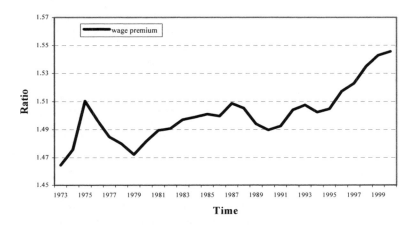

Source: Federal Office of Statistics Germany, Fachserie 16, various issues and own calculations. The wage spread is measured as the ratio of wages earned by employees at supervisory job positions to wage earners at lower job positions.

Figure 10.6   Wage spread, West-Germany, 1973-2000

As reported by Figures 10.5 and 10.6 the wage spread increases over time for both countries.[10] Why the wage premium increased over time can be explained largely by the hypothesis of so called skill biased technological change (SBTC).[11] However, concentrating on the relationship between educational efforts and the evolution of wage inequality, both negative and positive relations can be expected. The sign of this relation depends on the relative influence educational efforts have on the respective skill group. Table 10.4 shows the results of considering the relationship between educational expenditures and GDP as an explanatory variable of the educational wage spread. Furthermore, we analyse a second relationship raised by the SBTC hypothesis: that an increase in the number of skilled workers raises the wage premium.

Table 10.4 Education and the wage spread

	constant	Exogenous Variables	
		Educational Exp./GDP	high skilled/low skilled workers
US	0.0007	0.2821	
	(1.9342)	(2.0573***)	
	-0.0005		1.5781
	(-0.3120)		(15.0035***)
	-0.0058	0.0432	1.5516
	(-0.3805)	(0.7770)	(13.9547***)
Germany	0.0029	0.0896	
	(1.5390**)	(2.8878***)	
	-0.0027		-0.0240
	(-1.1697*)		(-0.4174)
	0.0035	0.0939	-0.0466
	(1.7617***)	(2.9842***)	(-0.9201)

Notes:
t-statistics in parentheses
Significance: ***=95%; **=90%; *=85%

The result of this regression analysis is obvious, additional expenditure on education leads to an increase in wage inequality in the US as well as, to a lower extent, in Germany. Furthermore, we obtain a positive correlation between the growth rate of the wage spread and the relative number of highly skilled workers in the US. However, for Germany we obtained a negative relation.[12] An expansion of the regression which includes both educational expenditures and the relative supply of skilled workers as explanatory variables leads to similar results. Furthermore, educational wage inequality is determined by a significant trend variable,[13] and in addition, educational efforts are positively correlated with the growth rate of the wage spread. Concerning the US, we observe that the growth rate of the relative supply of skilled workers is significantly related to the wage spread.

Besides the relation of wage inequality and educational indicators one has to consider the relation between educational efforts and participation in education. The results of the latter regression are reported in Table 10.5 below.[14]

For both countries we observe a positive correlation between educational expenditures and the supply of skills. However, the obtained parameter value for the US is twice as high as for Germany, where a non-significant parameter is obtained. Interpreting these results one may infer that an additional effort in education does not lead to a higher participation in education in Germany compared to the US.

Table 10.5 Educational efforts and supply of skills

	Exogenous Variable	
	constant	Educational Exp./ GDP
US	0.0050	0.1539
	(2.2623***)	(1.8836***)
Germany	0.0141	0.0929
	(1.9133***)	(0.7568)

Notes:
t-statistics in parentheses.
Significance: ***=95%; **=90%; *=85%.

Up to now we have looked at correlations only, but have not considered the evolution of a variable over time. Assuming that the wage spread reflects the 'market value' of an additional educational degree one can use an indicator of the productivity of an educational system by relating inputs in terms of relative expenditures to output in terms of relative wages or skilled workers.

Indicator I = Wage Spread / (Educational Expenditures / GDP)
Indicator II = Relative Number of high skilled workers / (Educ. Exp / GDP)

The hypothesis which has to be examined is that a (highly) productive educational system should lead to an increase of this indicator over time. A stationary relationship reflects a kind of 'constant returns' production of the educational system and a (non-stationary) decreasing pattern of the above defined variables indicates a 'low-productivity' system.

As shown by Figures 10.7 and 10.8 it is not clear if any series exhibit a stationary or a non-stationary pattern. In particular, one has to bear in mind that the German time series consists of 28 observations, only. In order to obtain more profound information on each series, we apply several tests for stationarity. In a first step we apply Dickey-Fuller tests (first two columns of Tables 10.6 and 10.7), augmented Dickey Fuller Test (ADF, columns three and four) and the Phillips-Perron Test (columns five and six).[15]

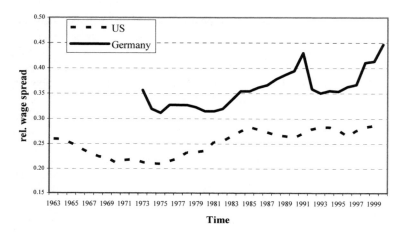

Source: own calculation.

Figure 10.7   Comparison wage spread/(educational exp./GDP), Germany and US, 1963–1999

As shown by Tables 10.6 and 10.7, the hypothesis of a unit root, that is, of non-stationarity, can not be rejected for both indicators and for both countries, if one considers both variables in levels (as shown by Figures 10.7 and 10.8). Applying the tests to first differences of each series the unit root hypothesis is rejected.

Considering the pattern of the series shown by Figures 10.7 and 10.8 one might expect a structural break in each series. The application of tests on the regression residuals points out that the series are characterized by a structural break in 1982 (US) and in 1986 (Germany), respectively. Therefore, we apply an augmented Phillips-Perron Test, which explicitly controls for the existence of a structural break. In particular, we assume that both series can be described by a 'jump' to higher level after the break. Assuming this pattern of a break leads to the results shown in Table 10.8.[16]

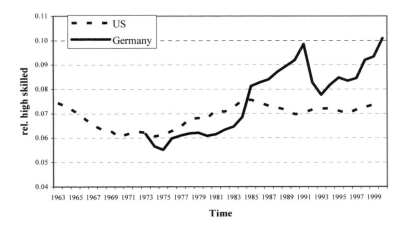

Source: own calculation.

*Figure 10.8   Comparison relative high skilled/(educational exp./GDP)
Germany and US, 1963–1999*

These results suggest rejecting the assumption of a unit root, and we may conclude that the educational systems of the US and Germany exhibit patterns of 'constant productivity'. However, the levels of the indicators as reported in Figures 10.7 and 10.8 indicate that the German system is, *on average*, more productive than the US one. The results shown in this section are still in line with the stylised facts reported in Tables 10.2 and 10.3. In particular, if we compare averages the German education system is more productive than the US one. On the other hand, Tables 10.2 and 10.3 also show that in the upper tail of highly skilled people, for example Ph.D. students, the US system produces more 'high potentials' than the German one.

However, one might argue that the indicator examined above only reflects private returns to (higher) education rather than social returns. Therefore, we consider the following indicator where we relate the output of researchers to educational expenditures.

Indicator III: Patents per Scientist and Engineer / Educational Expenditures per GDP

In order to ensure that our measure produces a comparable time series we concentrate on total public educational expenditures only.[17]

Table 10.6 *Unit root tests, indicator I*

	US					Germany				
	ADF	PP	a_0	a_2	γ	ADF	PP	a_0	a_2	□
	Test Statistics					Test Statistics				
White Noise	-	-	-	-	0.0024	-	-	-	-	0.0049
					(0.4943)					(0.4272)
R.W. + drift	-	-	0.0052	-	-0.0181	-	-	0.0584	-	-0.1594
			(0.4143)		(-0.3637)			(1.2102)		(-1.1693)
ADF	0.3430	-	-	0.4384	0.0015	0.8707	-	-	0.0101	-0.0707
				(2.7189)**	(0.3430)				(0.8707)	(-0.3655)
ADF	-0.9160	-	0.0111	0.4674	-0.0427	-1.1238	-	0.0619	0.0428	-0.1651
			(0.9547)	(2.8845)***	(-0.9160)			(1.1959)	(0.2001)	(-1.1238)
PP	-	0.3065	-	-	0.0024	-	0.4805	-	-	0.0049
					(0.4943)					(0.4273)
PP	-	-0.8171	0.0052	-	-0.01809	-	-1.2103	0.0584	-	-0.1594
			(0.4143)		(-0.3637)			(1.2102)		(-1.1693)

Notes: t-statistics in parentheses; significance levels: *** = 1%, ** = 5%, * = 10%; ADF = Augmented Dickey Fuller Test; PP= Phillips-Perron Test.

Regression for the ADF-test: $\Delta y_t = a_0 + \gamma y_{t-1} + a_2 t + \sum_{i=2}^{p} \beta_i \Delta y_{t-i+1} + \varepsilon_t$, the Phillips-Perron Test is based on: $y_t = a_0 + \gamma y_{t-1} + \varepsilon_t$, (cf. Enders (1995), chapter 4)

Table 10.7 Unit root tests, indicator II

	US					Germany				
	Test Statistics		a_0	a_2	γ	Test Statistics		a_0	a_2	$\square$
	ADF	PP				PP	γ			
White Noise	-	-	-	-	-0.0006 (-0.1422)	-	-	-	-	0.0191 (1.3926)
R.W. + drift	-	-	0.0041 (1.1022)	-	-0.0654 (-1.1101)	-	-	0.0033 (0.6214)	-	-0.0267 (-0.3557)
ADF	0.0928	-	-	0.44465 (2.8821)**	0.0004 (0.0928)	-	1.3752	-	0.00857 (0.4146)	0.0200 (1.3752)
ADF	-1.4813	-	0.0005 (1.4917)	0.4797 (3.1202)***	-0.0807 (-1.4813)	-	-0.7528	0.0057 (1.0267)	0.1249 (0.5952)	-0.0588 (-0.7528)
PP	-	-1.1422	-	-	-0.0006 (-1.1422)	1.3925	-	-	-	0.01910 (1.3925)
PP	-	-1.1101	0.0042 (1.1027)	-	-0.0654 (-1.1101)	-0.3557	-	0.0033 (0.6214)	-	-0.0267 (-0.3557)

Notes: t-statistics in parentheses; Significance Levels: *** = 1%, ** = 5%, * = 10%, ADF = Augmented Dickey Fuller Test; PP= Phillips-Perron Test.

The ADF Test is based on: $\Delta y_t = a_0 + \gamma y_{t-1} + a_2 t + \sum_{i=2}^{p} \beta_i \Delta y_{t-i+1} + \varepsilon_t$, the Phillips-Perron Test is based on: $y_t = a_0 + \gamma y_{t-1} + \varepsilon_t$, (cf. Enders (1995), chapter 4)

Table 10.8 Unit root tests, indicator III

	US				Germany			
	ADF	a_0	a_2	$\Box$	ADF	a_0	a_2	$\Box$
Indicator I	-3.2792***	-	0.1157	-0.9706	-3.1650***	-	0.0023	-0.6859
			(0.5133)	(-3.2792)***			(-0.0126)	(-3.1650)***
Indicator II	-4.2383***	-	0.1177	-1.0228	-3.6054***	-	0.1367	-1.1113
			(0.6676)	(-4.2383)***			(-0.0126)	(-3.6054)***

Notes: t-statistics in parentheses; Significance Levels: *** = 1%, ** = 5%, * = 10%.

The ADF Test is based on: $\Delta y_t = a_0 + \gamma y_{t-1} + a_2 t + \sum_{i=2}^{p} \beta_i \Delta y_{t-i+1} + \varepsilon_t$

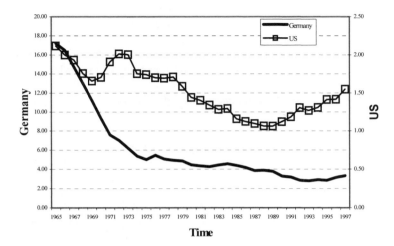

Source: Own calculation.

*Figure 10.9   Patents per scientist and engineer / (educational exp./GDP),
Germany and US, 1965–1997*

Although the level of the German research output (left scale) is still above
the US indicator, one observes a strong decline since the middle of the
1960s.[18] However, it should be noticed that the absolute level of the research
productivity still exceeds the productivity of U.S. researchers. Considering
the evolution over time only, both series behave quite similarly since the
middle of the 1980s. Since then, the US series shows a significant increase
whereas the German series has remained constant. An explanation of the
increasing pattern of the US series might be that the industrial revolution of
the introduction of information technologies at the end of the 1970s had a
higher impact on the 'productivity' of researchers in the US than in
Germany.[19] How the indicator above is determined by public educational
efforts of each country is analysed by a simple regression experiment.

Considering the above regression results we obtain also an important
difference between the US and Germany. In particular, we observe a
significant negative relation between public educational expenditures and the
output of scientists and engineers. However, we observe a positive relation
for the US economy. Particularly, if we consider a time lag of five years for
educational expenditures the positive parameter becomes highly significant.

Besides the 'returns' of educational systems one has to take a look at the
other side of the coin, the productivity of the research and development
system. As known from growth theory both human capital and R&D efforts

determine the long run growth rate. In particular, the R&D sector employs, in general, highly skilled workers like university graduates in order to develop new innovations. As already shown by Figure 10.4 above, the number of scientists and engineers increases over time for both countries. The question is, whether the increasing number of scientist generates new knowledge?

Table 10.9   Educational efforts and output of researchers

	constant	Educational Exp./GDP	Constant	Public Educational Exp./GDP,
US	0.0110	0.1344	−0.0095	0.4884
	(0.9686)	(0.6663)	(−1.1007)	(3.1654***)
Germany	0.2962	−4.8223	0.1339	−1.7764
	(9.1714***)	(−7.3587***)	(−4.2910***)	(3.1654***)

Notes: t-statistics in parentheses; Significance: ***=95%; **=90%; *=85%.

Following Griliches (1990) we apply the number of national patent applications as an indicator of innovations and the production of new knowledge. Furthermore, we weight the number of patents with the respective measure of inputs in order to follow our 'input - output' approach, that is, we assume that the productivity of a country's knowledge production is given by[20]

Indicator IV: Patents per S&E / (R&D / GDP).

The evolution over time of the above mentioned indicator is presented in Figure 10.10.[21] There, it is shown, that Germany exhibits a large decline of research productivity compared to the US during the last 30 years.[22] However, notice that in 1997 the efficiency measure of German R&D expenditures are on a similar level with the U.S.. Figure 10.10 shows, that although the efficiency of German research expenditures declines the efficiency level is still able to compete with the U.S.. The result of Figure 10.10 is supported by the following regression analysis where we relate our measure of research productivity to relative R&D expenditures.

On the one hand the results reported by Figure 10.10 and Table 10.10 are in line with the assumption of economic growth without scale effects as, for example, pointed out by Jones (1995), Segerstrom (1998), or Young (1998), which states that the growth rate of an economy does not depend directly on the number of scientists and engineers and, furthermore, that the research process exhibits decreasing returns to scale. On the other hand, the above results indicate large deficits of the productivity of the German research sector in comparison to the US. For example, as reported by Table 10.10 the efficiency of non-defence related R&D expenditures of the US (U.S. non-def.) is 8 times higher than in Germany. However, for both countries the results show a highly significant intercept term which represents a strong relation of R&D efforts and patents.

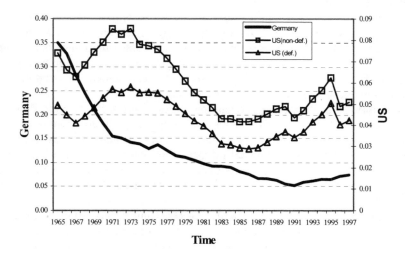

Source: Own calculation.

Figure 10.10 Patents per S&E/(R&D/GDP), Germany and US, 1965–1997

Table 10.10 R&D efforts and knowledge production

	Exogenous Variables	
	constant	R&D Exp./ GDP
US	0.1486	–0.0169
(incl. Defense)	(3.7466***)	(–1.0697)
US	0.1819	–0.0419
(excl. defense)	(5.5058***)	(–2.2978***)
Germany	1.0669	–0.3355
	(5.5058***)	(–2.2978***)

Notes: t-statistics in parentheses; Significance: ***=95%; **=90%; *=85%.

10.4   CONCLUSION

Although our measures and indicators only highlight a few aspects of educational and research systems, we give some evidence why the US economy exhibits higher long run growth: The US universities produce a higher number of doctorates in S&E who are, in addition, more productive than their German counterparts.

Our results suggest that it might not be sufficient only to concentrate on general educational levels, for example to raise the number of students at colleges and universities. It seems obvious that the distribution of skill groups as well as their educational level, for example college vs. doctorate degrees, might be a more important determinant of technological innovations and economic growth than recent discussions suggest.

A further result is that aggregate measures of productivity and efficiency of educational and research systems are still missing.[23] It goes without saying that the 'quality' of research and education does not depend on expenditures only. Educational or intellectual infrastructure, the quality of teachers, class sizes, and so on, are further important factors in the returns to education or research and development (see, for example, Sianesi and Van Reenen (2003), p.181).

Another point is that, in particular for Germany, a detailed theoretical and empirical analysis of the productivity of its research and educational system is still missing. In order to derive detailed insights into the pattern of economic growth of Germany as well as of Europe such an analysis, from our point of view, might be necessary. Furthermore, assuggested by our study, concentrating on aggregate numbers only, like the ratio of students to employees or R&D expenditures to GDP,may not not be sufficient to derive policy instruments for economic growth. Up to now, a detailed analysis of the structure and efficiency of educational and R&D systems and their importance for economic growth is still missing. Therefore, our results should be seen as a first look on an important topic for future research.

NOTES

1. Average growth rates of real GDP. Own calculations with data taken from Sachverständigenrat (2003). See also OECD (2003b) for a detailed survey of the pattern of economic growth across OECD countries.
2. PISA: Programme for International Student Assessment, organized by the OCED in 2000.
3. See, for example, Greiner et al. (2001) for a discussion of the new growth theory from a time series perspective.
4. Own calculations based on the Annual Statistical Abstract of the United States 2000 and the Datenreport 2002 published by the Federal Statistical Office Germany. Concerning the

amount of German private educational expenditures one should point out that these expenses are almost all carried out by firms which are involved in the apprenticeship system.

5. Own calculations based on Datenreport 2002, published by the Federal Statistical Office, Germany.
6. See OECD *Education at a Glance*, various issues, OECD, Paris.
7. The definition of science and engineering captures: Engineering, Mathematics, Natural Sciences, Computer Sciences, Social Sciences.
8. Because of reorganizations of the OECD Main Science and Technology Indicators Database, this index can only be calculated until 1997. Cf. Jones (1995) for a similar indicator capturing the number of scientists and engineers engaged in R&D.
9. Ingram and Neuman (2000) show also that the returns to education vary across different types of education. For example, they show that the return to mathematical skills has doubled since the middle of the 1980s whereas the return to manual skills declined.
10. Comparing the results of Figure 10.6 with the German wage inequality reported by the OECD (1993, 1996) one should expect a decline in German wage inequality. But, if the West German manufacturing sector is considered (as here), or, referring to Fitzenberger (1999), the establishment panel is applied, one observes an increase in educational wage inequality for Germany.
11. Recent studies on the hypothesis of skill biased technological change and the returns to education are, for example, Greiner et al. (2004), Sianesi and Van Reenen (2003) or Rubart and Semmler (2004).
12. Note that all regression results reported in Table 10.4 are based on growth rates rather than level variables.
13. See, for example, Rubart and Semmler (2004) for an evaluation of labour market institutions as factors explaining the trend of wage inequality. Furthermore, a recent discussion of the skill-bias can be found in Card and DiNardo (2002).
14. Note that we only consider data of the German manufacturing sector.
15. All tests are computed with EViews. Detailed descriptions of the test procedures can be found in Enders (1995), ch.4 or Hamilton (1994), ch. 17.
16. See Enders (1995), Ch. 4, for a detailed discussion of the augmented Phillips-Perron Test applied in this section. The break is captured by a dummy variable which describes the higher level of each series after the structural break. Afterwards, a Phillips-Perron Test is applied to the regression residuals.
17. The application of both public and private educational expenditures would lead to a similar shape for the US series.
18. Applying time series tests on the indicator shown by Figure 10.10 (not reported here), gives the result that the German series is stationary whereas for the US series a Unit root is reported. Furthermore, there are no hints of structural breaks.
19. See, for example, Greenwood and Yorukoglu (1997) or Jorgenson and Stiroh (2000) for a seminal discussion of the IT-revolution as a source of economic growth.
20. The assumption of patents as an indicator of technological change (innovations) is problematic, but as pointed out by Griliches (1990) patents exhibit all patterns needed for such a measure. Cf. Griliches (1990, p. 1671).
21. For the US we distinguish R&D expenditures including and excluding defence related efforts.
22. A similar decline is obtained if one considers patents per scientist and engineer.
23. A notable exception in this area is Lazear (2001).

REFERENCES

Aghion, P. and P. Howitt (1998), *Endogenous Growth Theory* (1st ed.), Cambridge, Mass: The MIT Press.

Card, D. and J.E. DiNardo (2002), 'Skill-biased technological change and rising wage inequality: some problems and puzzles', *Journal of Labor Economics* **20** (4), pp. 733–83.

Enders, W. (1995), *Applied Econometric Time Series* (1ˢᵗ ed.), New York: John Wiley & Sons.

Fitzenberger, B. (1999), *Wages and Employment Across Skill Groups – An Analysis for West Germany*, Heidelberg: Physica Verlag.

Greenwood, J. and M. Yorukoglu (1997), *Carnegie-Rochester Conference Series on Public Policy*, **46**, pp. 49–95.

Greiner, A., J. Rubart and W. Semmler (2004), 'Economic growth, skill-biased technical change and wage inequality: A model and estimations for the US and Europe', *Journal of Macroeconomics*, **26** (4), pp. 597–621.

Greiner, A., W. Semmler, J. Rubart and G. Gong (2001), 'Economic growth in the US and Europe: the role of knowledge, human capital, and inventions', in J. Gabriel and M. Neugart (eds), *Ökonomie als Grundlage politischer Entscheidungen*, Leverkusen: Leske & Budrich, pp. 27–59.

Griliches, Z. (1990), 'Patent statistics and economic indicators: a survey', *Journal of Economic Literature*, **28**, pp. 1661–1707.

Hamilton, J.D. (1994), *Time Series Analysis* (1ˢᵗ ed.), Princeton, New Jersey: Princeton University Press.

Ingram, B.F. and G.R. Neumann (2000), 'The returns to skill', mimeo, University of Iowa, May.

Jones, C.I. (1995), 'Time series tests of endogenous growth models', *Quarterly Journal of Economics*, **110**, pp. 495–525.

Jorgenson, D.W. and K.J. Stiroh (2000), 'Raising the speed limit: US economic growth in the information age', *Brookings Papers on Economic Activity*, **1**, pp. 125–211.

Krueger, D. and K.B. Kumar (2004a), 'Skill-specific rather than general education: a reason for US–Europe growth differences?', *Journal of Economic Growth*, **9**, pp. 167–207.

Krueger, D. and K.B. Kumar (2004b), 'US–Europe differences in technology-driven growth: quantifying the role of education', *Journal of Monetary Economics*, **51**, pp. 161–90.

Lazear, E.P. (2001), 'Educational production', *Quarterly Journal of Economics*, **66** (3), pp. 777–803.

Lucas, R.E. (1988), 'On the mechanics of economic development', *Journal of Monetary Economics*, **22**, pp. 3–42.

Nelson, R.R. and E.S. Phelps (1966), 'Investment in humans, technological diffusion, and economic growth', *American Economic Review*, **61**, pp. 69–75.

OECD (1993), *Employment Outlook*, Paris: OECD Publications.

OECD (1996), *Employment Outlook*, Paris: OECD Publications.

OECD (2003a), *Education at a Glance 2003*, Paris: OECD Publications.

OECD (2003b), *The Sources of Economic Growth in OECD Countries*, Paris: OECD Publications.

OECD (2004), *Education at a Glance 2004*, Paris: OECD Publications.

Romer, P.M. (1990), 'Endogenous technological change', *Journal of Political Economy*, **98**, pp. 71–102.

Rubart, J. and W. Semmler (2004), 'Technical change, labor market institutions and wage inequality: a comparison of the US and Europe', mimeo, Darmstadt University of Technology and University of Bielefeld, March.

Sachverständigenrat (2003), *Staatsfinanzen konsolidieren – Steuersystem reformieren. Jahresgutachten 2003/2004*, Wiesbaden, November.

Segerstrom, P.S. (1998), 'Endogenous growth without scale effects', *American Economic Review*, **88** (5), pp. 1290–310.

Sianesi, B. and J. Van Reenen (2003), 'The returns to education: macroeconomics', *Journal of Economic Surveys*, **17** (2), pp. 157–200.

Temple, J. (2000), 'Growth effects of education and social capital in the OECD', mimeo, University of Oxford, April.

Young, A. (1998), 'Growth without scale effects', *Journal of Political Economy*, **106** (1), pp. 41–63.

Young, A. A. (1928), 'Increasing returns and economic progress', *The Economic Journal*, **38**, pp. 527–42.

COMMENT

Ulrike Stierle-von Schütz

The chapter of Caspari, Rubart and Rehme investigates two well known factors of the growth process coming from the endogenous growth theory, namely human capital and R&D efforts. They focus particularly in their time series analysis on the input and output side of the German and US educational and research system at a macroeconomic level in order to detect determinants of the growth differentials between both countries.

By conducting a descriptive analysis of both systems, including tertiary education and college and university degrees in science and engineering, the authors summarize the well known fact that in Germany spending on R&D and education are lower than in the US. In addition, they point to a very interesting observation, namely the different distribution of skill groups as well as their educational level.

In their empirical examination the authors construct several indicators of efficiency and carry out regression analyses linking input (spending as a share of GDP) and output factors (relative numbers of white collar workers) of the educational and research systems to the wage spread as an indicator of return to education. It turns out that both additional effort in education and a higher number of highly skilled workers are negatively correlated to the wage spread in Germany but positively in the US. Also it seems that higher spending in education does not lead to a higher supply of skilled workers in Germany in contrast to the US. Regarding the development of productivity of both educational systems the authors show that on average, interestingly, Germany has a kind of leadership but obviously not in the production of high potentials, meaning the structure of the output seems to be important. In order to evaluate the productivity of the R&D system at a basic level, the authors use a weighted number of national patent applications in relation to the R&D spending as a share of GDP. Their short analysis illustrates that the German system suffers from a largely decreasing productivity performance relative to the US.

The chapter gives a concise introduction to a very important topic – the search for determinants of growth differentials. In this way it fits well into the discussion about the catching up process of Europe in relation to the United States.

Although these first tests and thoughts are far from being comprehensive as the authors already indicate, some shortcomings should be mentioned in order to give the future research an appropriate direction. Some important data explanations and measurement issues are missing. One important aspect seems to be the distinction between private and public actors: in order to evaluate expenditure on education and R&D, one should be clear about the sources of spending. As Peter Nijkamp notes, (see chapter 3 in this volume), from a meta-analysis public expenditure on education and research is especially growth enhancing. On the output side of R&D, for the comparison of productivity measures in both systems, this distinction should be made in order to capture differences adequately. Investigating the impact of education on R&D and growth at a macro level should include the search for the social return of education because of, for example, externalities and individual differences in the private return (Temple, 2001). Therefore, relying only on wage differentials might not capture the whole effect of education.

One should be careful about data quality, as de la Fuente and Domenech (2000) point out, since studies from the mid-1990s often discovered a negative relationship between education and productivity growth (see, for example, Benhabib and Spiegel, 1994, or Pritchett, 1996).

Some caution is also needed in drawing policy conclusions from this chapter. The empirical analysis with just some tests without the backing of a clear theoretical model and no other control variables might lead to arbitrary positions, especially because comparisons are only made between two countries with very different education and research systems.

In the same line some conclusions given by the authors are not very transparent in their recommendation. On the one hand, a system producing a high number of PhD scientists is said to be productive, so policy makers should pay attention to the output of their education system; on the other hand the results indicate that a growing number of scientists and engineers does not directly lead to a higher growth rate. Here the authors should make clear how both results fit together.

Finally the research focus is very interesting and further investigations should also include a more in-depth analysis of efficiency and quality of education and research as well as an evaluation of the social benefits of education.

REFERENCES

Benhabib, J. and M. Spiegel (1994), 'The role of human capital in economic development: evidence from aggregate cross-country data', *Journal of Monetary Economics* **34**, pp. 143–73.

de la Fuente, A. and R. Domenech (2000), 'Human capital in growth regressions: how much difference does data quality make?', CEPR Discussion Paper no. 2466, London.

Pritchett, L. (1996), 'Where has all the education gone?', World Bank Policy Research Working Paper No. 1581, Washington.

Temple, J. (2001), 'Growth effects of education and social capital in the OECD countries', OECD Economic Studies, No. 33, 2001/2, pp. 57–101.

Index